AROUND MAGHULL & LYDIATE

THROUGH TIME

John K. Rowlands

AMBERLEY PUBLISHING

Acknowledgements

I am especially grateful to the people of Maghull and Lydiate who have, over the years, given me permission to use their photographs, for this book could not have been done without their help.

I am indebted to Patricia and Ray Spray, Rhona Simon, Lara Mason for her photographs and Simeon Clow for his computer skills.

To Cathy for her support, encouragement and, above all, patience

First published 2010

Amberley Publishing plc
Cirencester Road, Chalford,
Stroud, Gloucestershire, GL6 8PE

www.amberley-books.com

ISBN 978-1-4456-0209-7

British Library Cataloguing in Publication Data.
A catalogue record for this book is available from the British Library.

Typeset in 9.5pt on 12pt Celeste.
Typesetting by Amberley Publishing.
Printed in the UK.

Introduction

Early one morning in April 1974, I arrived at a busy Euston Station to travel to Liverpool for an interview in Maghull which, until a few days earlier, I had never heard of. The Liverpool train was packed, and I later learnt that I was on the train taking excited race goers to the Grand National.

That day I was quickly attracted to Maghull and Lydiate and their surrounding countryside. The canal, with the unique bridges, seemed to be at every turning. I can still remember how stunned I was at my first sight of the ancient, thatched Scotch Piper. I was entertained at the old vicarage in Lydiate, where we watched Red Rum win, and I was told of the link between Maghull and the Grand National. All the above are described in the book, which is a journey through the two towns, starting at the Lydiate and Downholland boundary and ending at Melling Lane, heading towards the M58. I spent many years, both day and night, driving around the area and this book is the result of the hours spent exploring the towns and recognising the changes through time.

Maghull is thought to have begun near Male Green, now covered by Buckingham Road. The change from an agricultural community with over thirty farms was due, in the main, to advances in transport. There had long been a road between Liverpool and Preston passing through the villages, and the first coach on the Liverpool and Preston Trust Turnpike passed through in June 1774. This led to the building of coaching inns and stables, with businesses such as beer houses and blacksmiths being established, particularly close to the boundary with Lydiate.

The local section of the Leeds-Liverpool Canal was opened at the same time and as well as beer houses and inns being opened near the local bridges, cottages for the canal workers were erected near the Red Lion Hotel. The railway linking Liverpool and Preston was opened in 1850, and the proximity to Maghull led to building of substantial houses close to the station to accommodate businessmen commuting from Liverpool. A second railway, which passed through Lydiate, was later opened but had little impact upon the community.

Lydiate seems to have been less influenced by the transport developments and had grown in a linear pattern, reliant upon farming; but since the last war, domestic housing has filled many of the open fields.

However, wealthy businessmen were already building large houses in Maghull in the nineteenth century and they played their part in its history. Moss Side House was sold and led to the opening of the recently demolished Moss Side Hospital. The present Quarry Brook was built on the site of a house of the same name and is now a convent.

Maghull has been the home for many distinguished men whose achievements are described in *The Dictionary of National Biography*. Perhaps the most famous resident was John Lennon, who lived with relatives in Cedar Grove. There is a plaque on the supermarket on the site of the Albany cinema where the Beatles performed.

During the last war it was a place of safety for refugees from the Liverpool Blitz, and many children from Liverpool were evacuated to the area. Wooden hutted camps, which were built to house the refugees, eventually billeted American soldiers. When they left for D-Day, the camps were taken over by Polish forces and later used for returning soldiers and their families. There is no trace of this period of history.

The boom in house building in Maghull, halted by the Second World War, was soon restarted and the former village life vanished forever.

On reflection, the changes through time have mainly been additions, either by razing farms or acquiring farm land for building. The canal is now a place of peace and beauty. The road system, including the country back lanes, is as it has been for centuries. There has been no destruction of large areas of housing or factories as in the large towns. One of the attractions of Maghull and Lydiate is that there is open countryside within ten minutes of any house, as it has been for centuries.

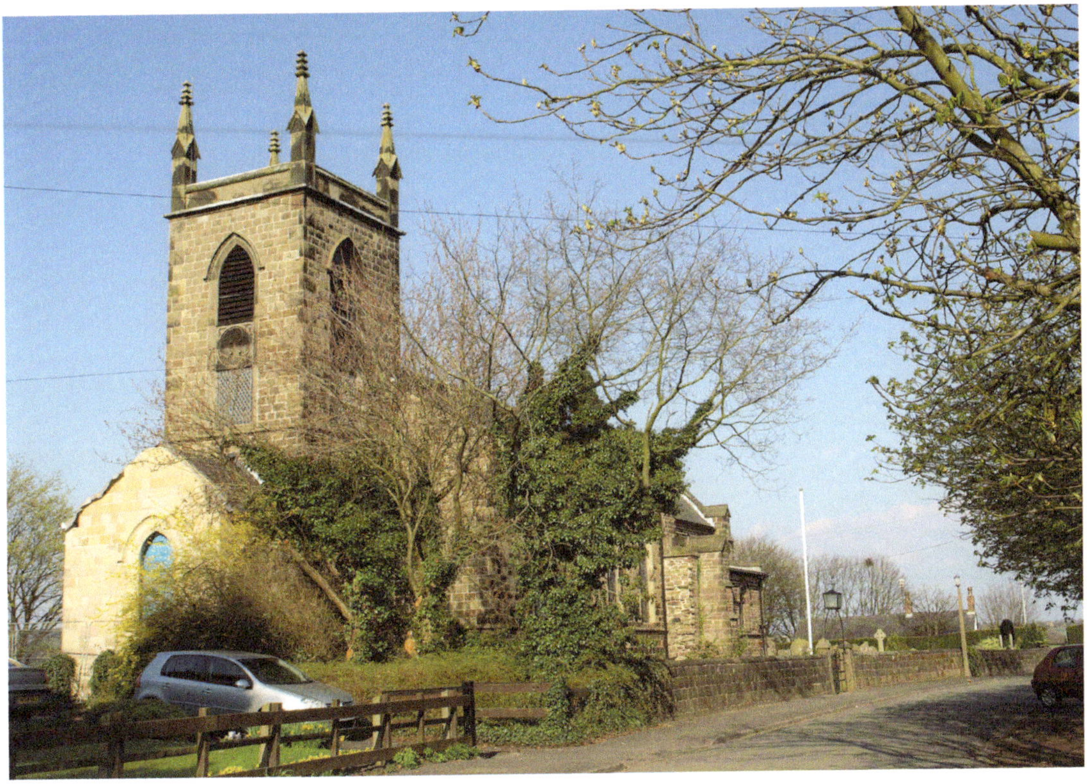

Church Lane

Consecrated in 1841, St Thomas' church stands beyond the Lydiate Brook, the parish boundary, and is glimpsed amid the trees on the approach to Lydiate from the north. The photograph was taken after the chancel and vestry were added in 1913, and there have been recent extensions to the tower.

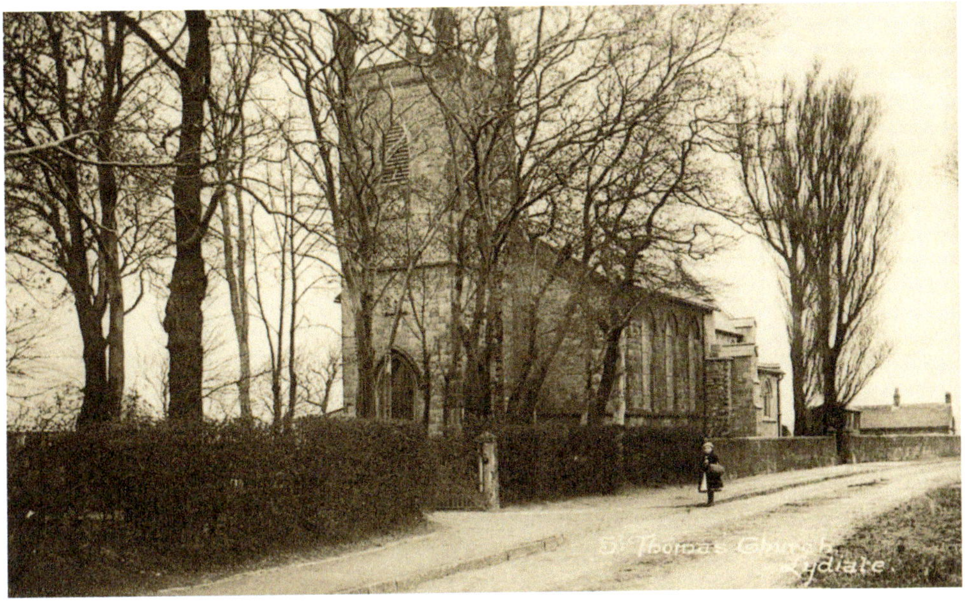

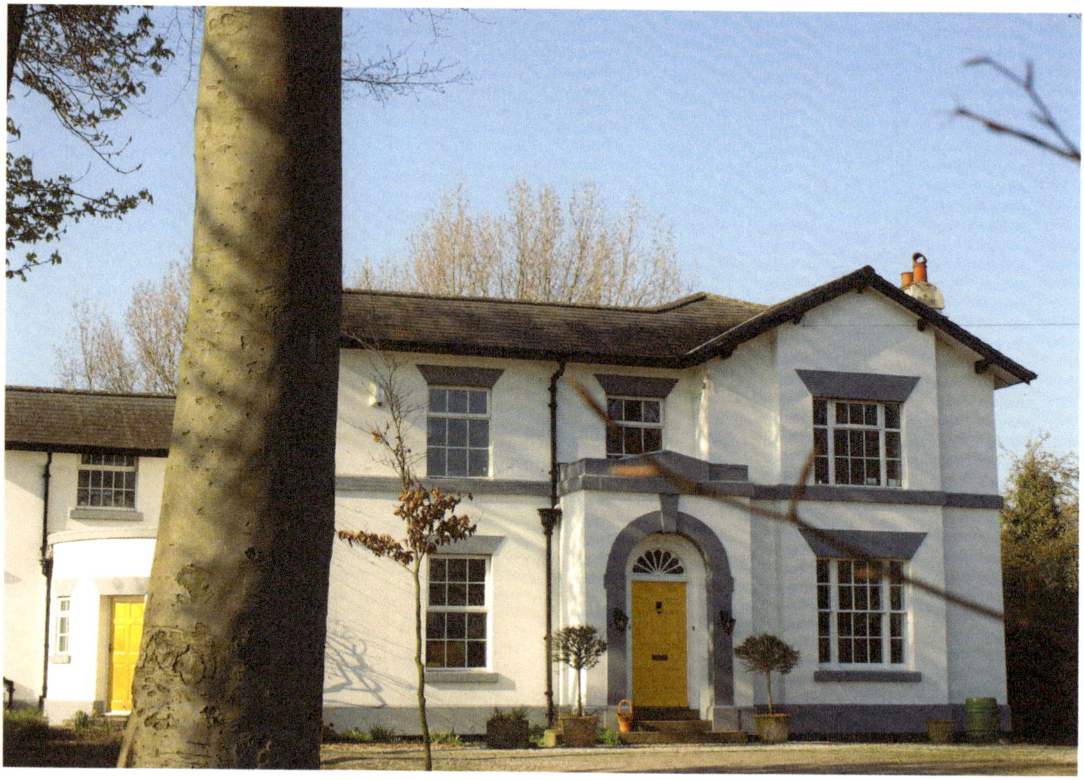

St Thomas' Vicarage

The original vicarage was sold in 1962 and became a private residence. It has been extended, and the change to the direction of the driveway makes an exact comparison difficult.

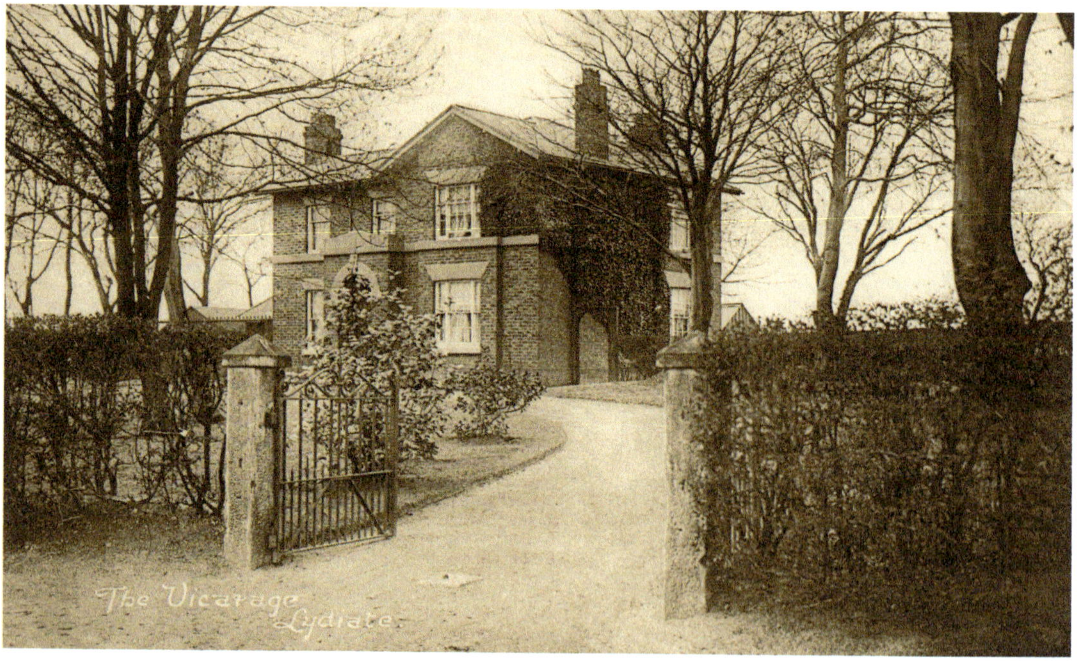

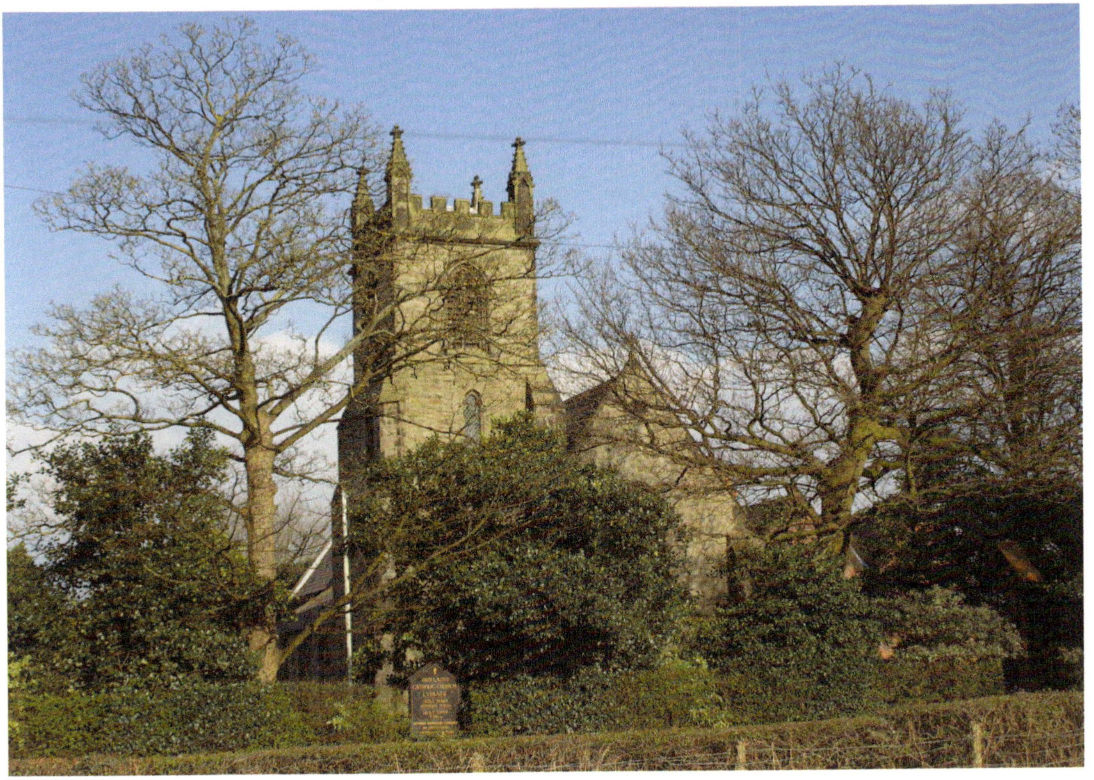

The Southport Road junction with Hall Lane

Our Lady's Roman Catholic church was opened in 1854. The trees still frame the church, but the ivy has been removed from the walls. The spire became unsafe and was taken down in the 1930s.

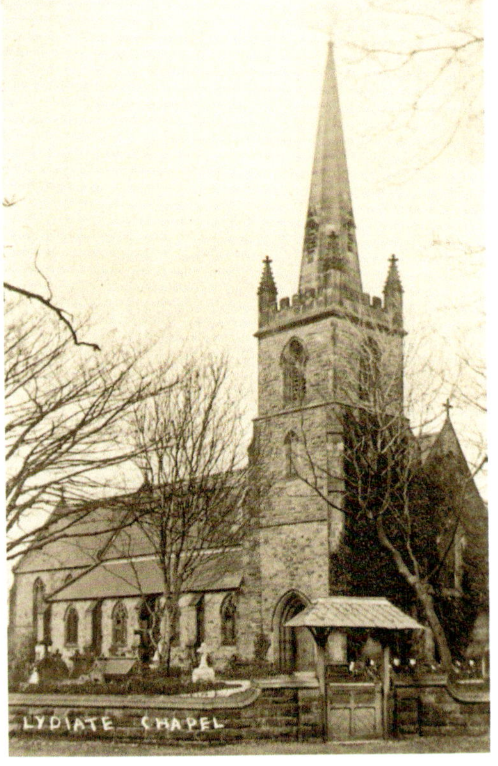

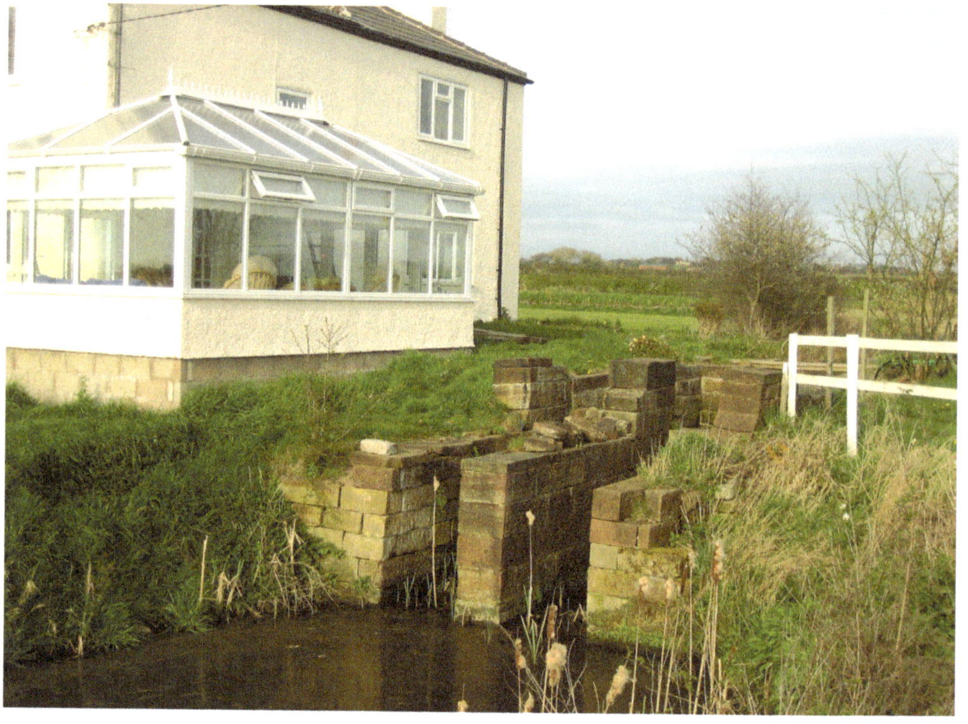

Seven Centuries of History

Situated in Eager Lane, in the lovely open countryside, is the watermill, which has been in the part of Lydiate known as Eggergarth for several centuries. The mill race dried up some time ago and although the waterwheels have gone, the foundations still stand. The Mill House has recently been renovated and the farm outbuildings converted into houses.

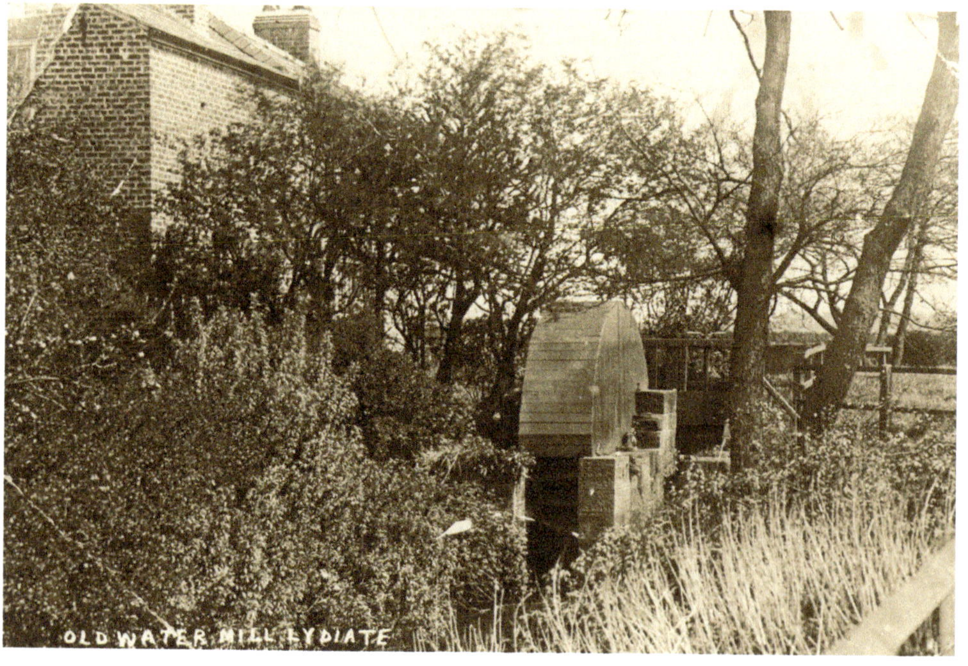

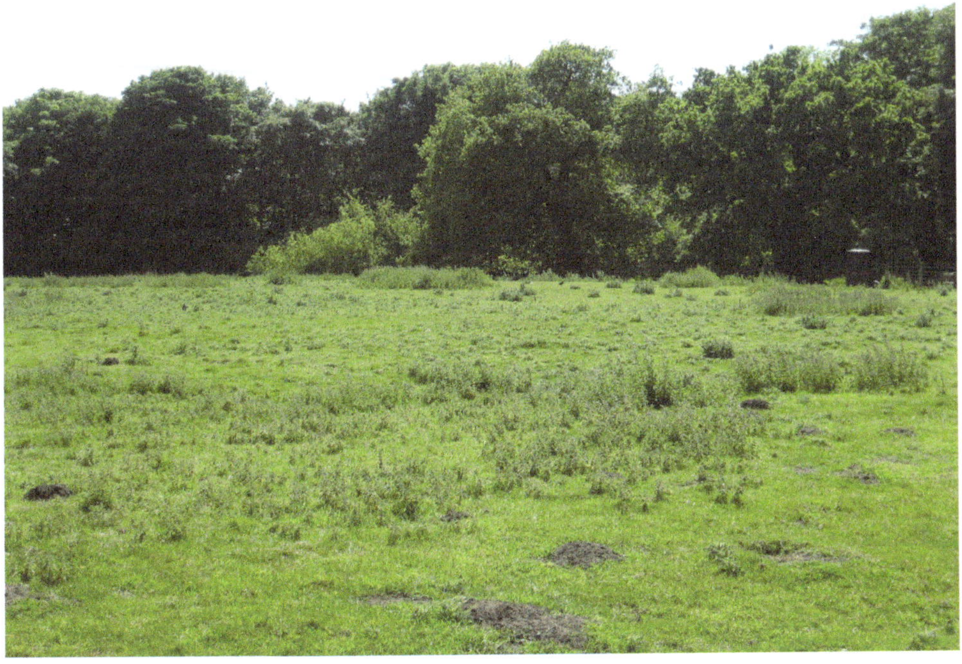

Lydiate Hall

Hidden amongst the trees, so that they are almost impossible to see from the road, are the ruins of the hall built in the first half of the sixteenth century. It is hard to imagine that such a magnificent timbered building existed in the village. Sadly, it fell into ruins during the nineteenth century and was abandoned. A few years ago, with the help of several grants, it was repaired and made safe.

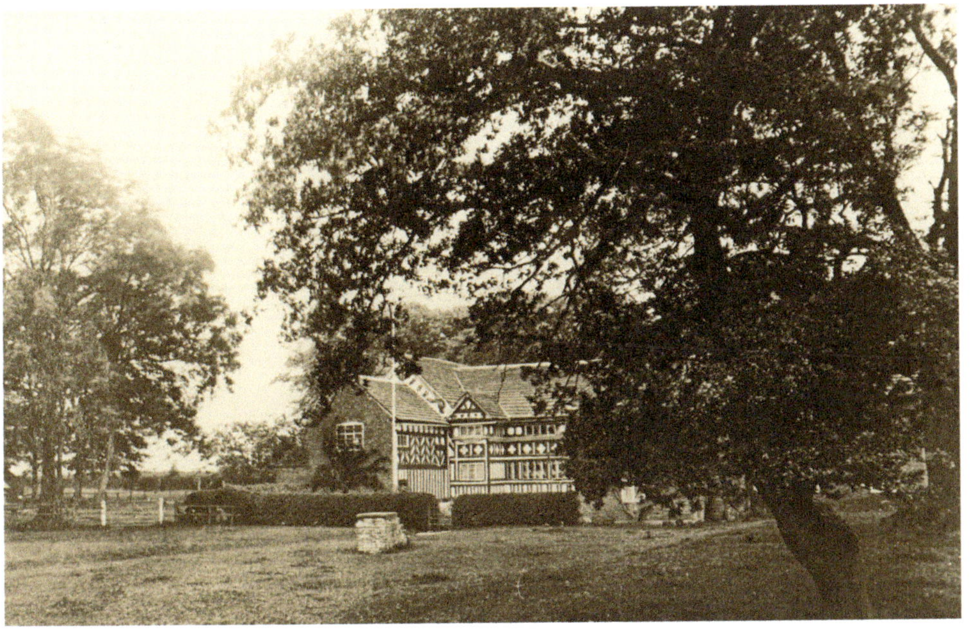

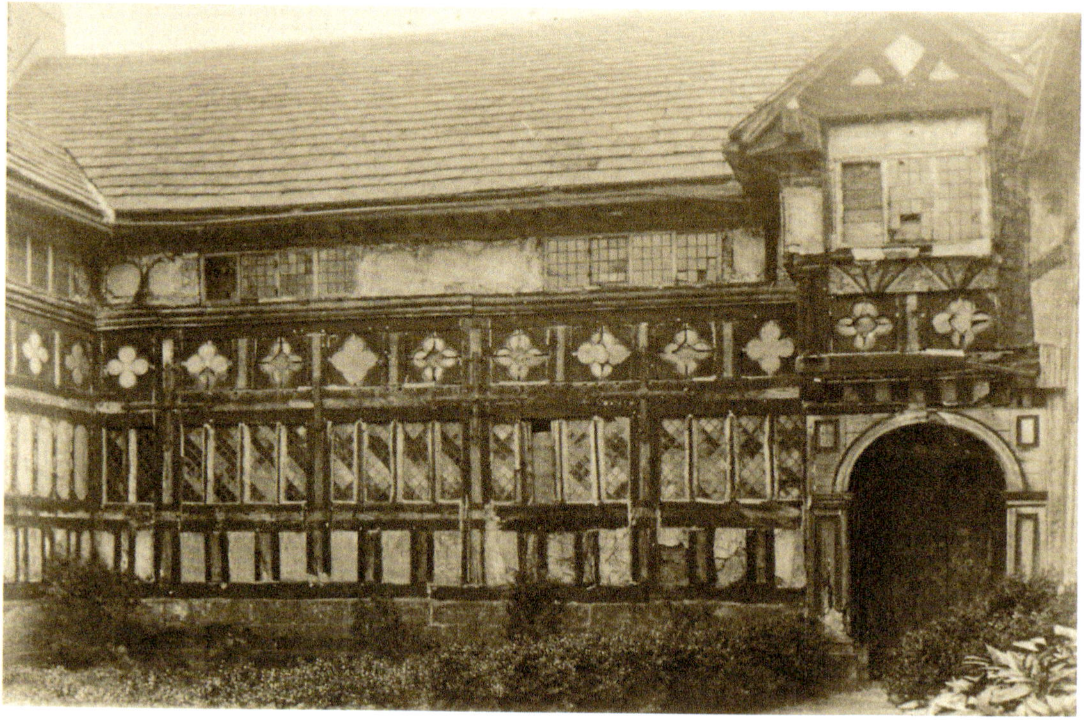

A Grand Day Out

This 1892 photograph, which would fascinate a sociologist, appears to be of a photographic society visiting Lydiate. However, it has proved impossible to work out where the photograph was taken. There are few walls in Lydiate, especially one so well built, with such a fine gate. The top picture of Lydiate Hall was taken in 1895 by George Harrison, a keen amateur photographer.

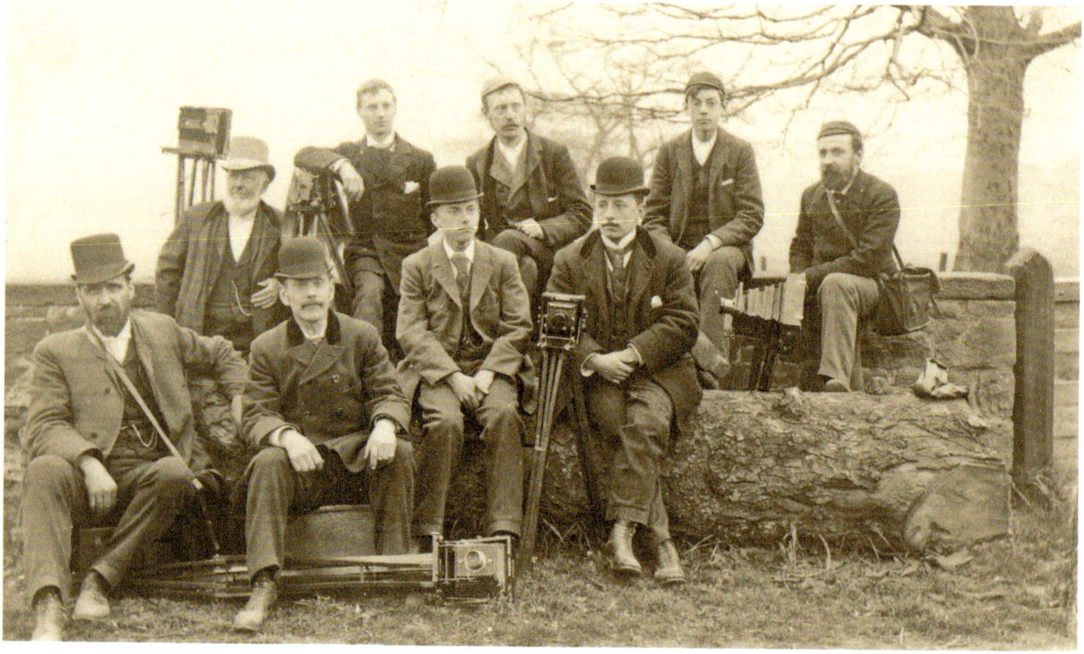

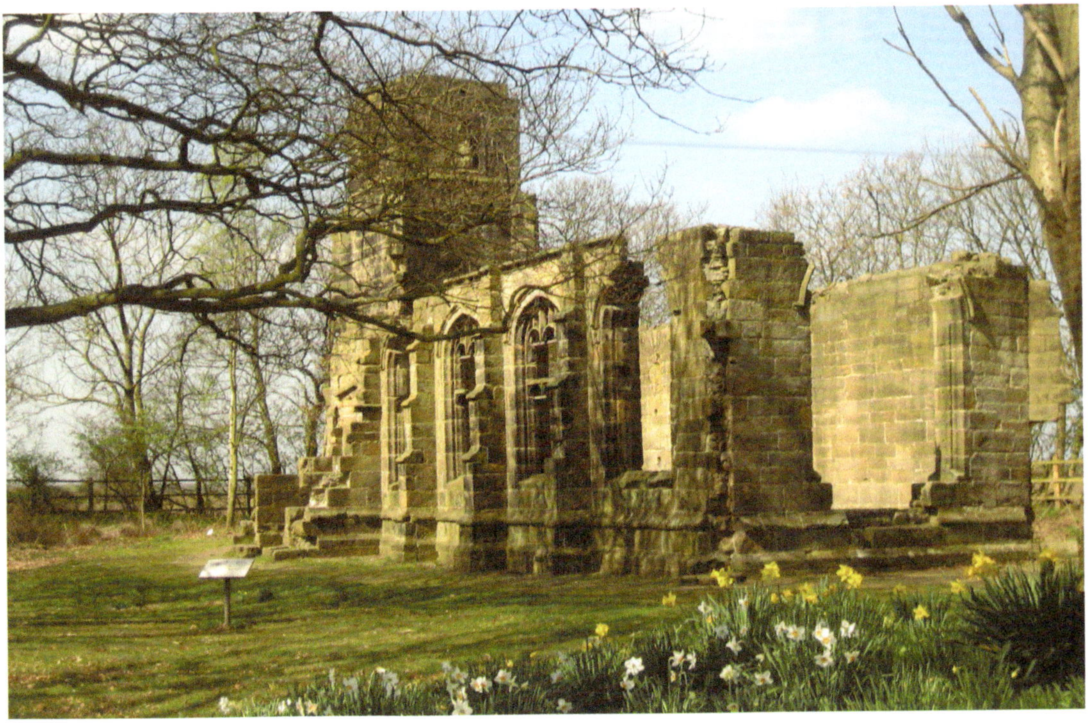

The Ruin that Came to Life

Standing in splendid isolation, St Catherine's chapel, known locally as Lydiate Abbey, is some distance from the hall to which it was the private chapel for the Ireland family. Derelict for centuries, it has been repaired and the grounds opened for visitors. In recent times the abbey has been the popular venue of open-air theatre.

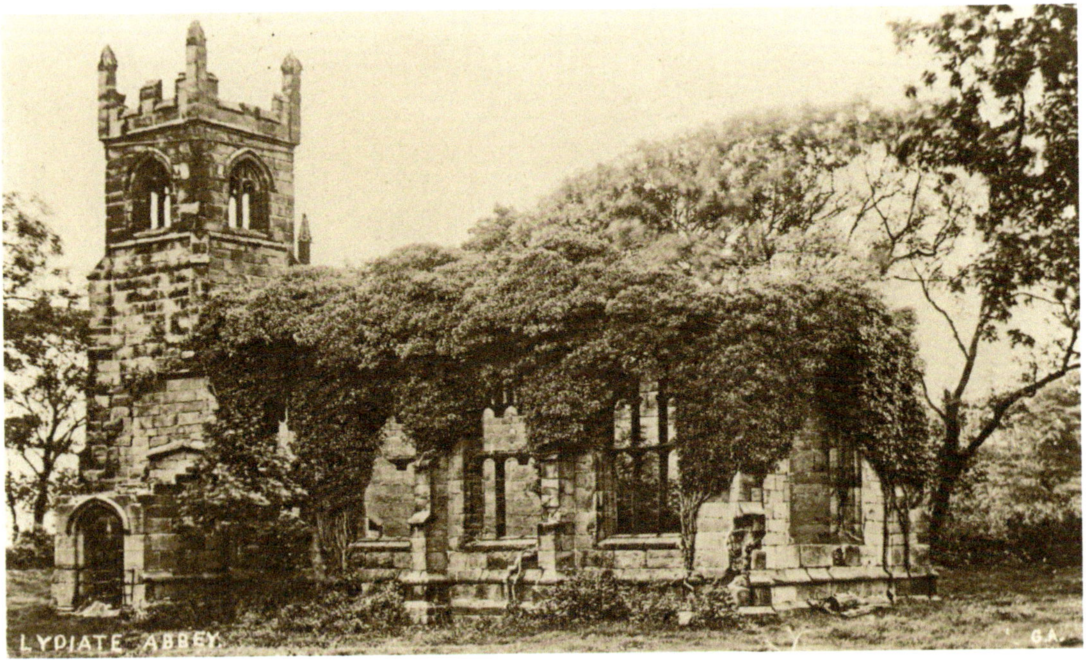

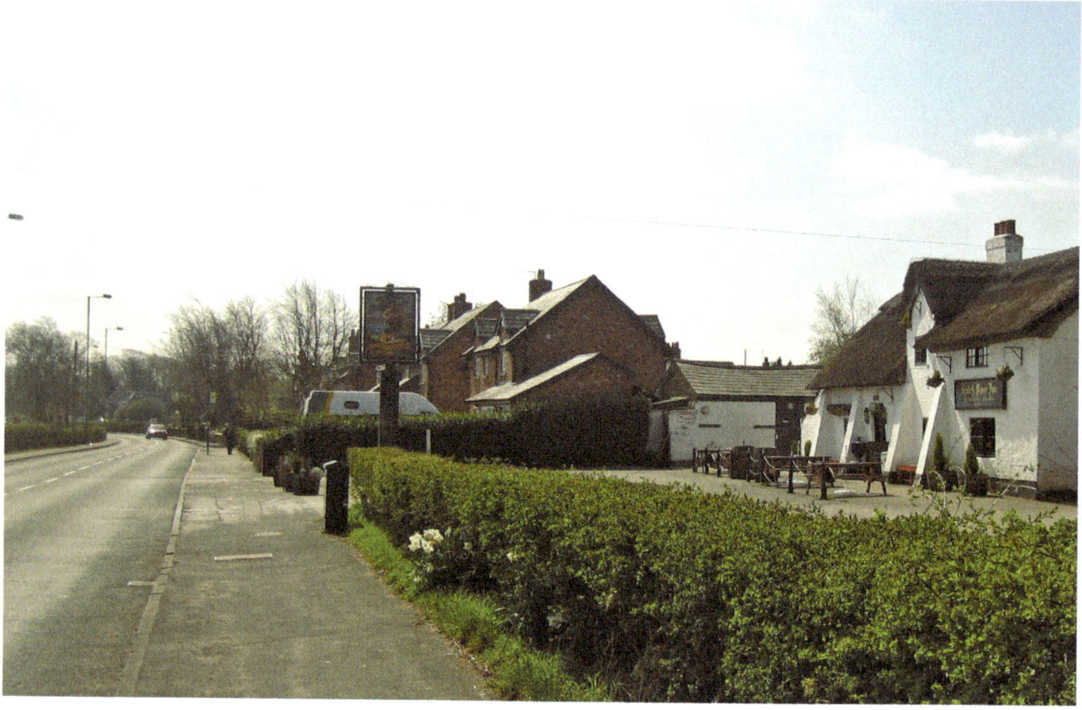

A Jewel of Lydiate

The older view of the Scotch Piper is blocked by houses standing on the open land, which at one time had a garage on it. Thought to have been built in the early sixteenth century, it is one of the oldest public houses in Lancashire and has changed very little over the years.

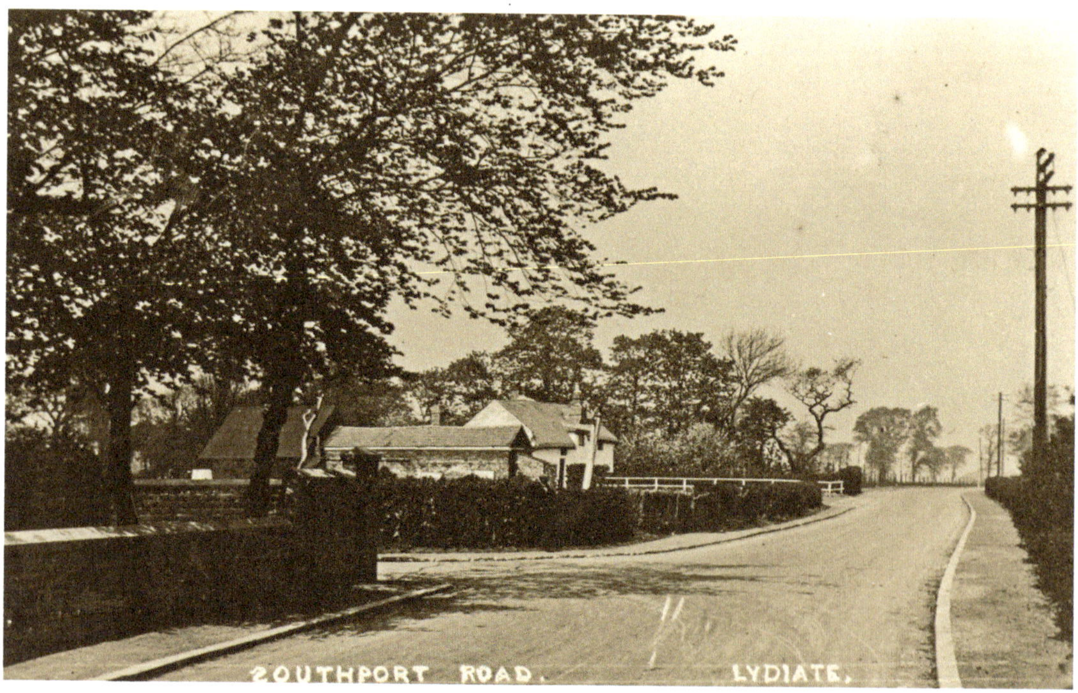

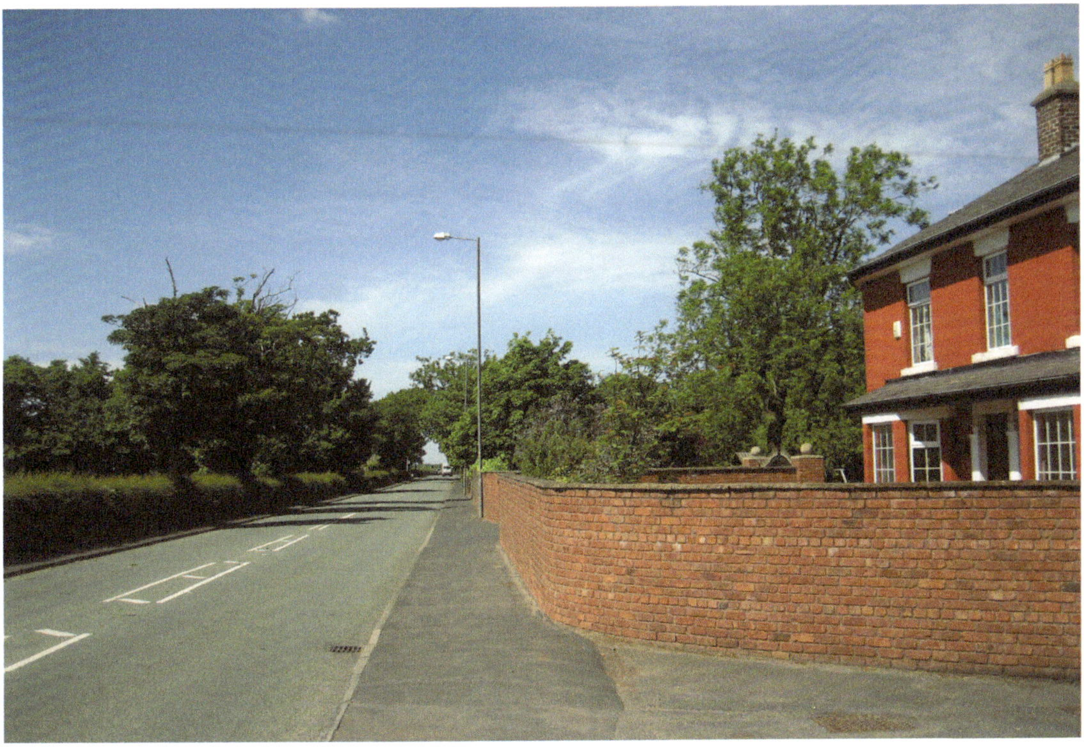

The Open Road to Halsall

A view from close to the Scotch Piper. The trees and hedges now obstruct the view of Our Lady's church and the Presbytery. Oak House is now surrounded by a large wall.

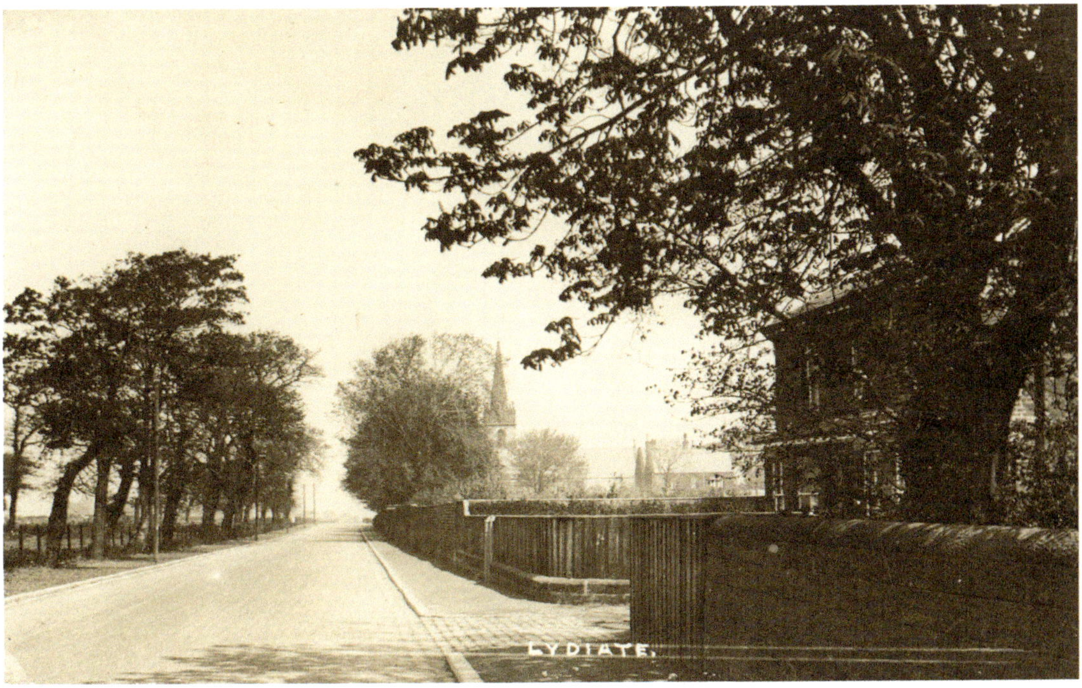

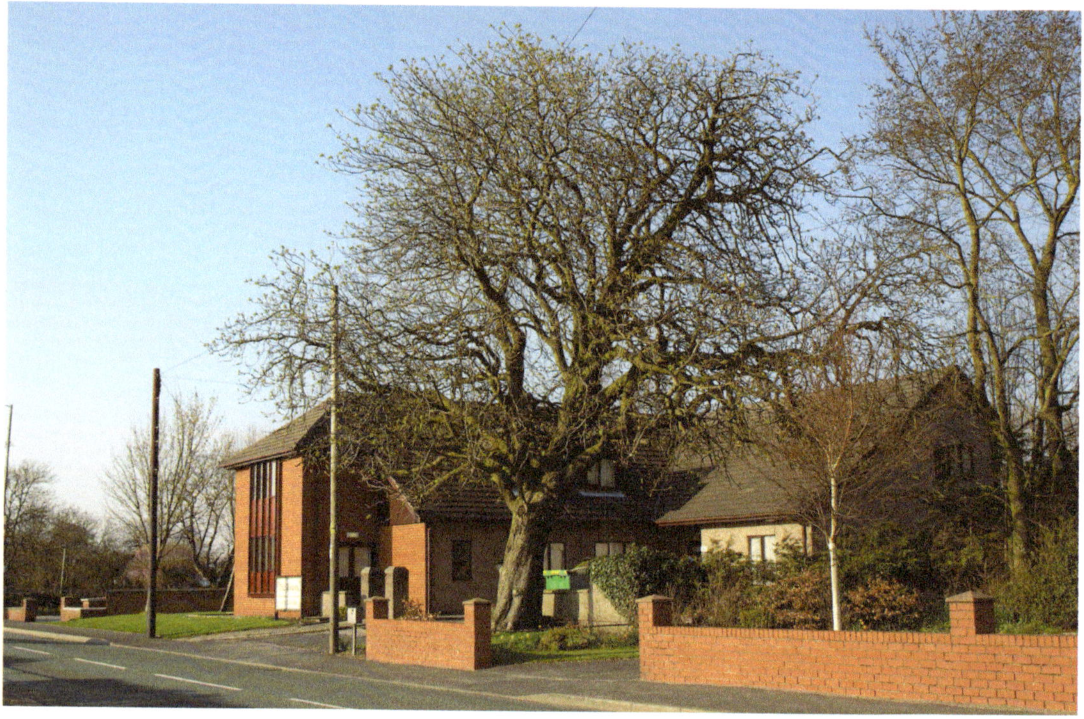

A Village School

St Thomas' Church of England School, with the headmaster's residence to the right, was erected by public subscription in 1839. All but a small wall was demolished about 150 years later, and the Shieling Care Home was built on the site. However, the tree still faithfully guards the entrance, behind the brick wall that has replaced the fine hedge.

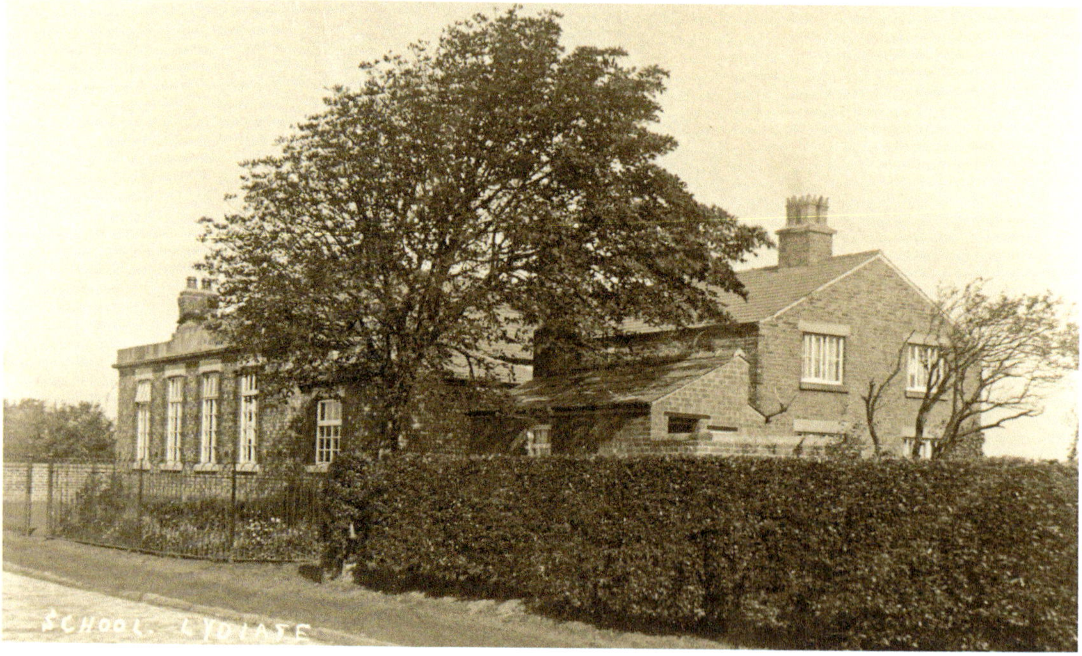

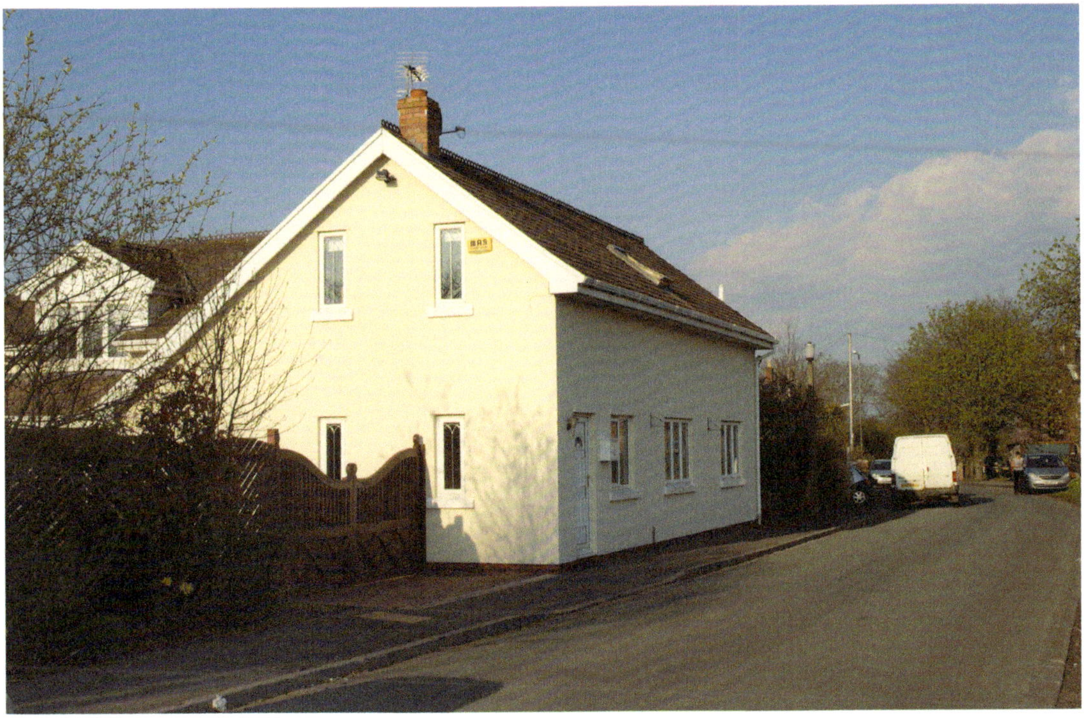

Station Road

Comparing this view of Rose Cottage at the turn of the century to the same location today, it may appear as if the original building still exists. However, when the cottage was renovated, only a very small part was retained. The classic bonnets worn by the ladies, which once upon a time were normal headwear in the area, have also vanished.

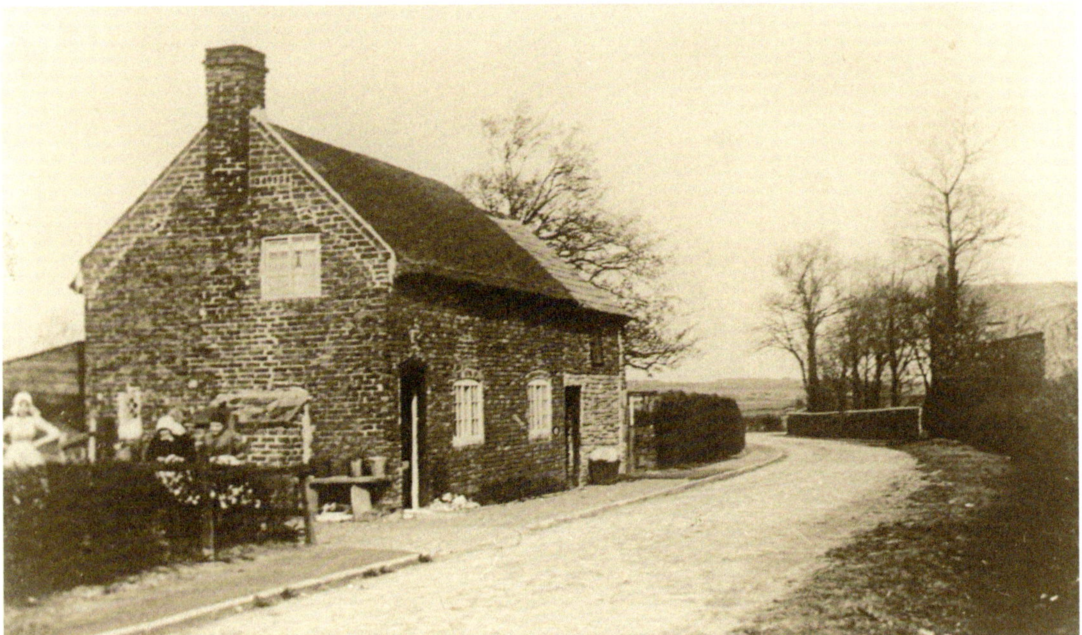

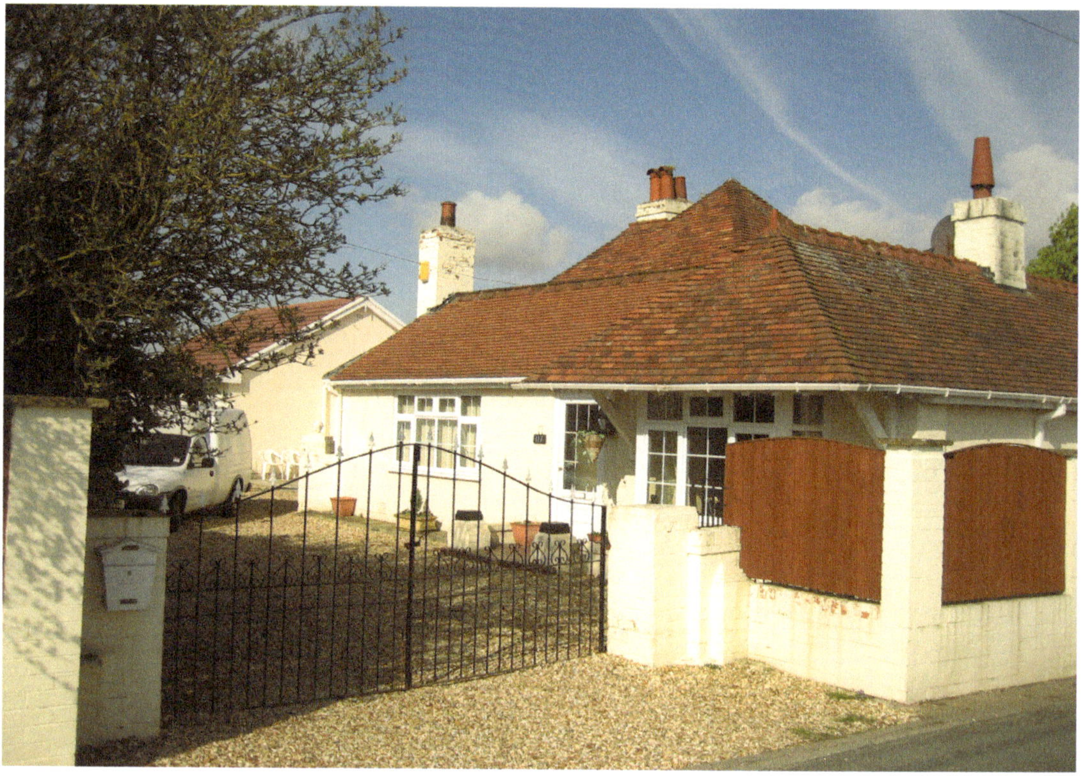

Pilling Lane

The hedge in front of Swift's Cottage has been replaced by a large wall which makes it difficult to see the original building, but it is apparent that some of the original structure still exists in the extension.

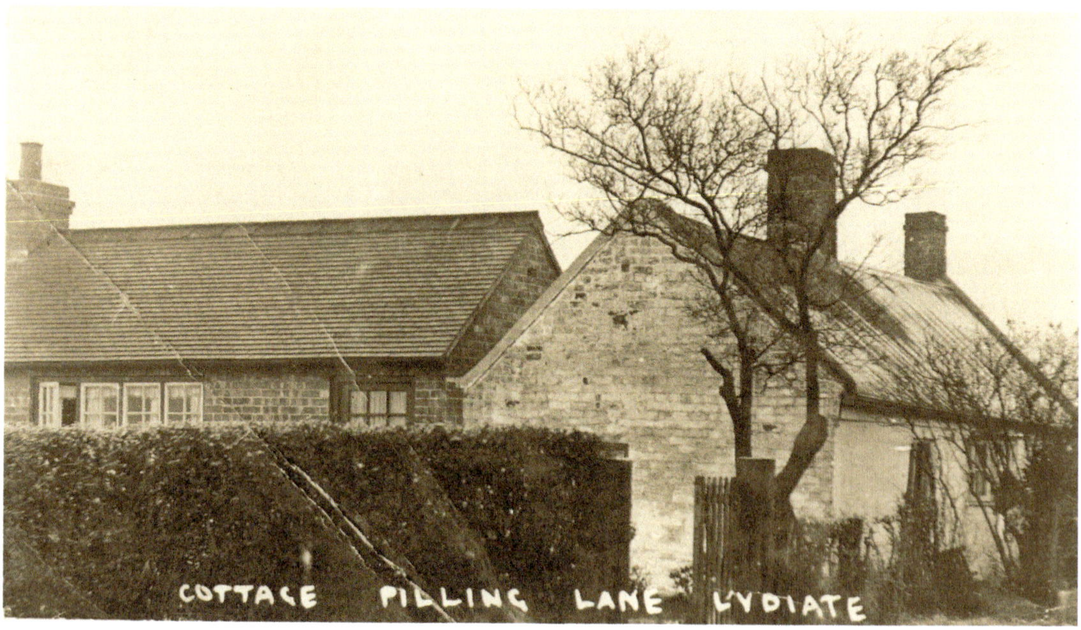

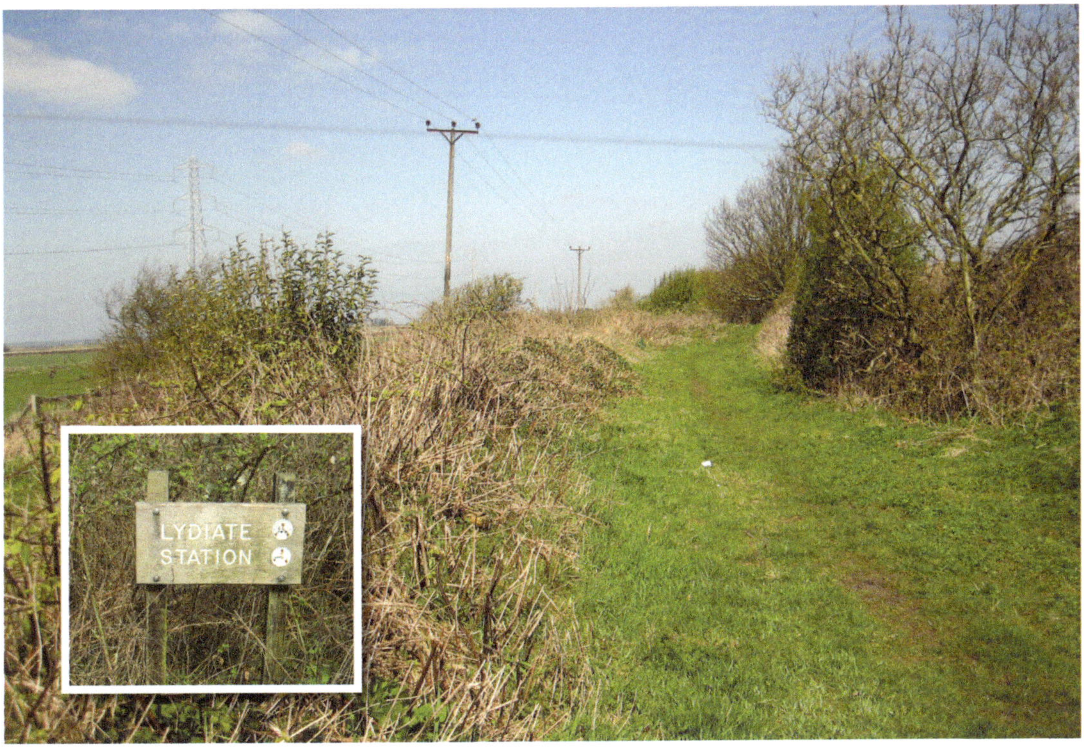

Lydiate Station

The station was actually in Altcar and opened in 1884 on the Southport & Cheshire Lines Extension Railway. It remained in use until the line closed in 1952. Today, apart from the staff cottages, nothing exists of the station and the lines and the area is covered by overgrown bushes. The Trans-Pennine Trail passes along the route of the former line.

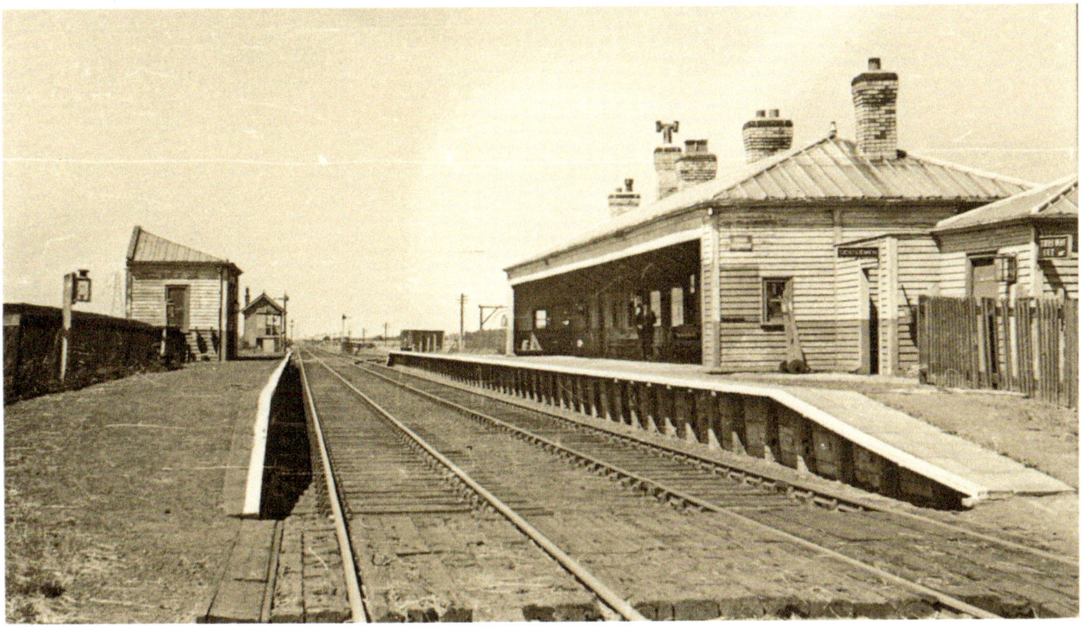

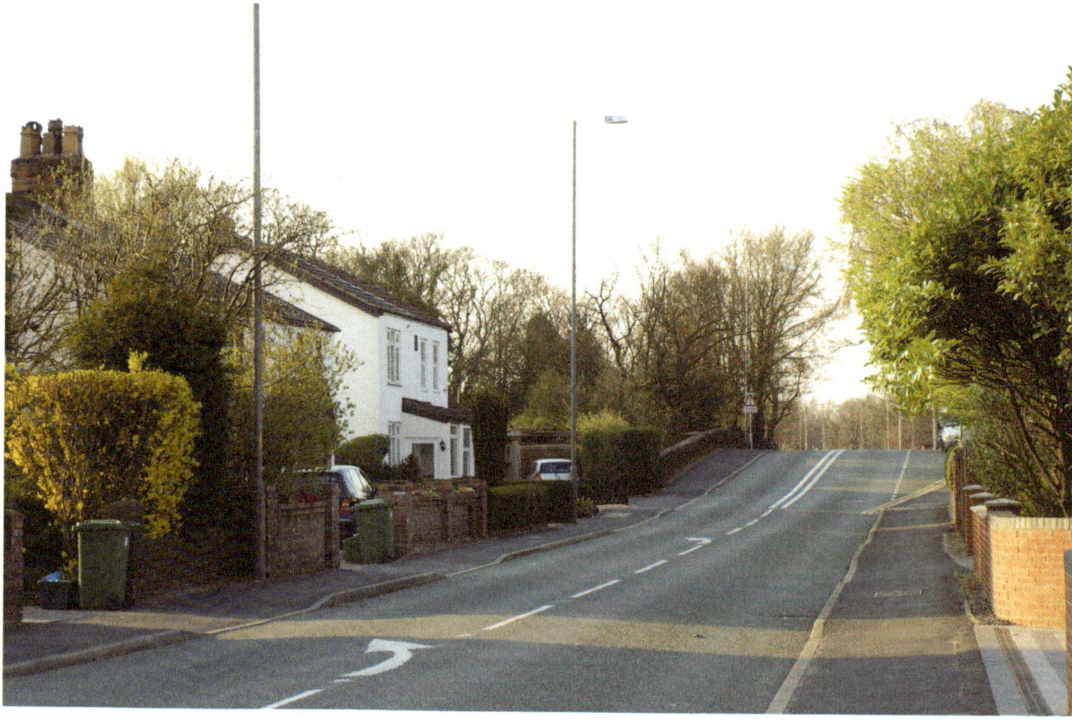

Southport Road Approaching the Canal Bridge from Maghull

The volume of traffic has led to the road being widened, especially at the bridge, which was renovated in 1930, and a pavement is now on both sides. The house standing on its own is now one of a row of houses, and they are hidden behind the trees.

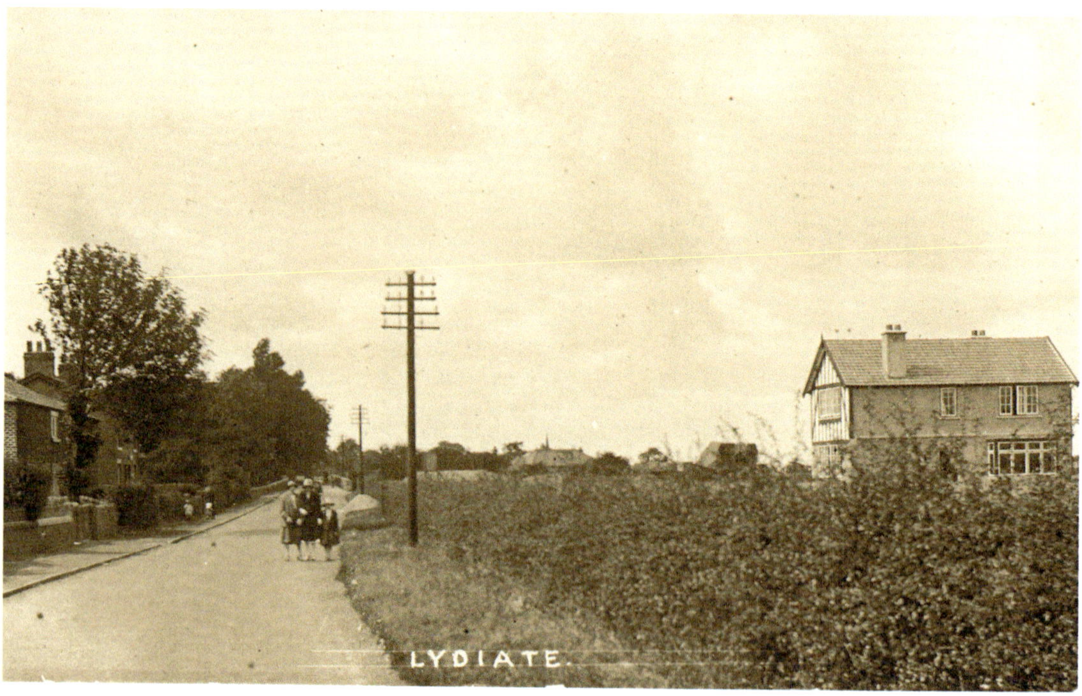

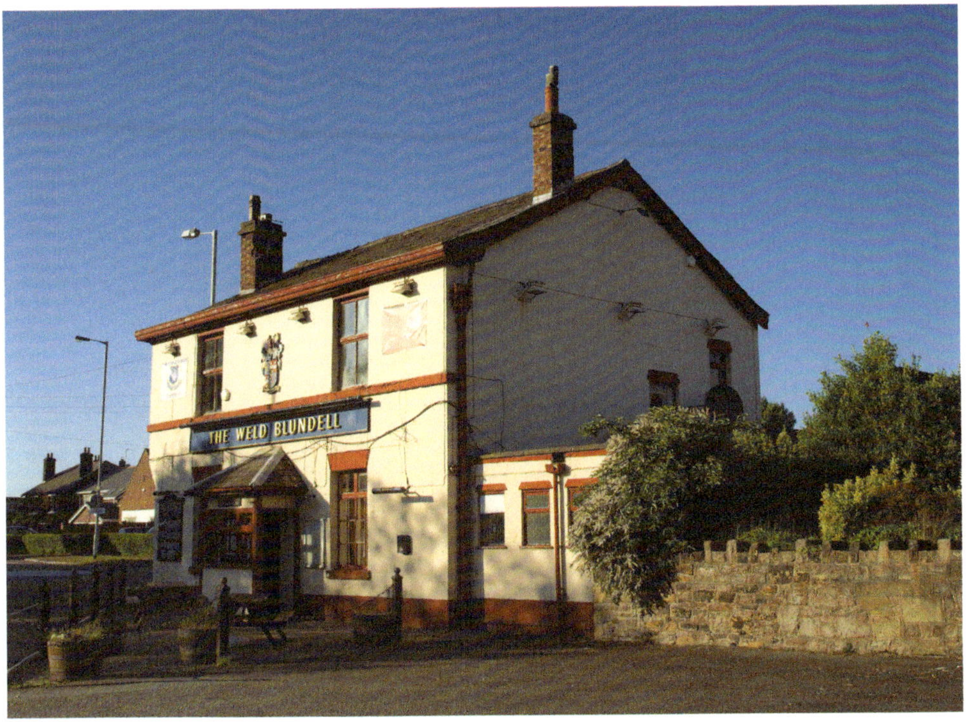

The New Lollie

Almost unchanged for over 150 years, The Weld Blundell Arms, known locally as the New Lollie (while the Scotch Piper is the Old Lollie) is situated in Southport Road opposite the small village green. It has become a typical example of modern tastes and advertising, so it has lost most of its simple charm.

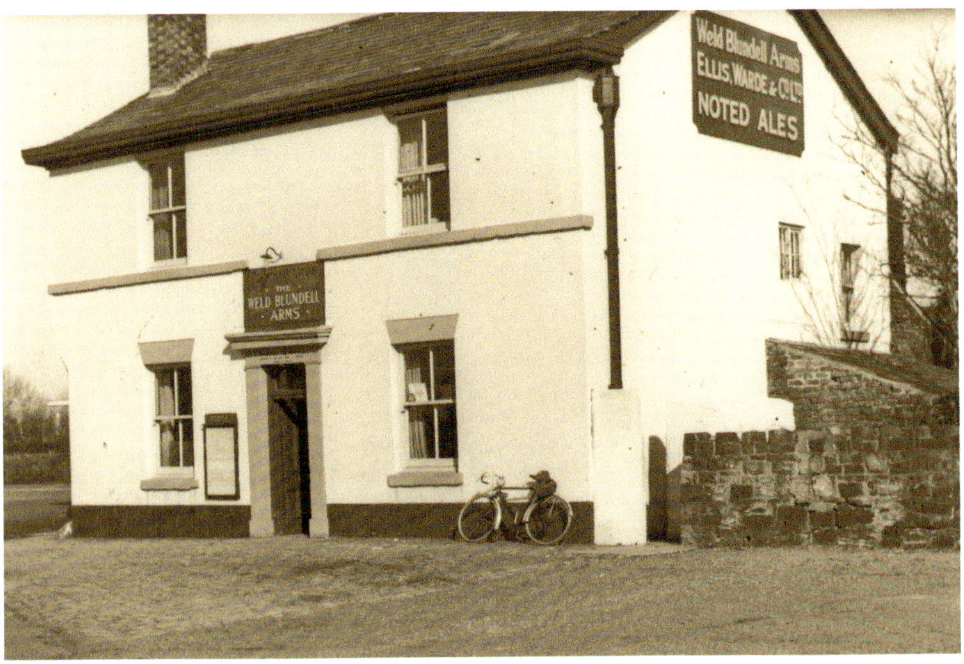

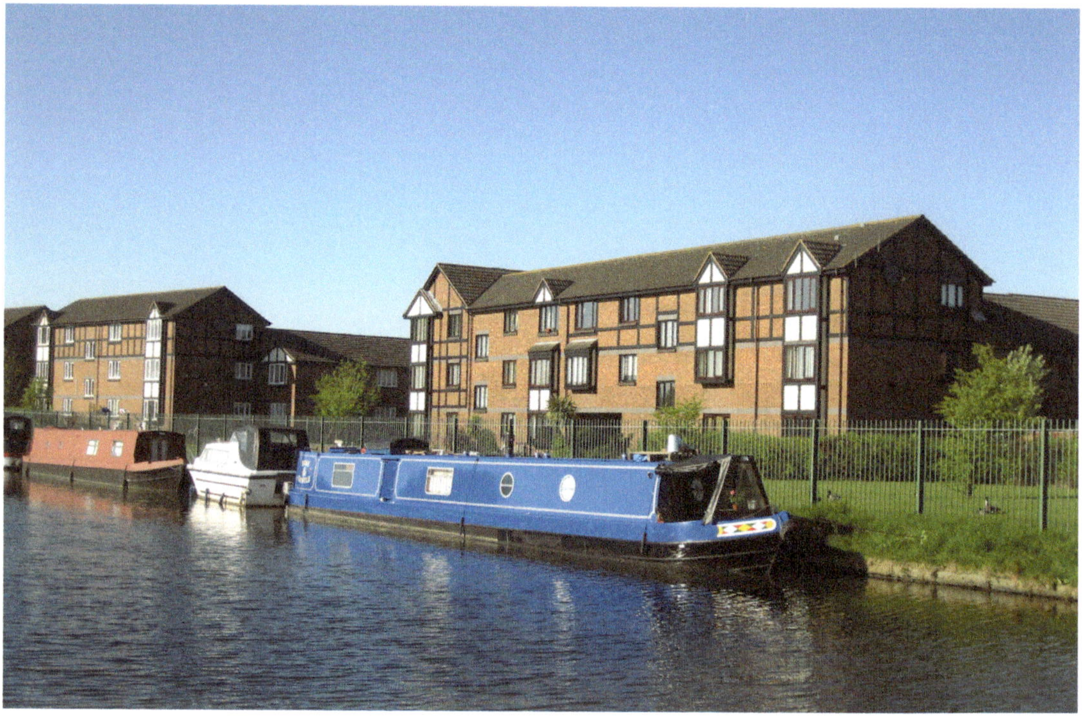

Industrial Lydiate

During the last war, a large area of land between the canal and Southport Road was occupied by many thousands of oil drums, which were cleaned by the Universal Oil Company that had moved from Liverpool to avoid the bombing. The site was eventually cleared, and The Moorings Estate built upon the land.

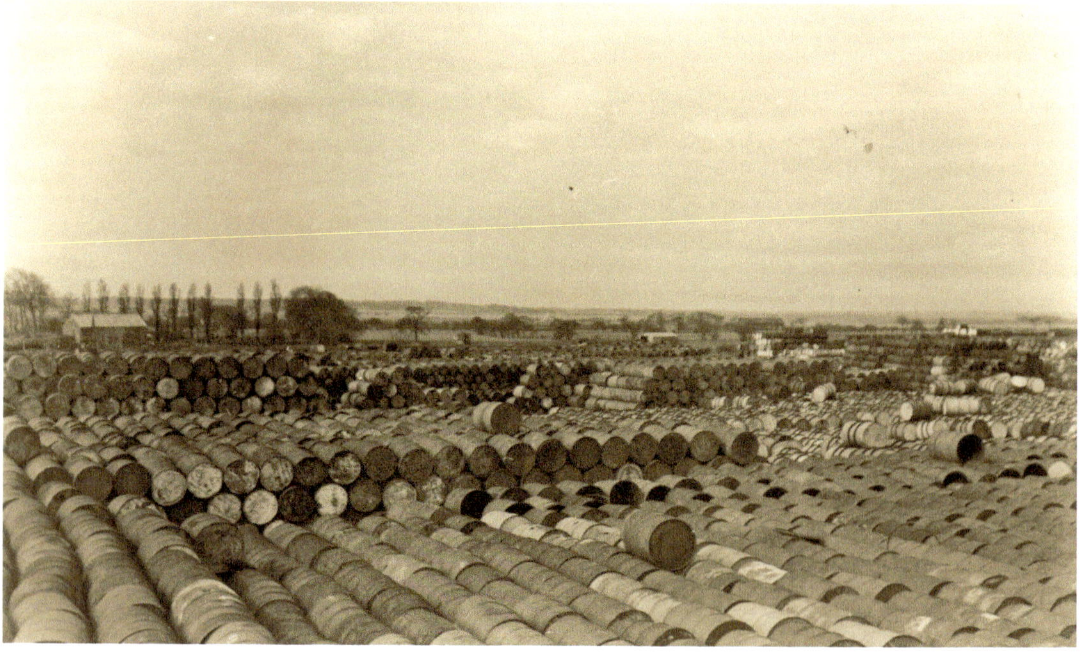

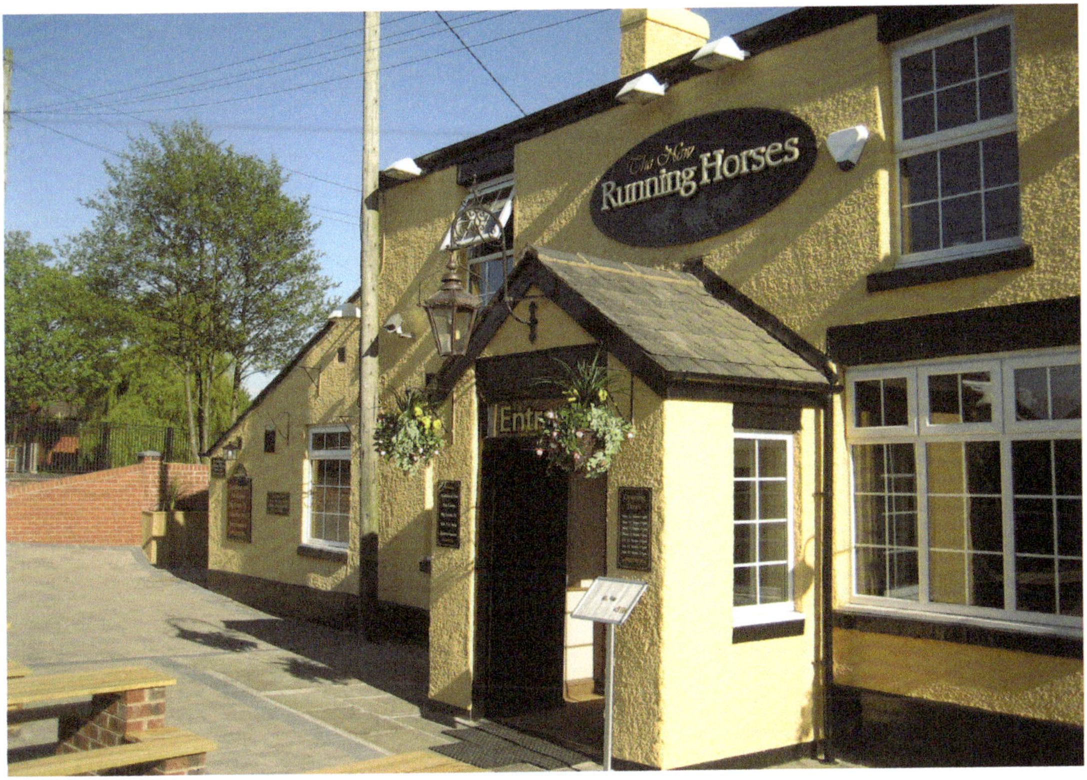

A Relic of the Canal Heydays

The Running Horses Inn is a reminder of the days when horses were an essential part of canal life. The landlord's family are seen outside of the public house in the 1920s, and the scene can be easily recognised despite a recent major renovation.

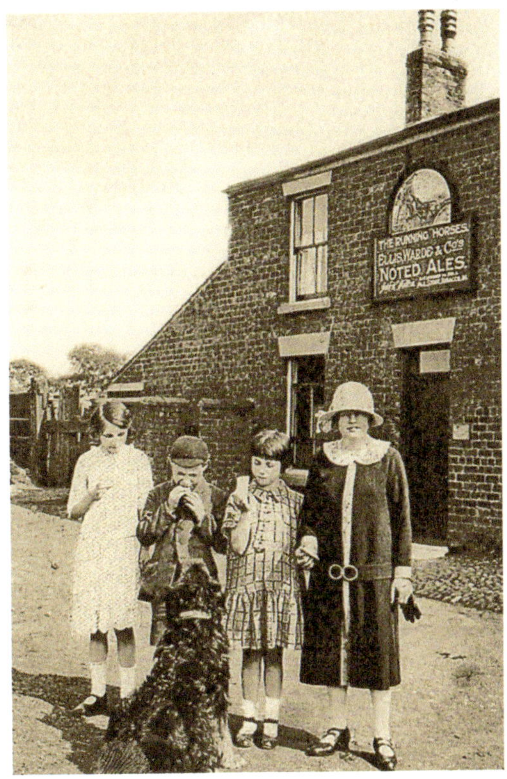

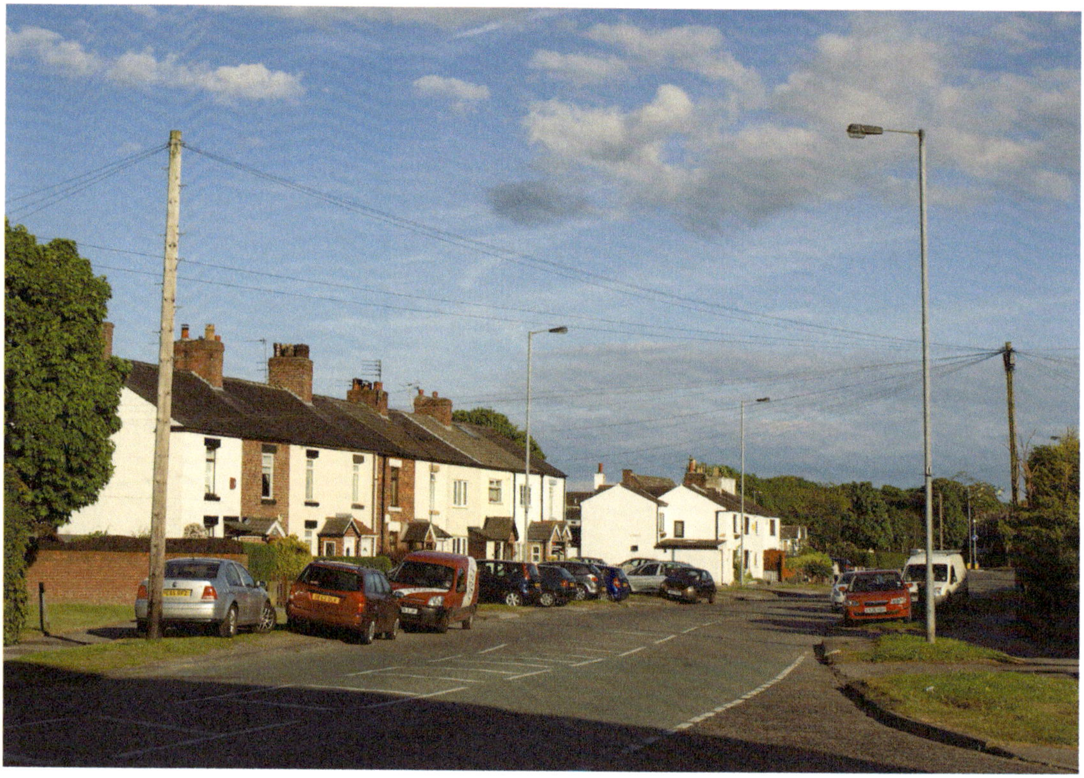

The Junction of Southport Road and Bell's Lane

The bend in the road has been straightened and grass verges added in front of the terrace of Pye's Cottages, most of which appear to have new porches, to allow cars to park.

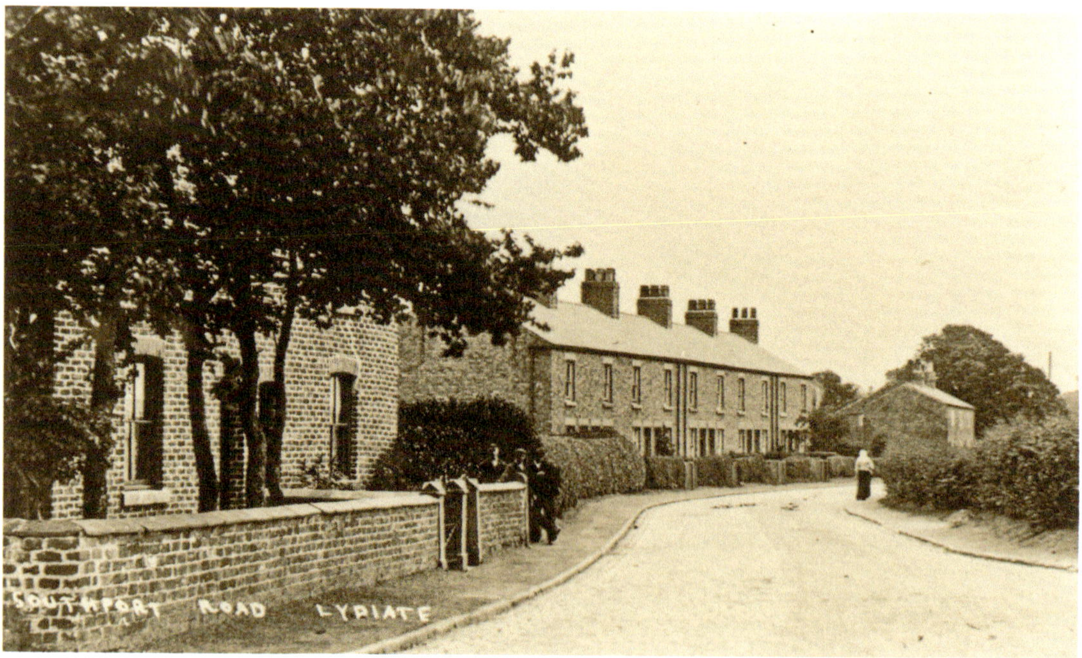

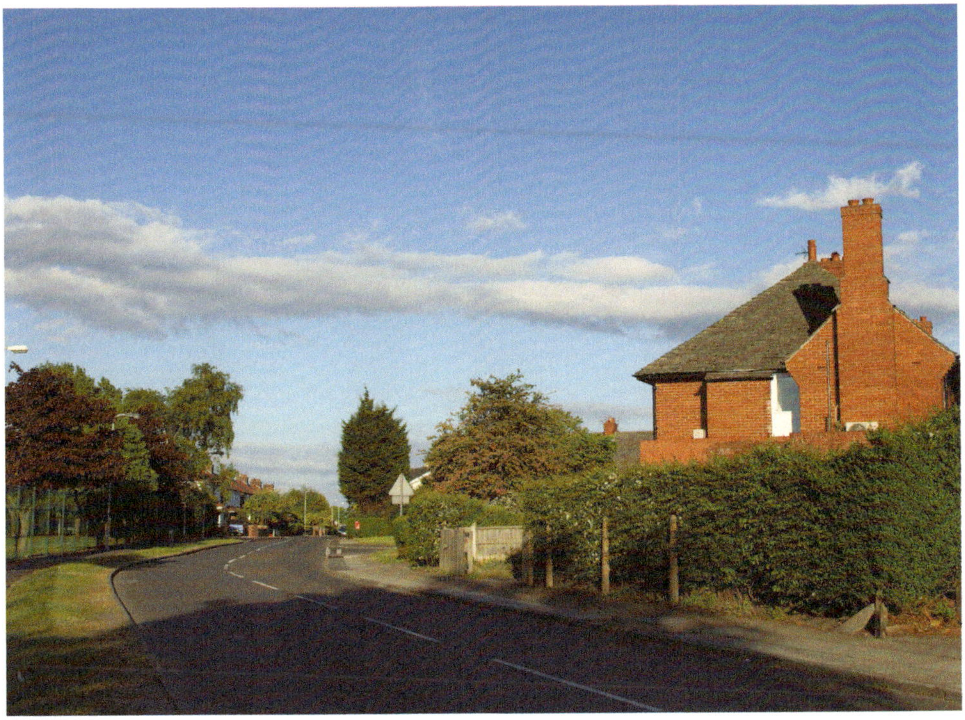

Lambshear Lane

The schoolgirls are probably returning from Lambshear Lane School to the new estate, the entrance to which is obscured. There is a new traffic sign and the telephone box has gone. The hedge on the left has been replaced by a pavement, with a wire fence surrounding the field of the St Gregory's Catholic Primary School.

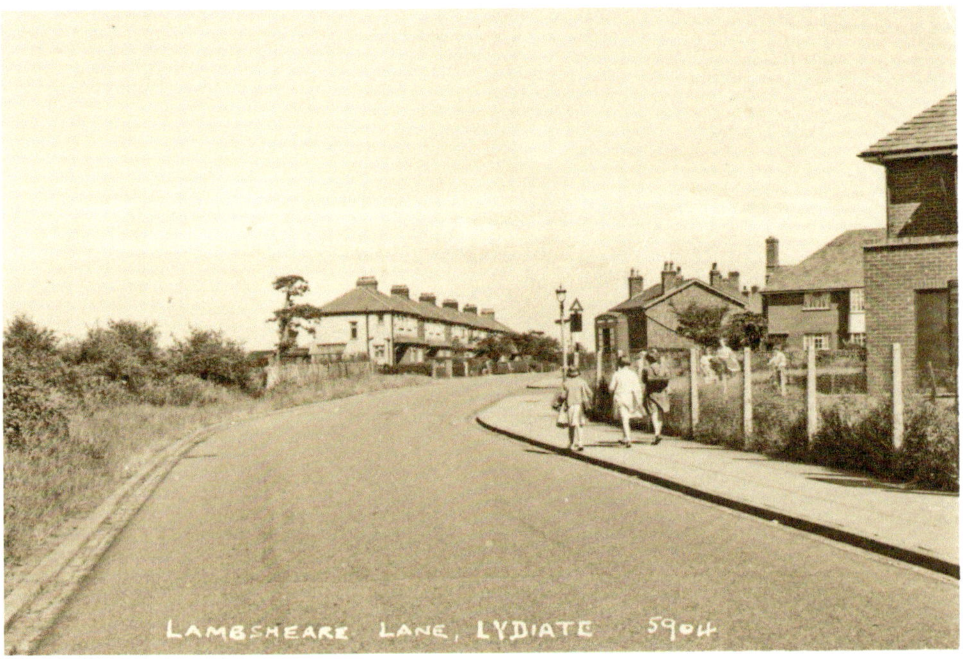

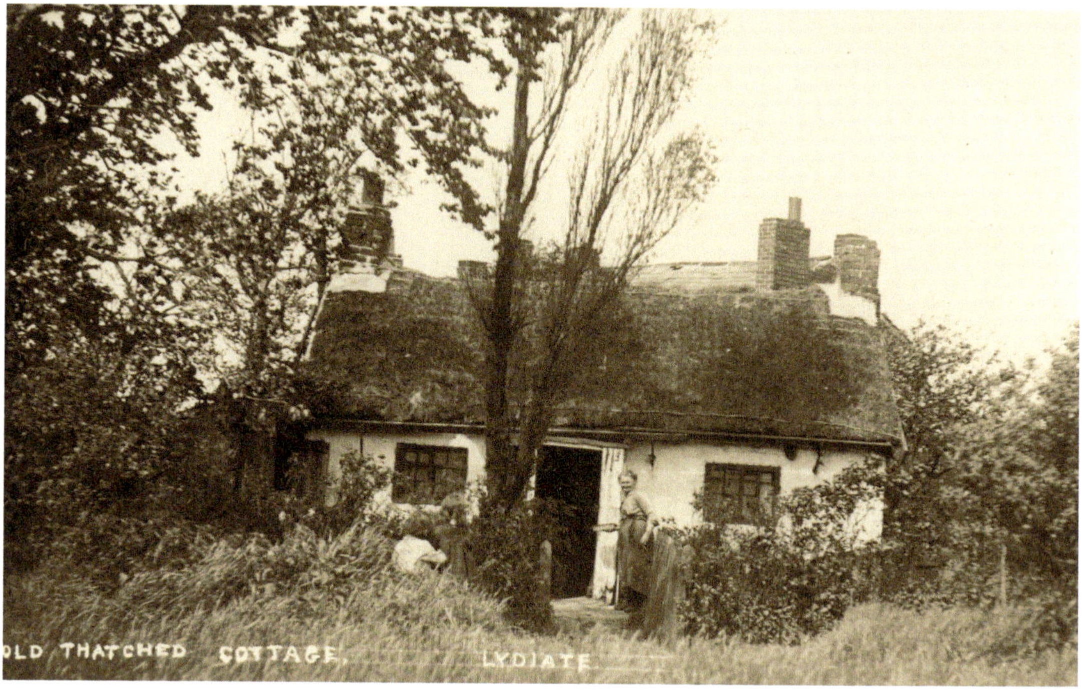

Sandy Lane *c.* 1900

These two contrasting homes were both on Sandy Lane. The thatched cottage with the two mischievous girls almost hidden in the long grass has been demolished. The former farm has been extended and is almost unrecognisable.

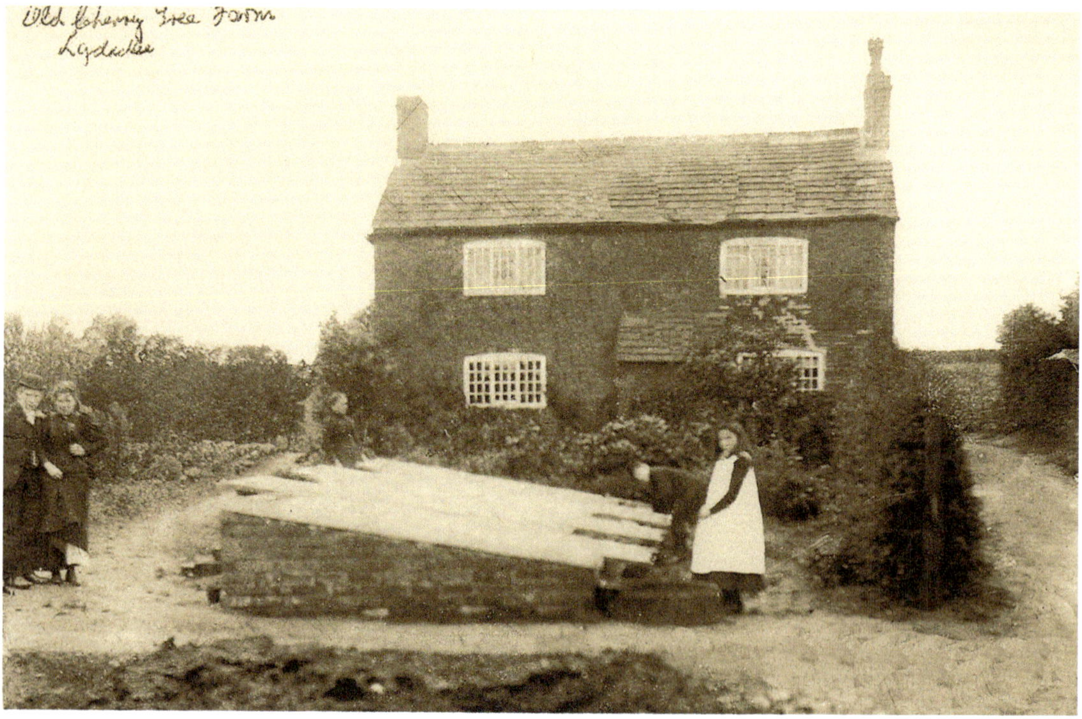

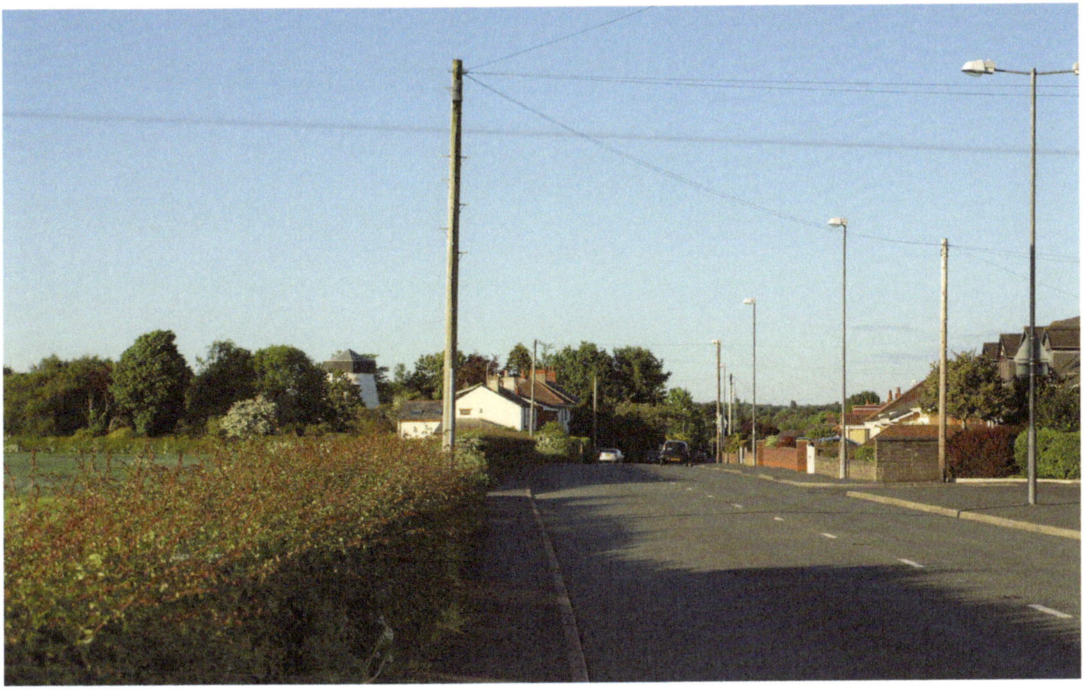

The Turnpike Road to Ormskirk

The windmill standing close to Liverpool Road as it sweeps towards the town boundary is just visible amongst the mature trees. Bungalows close to the site of the turnpike toll bar now occupy the land to the right.

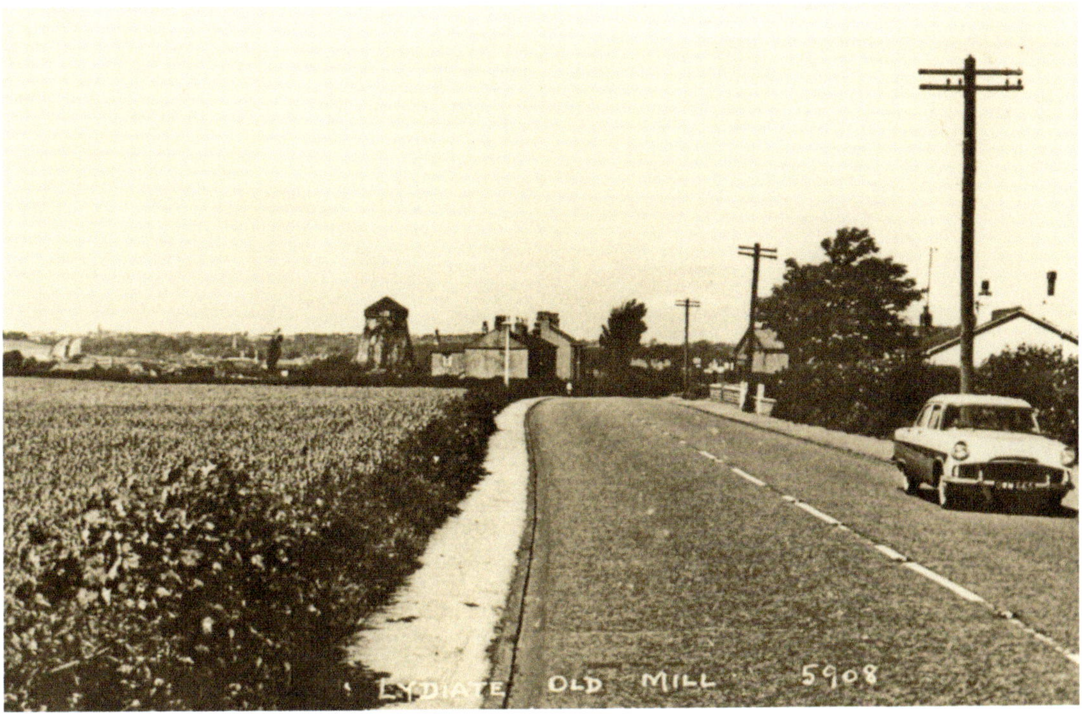

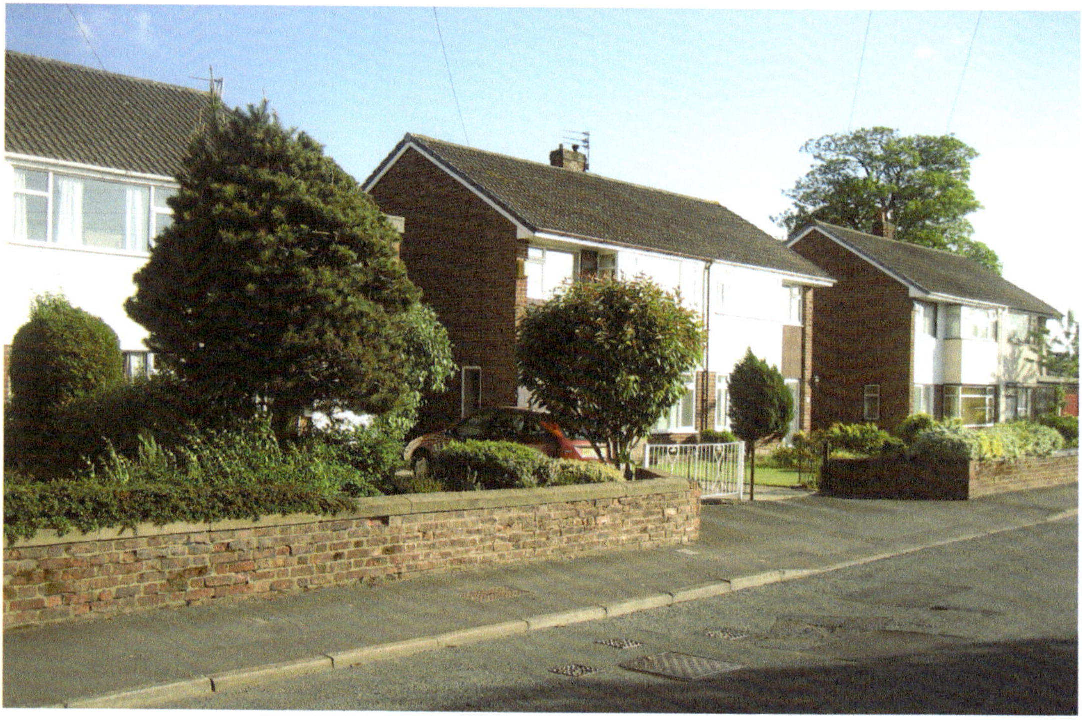

Oakhill House

Previously standing a short distance from the windmill, the house was built by a wealthy stagecoach proprietor opposite his company's stables. It became a nursing home and insurance office before being flattened after the last war. All that remains is the brick garden wall.

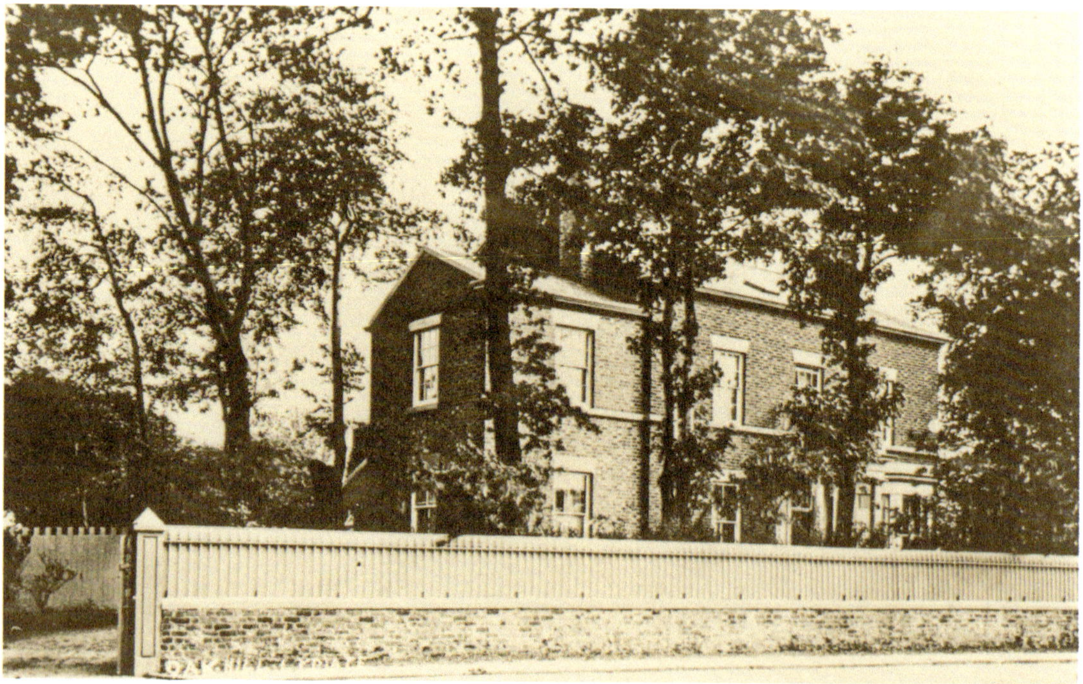

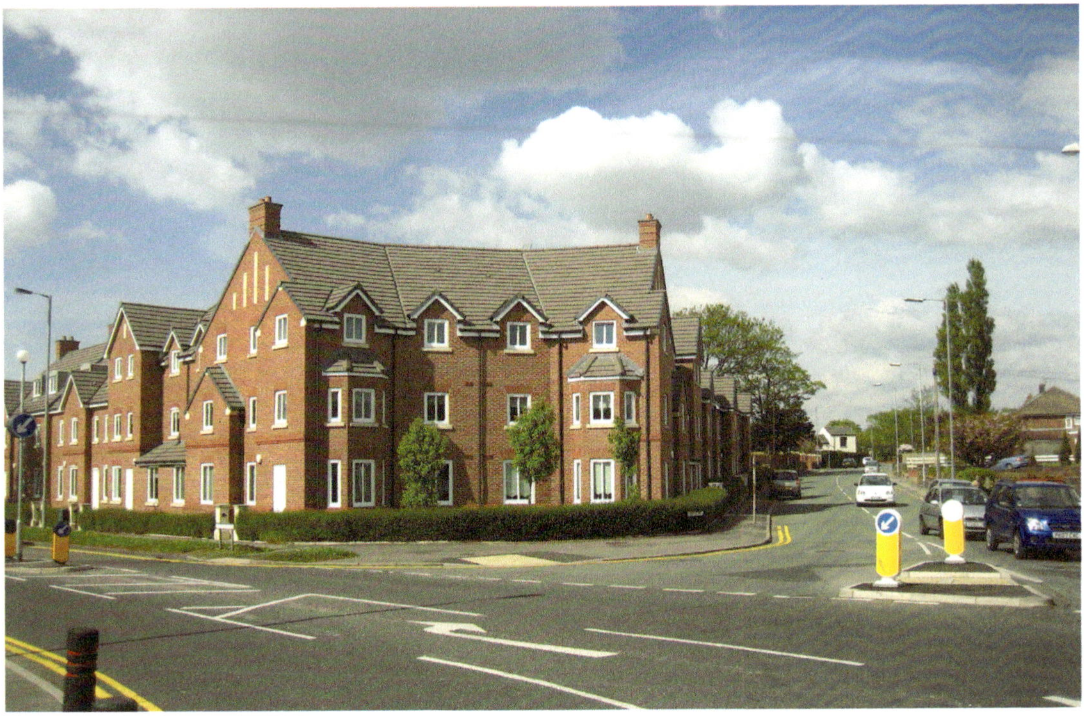

The Corner of Southport Road and Liverpool Road

The town boundary, Maghull Brook, behind which the boys are standing, is now underground. The row of cottages was replaced by a small garage, which expanded until eventually it covered the whole site. However, the erection of a modern block of flats, Aster Court, has left no trace of the garages.

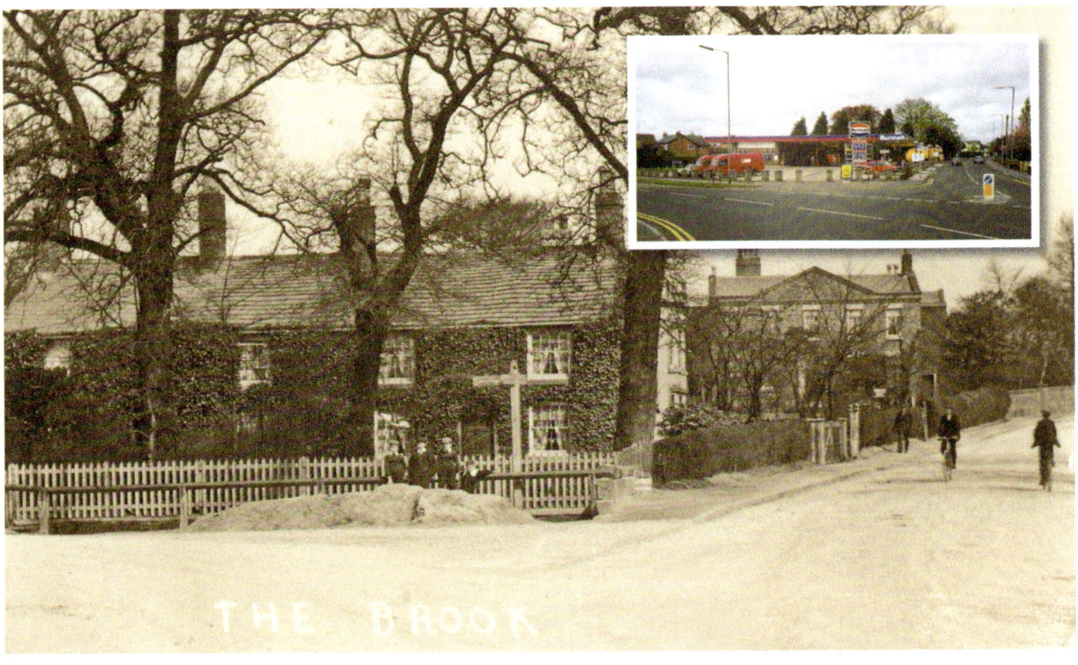

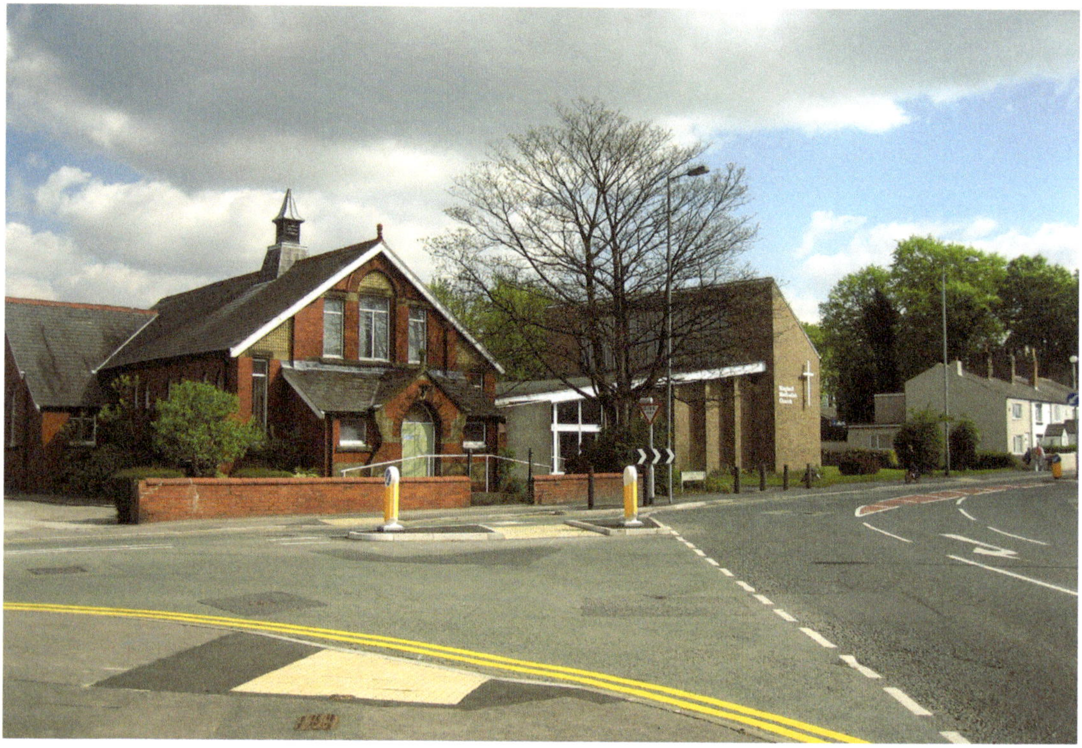

The Methodist Chapel

The first building welcoming the traveller entering Maghull is the chapel, built in 1896 to replace the small nearby hut where services were held. In 1965 an extension of a modern design was built to the chapel, and the original building is now used as a meeting hall.

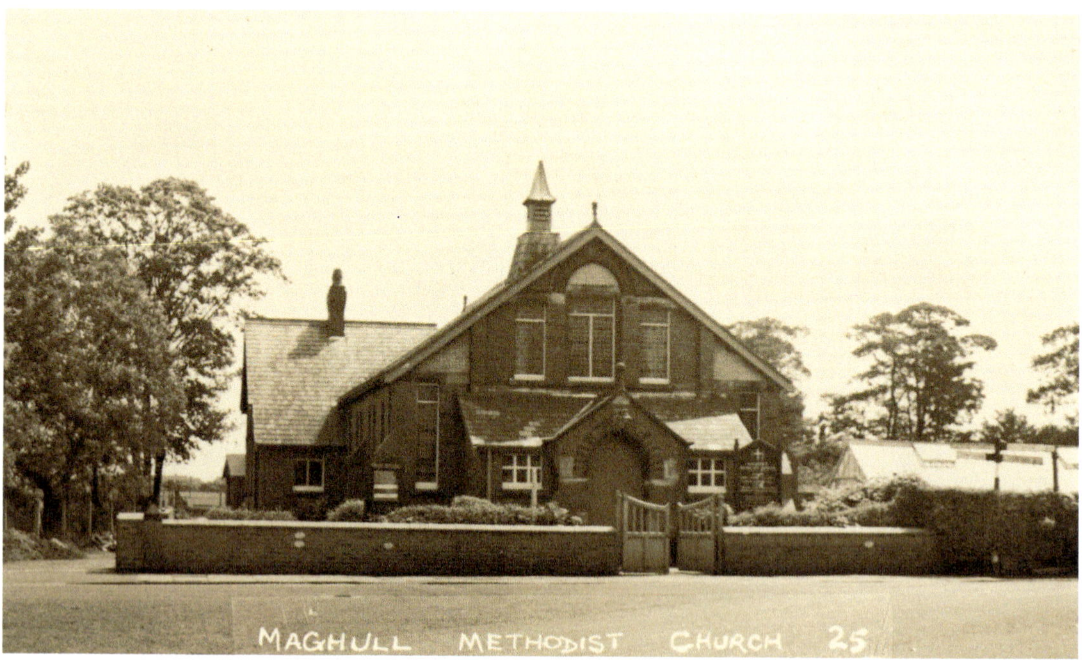

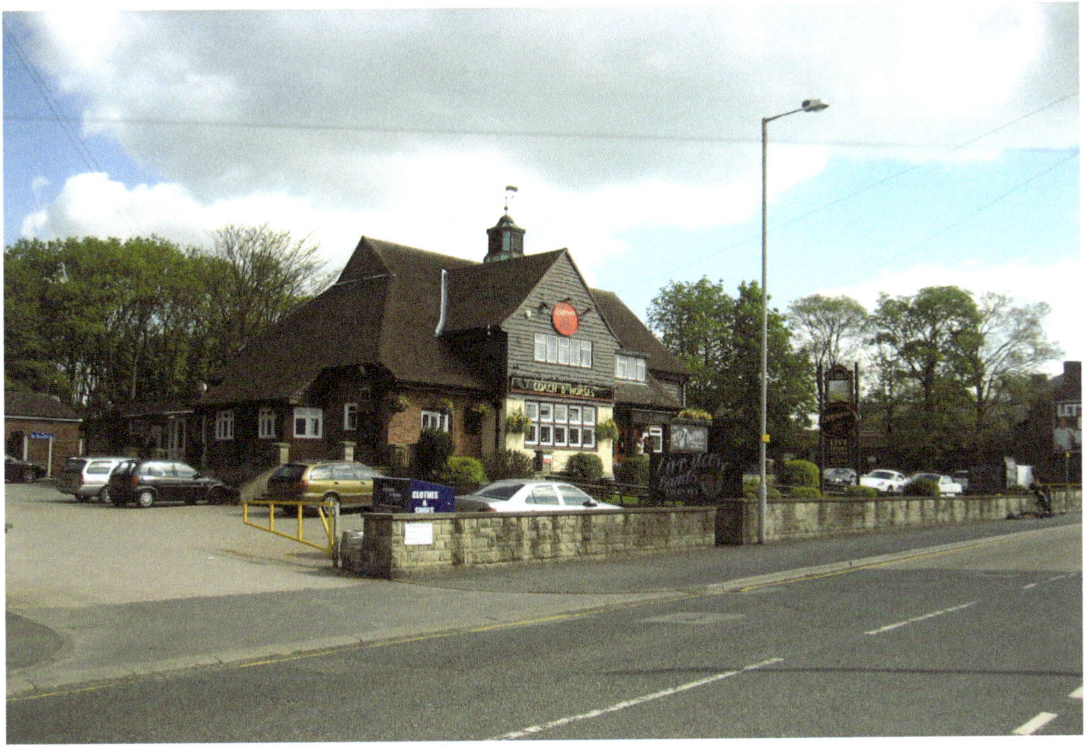

The Gentleman's Residence

The impressive house known as Woodland Mount was demolished in 1961, and the new Coach and Horses Hotel was built on the raised land from which the original house got its name. The hotel is still surrounded by the same beautiful trees.

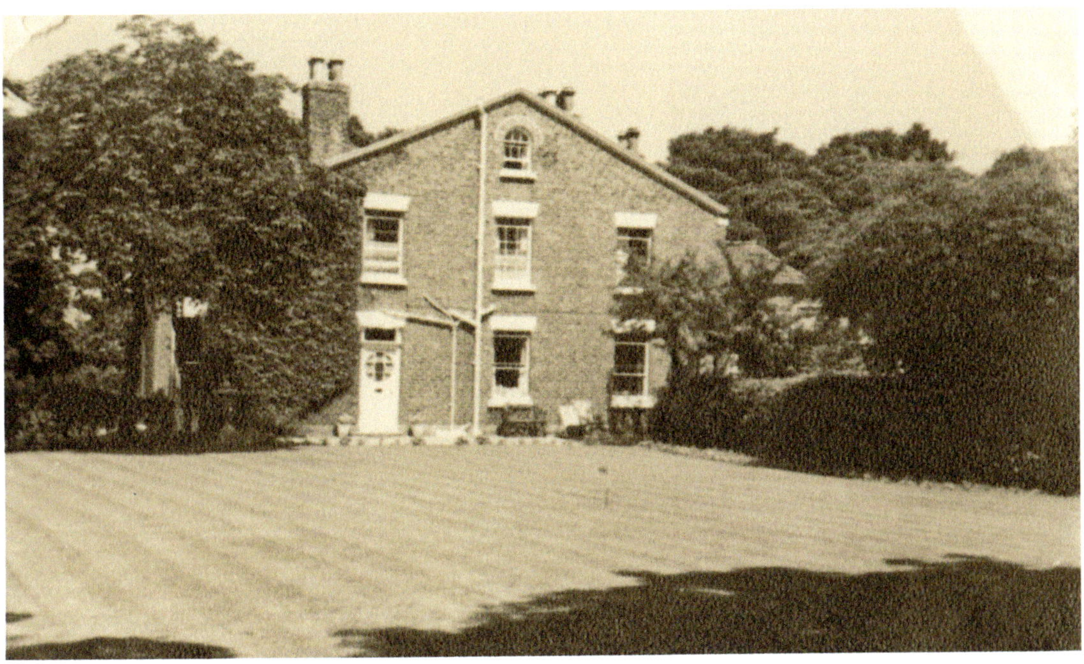

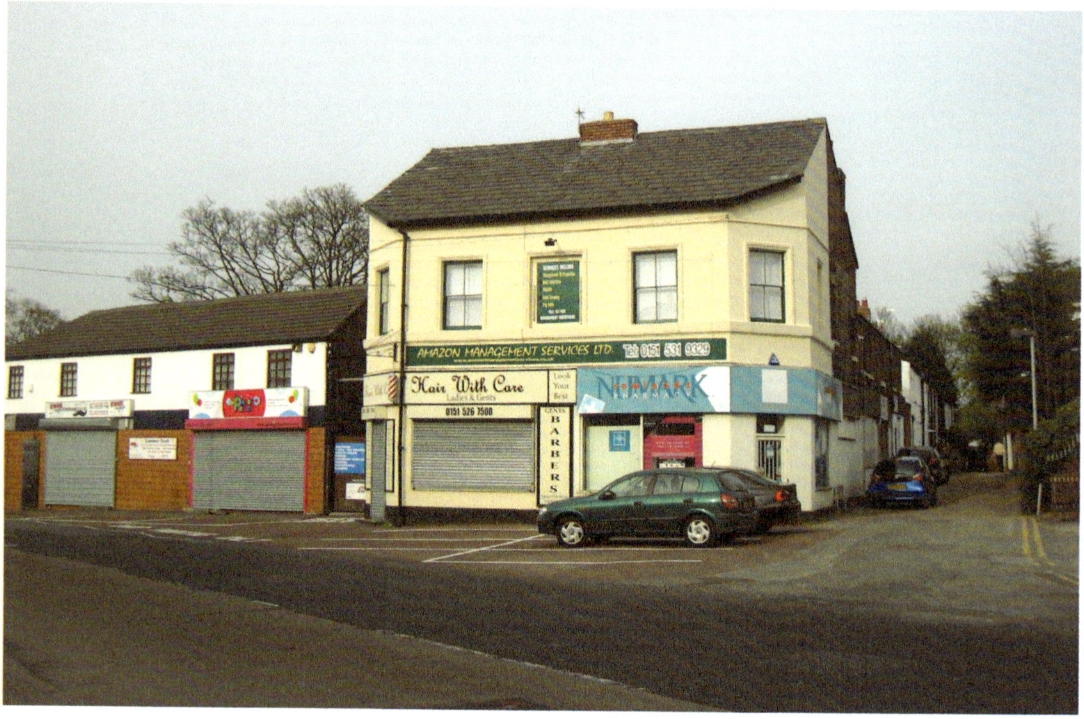

The Original Coach and Horses Hotel

The name recalls the mail coach days when the Liverpool to Preston Turnpike passed through the two towns. Almost 200 years old, the original hotel, which has been owned by many different local breweries, was converted into shops when the licence was transferred to the new hotel with the same name.

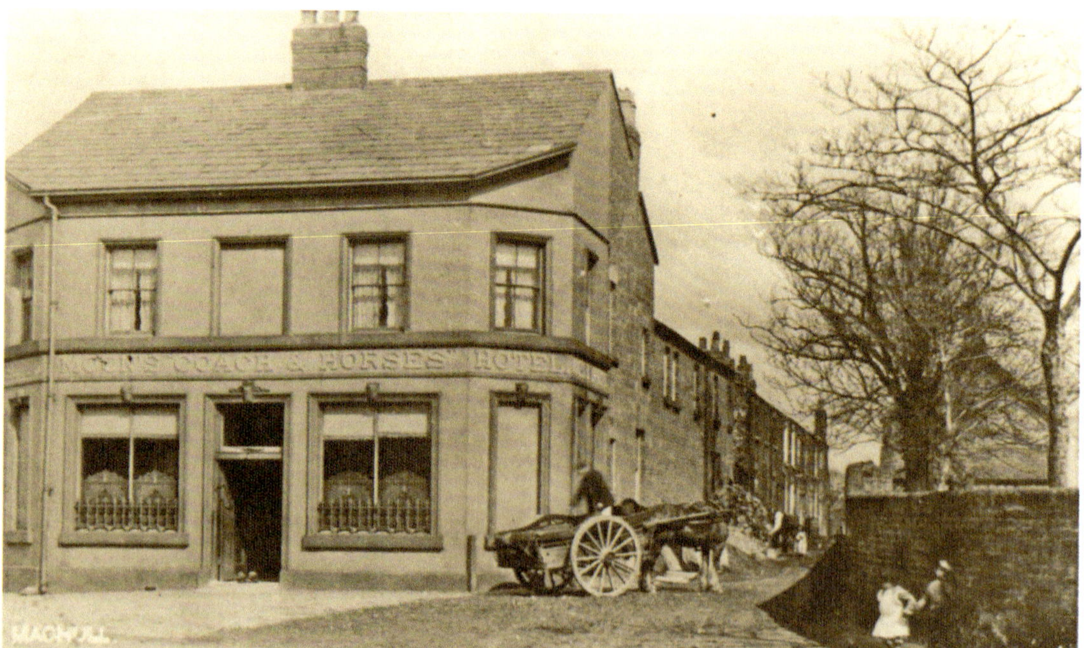

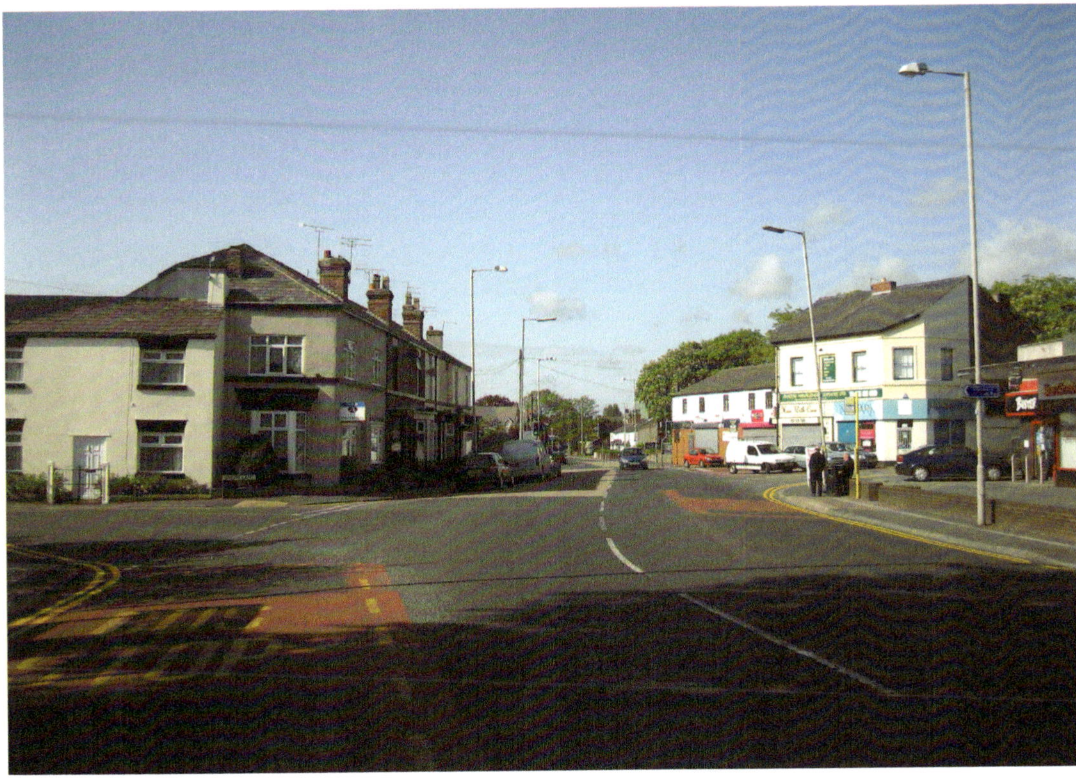

The Junction of Liverpool Road North and Green Lane

The widest part of the old turnpike seems to be little changed. The field wall on the right has been demolished, and shops erected on the field.

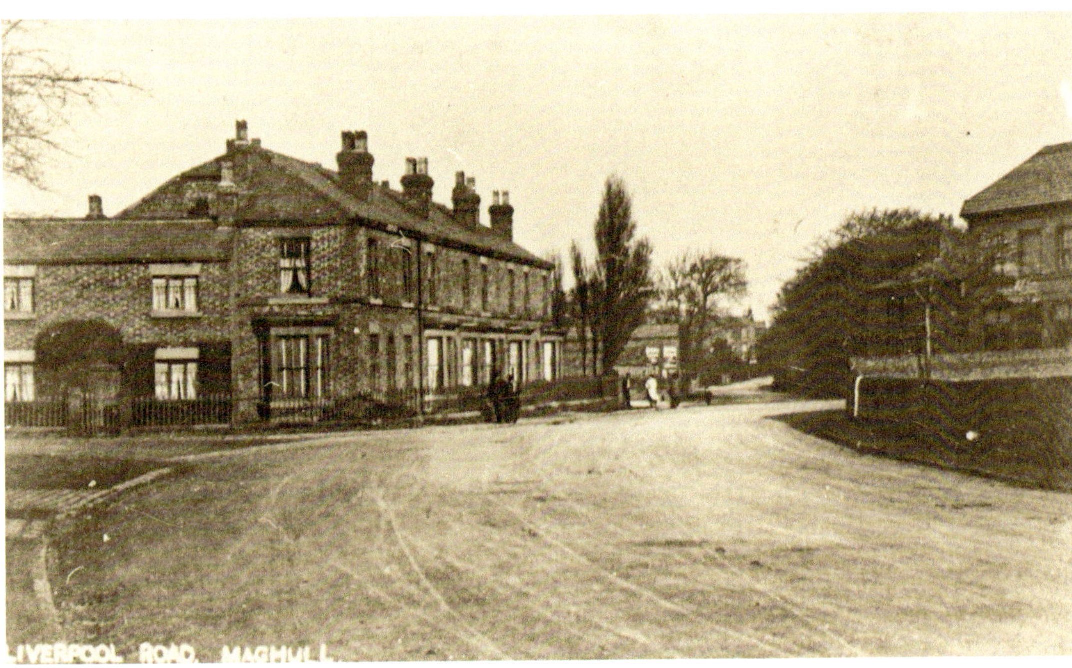

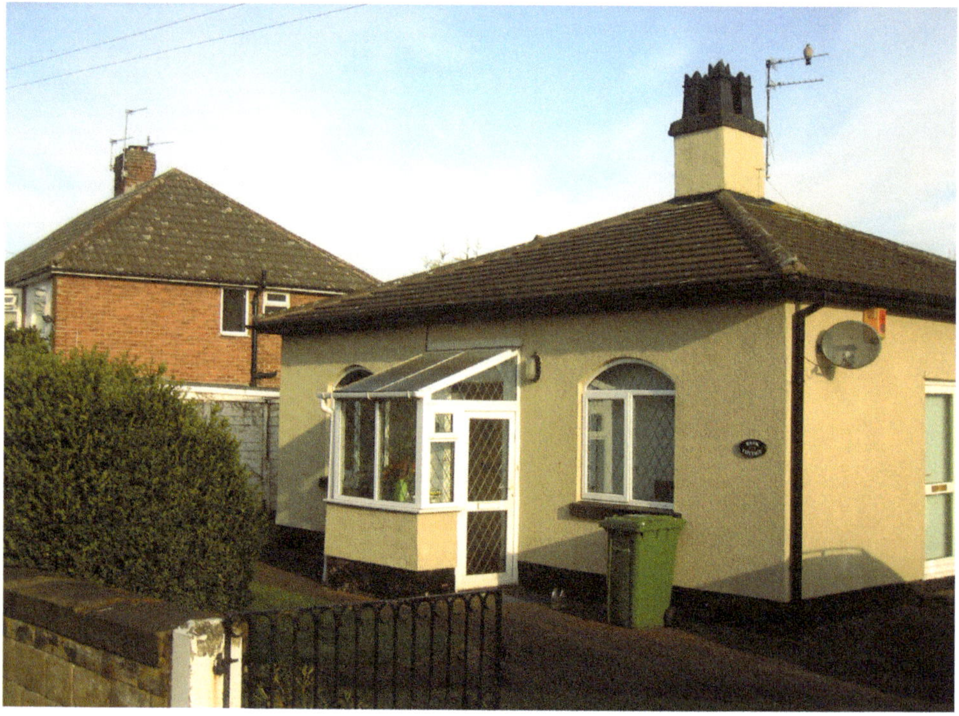

Green Lane

Bank House was situated in the beautiful country lane on the edge of Maghull, and the former site is now occupied by Rigby Road. Bank Cottage, which stood at the entrance to the estate, survives with a modern porch and windows.

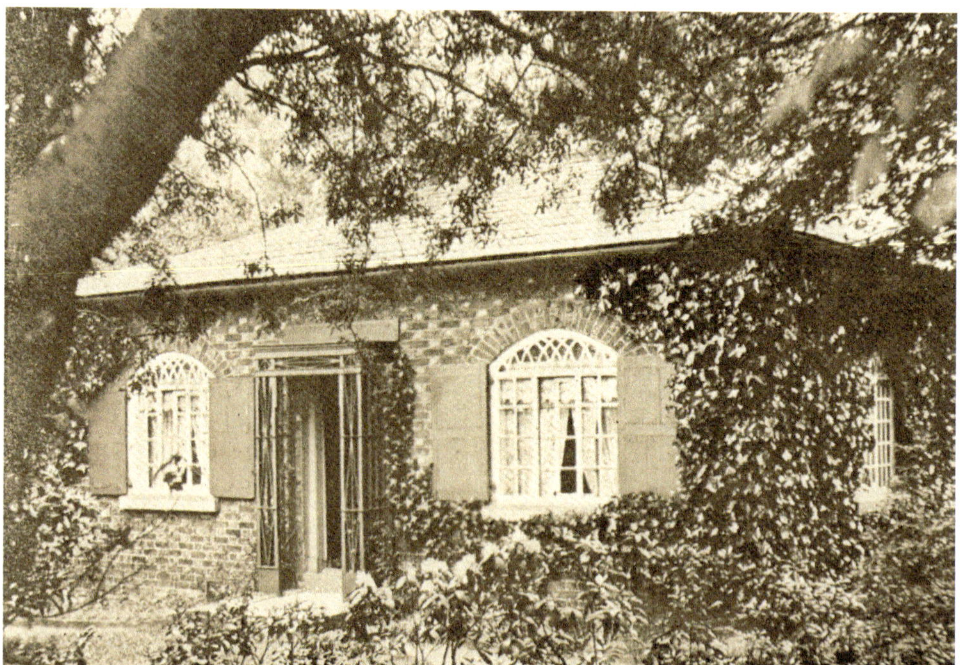

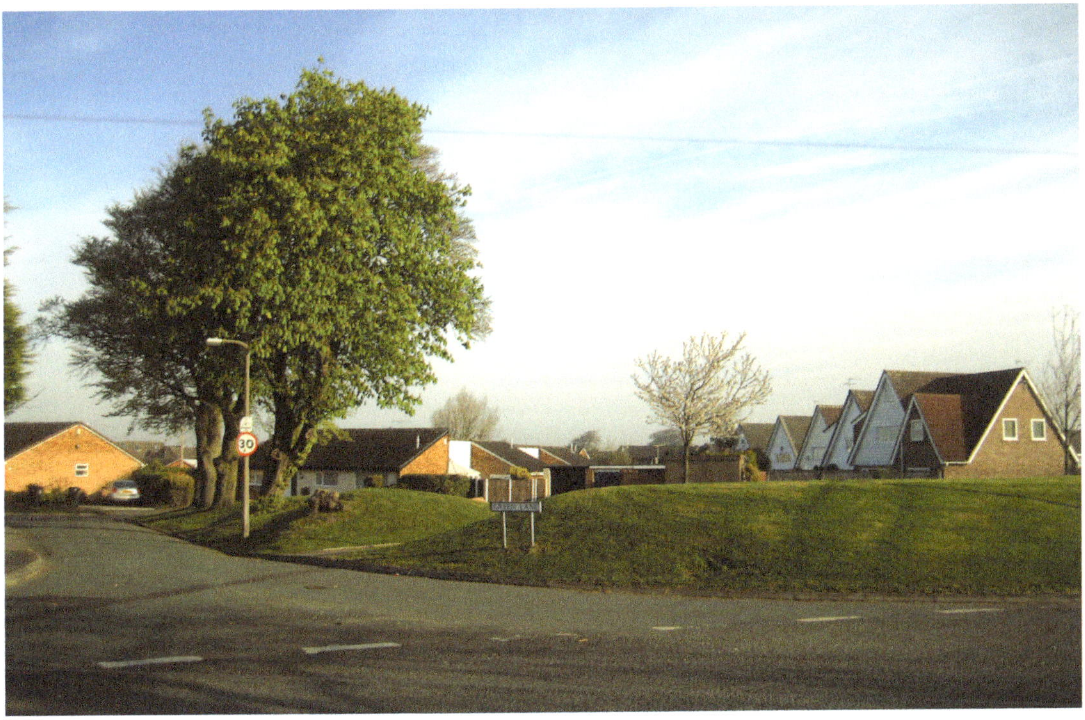

The Result of New House Building

One of the over thirty farms that were thriving in Maghull during the nineteenth century, the impressive Stone Barn Farm was demolished when the Green Park Estate was planned during the 1960s, and all that remains is a short road leading to a small mound.

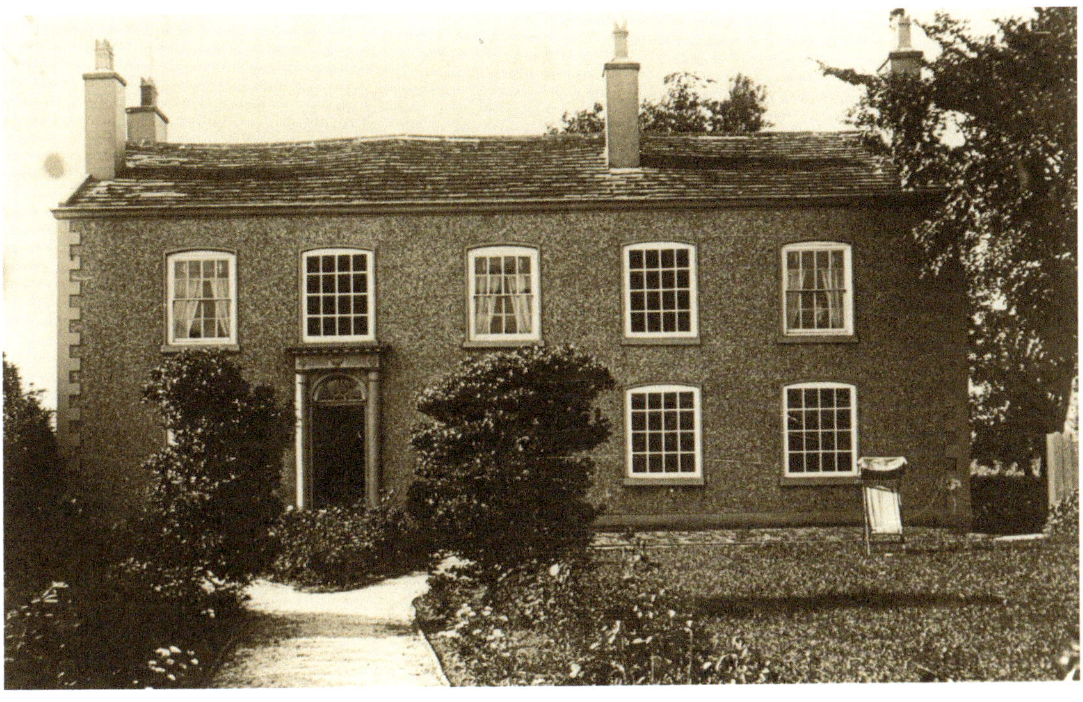

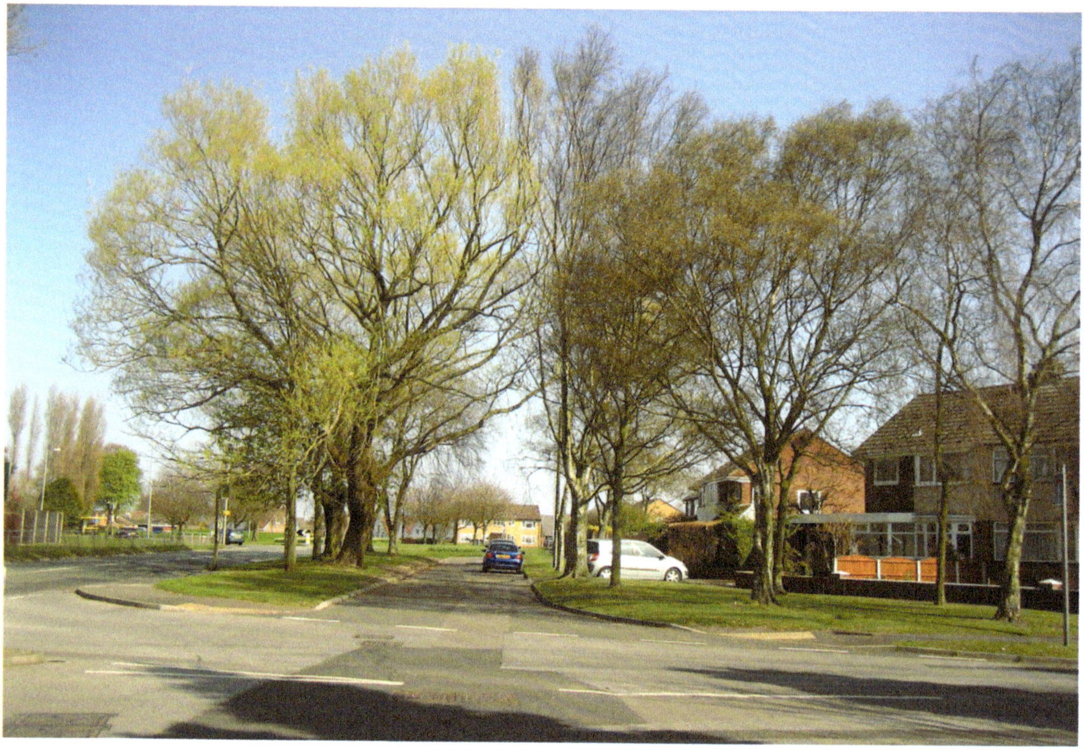

The Junction of Green Lane with Shop Lane

The land on which the old house, Lime Cottage, and adjacent shop, which gave the name to Shop Lane, stood has had a new road driven through, and the original Green Lane is now a slip road.

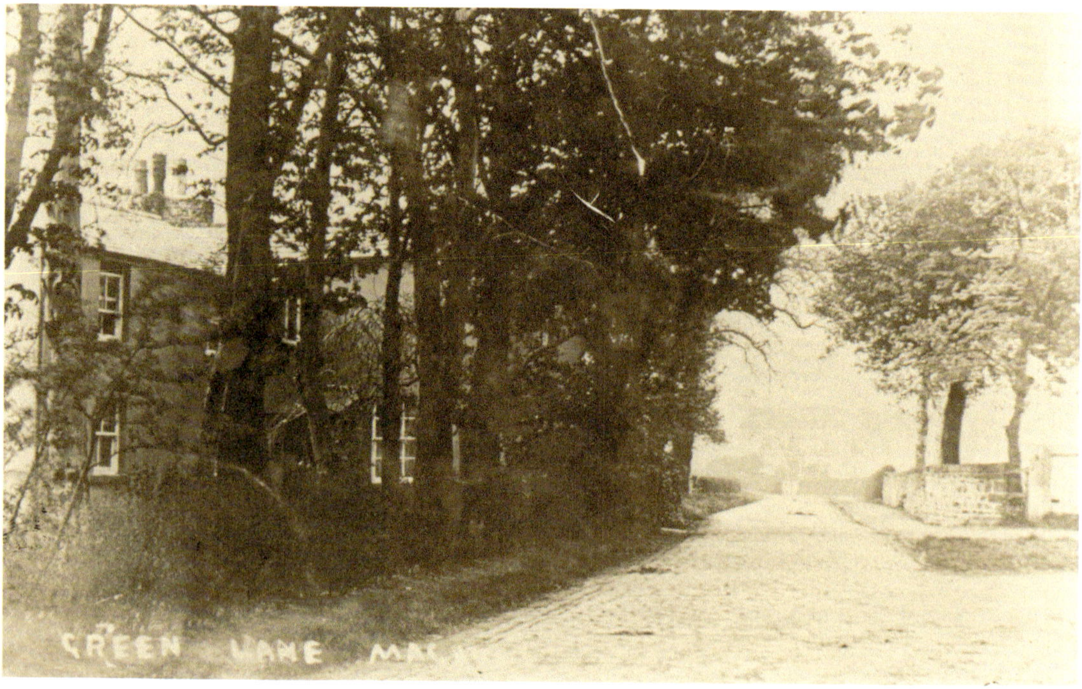

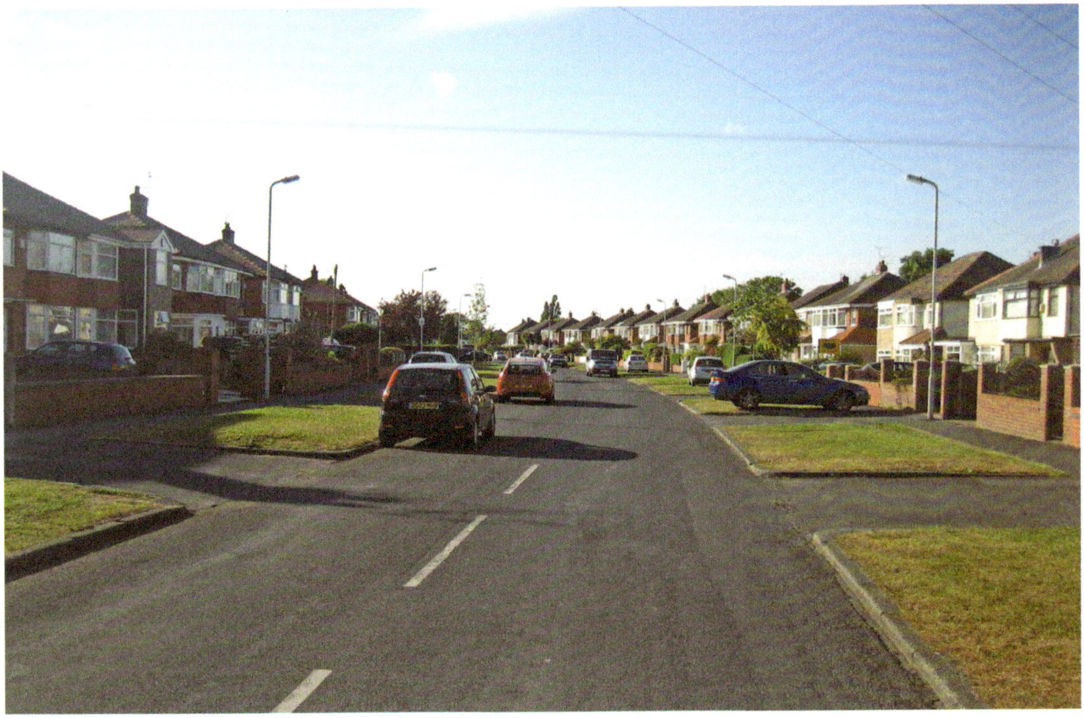

The End of the War

At this merry party, the residents of Clent Avenue are celebrating Victory in Europe during the summer of 1945. The tidy grass verges still line the road, and the garden walls which are visible seem unchanged. I wonder what became of the young man making the 'V' sign.

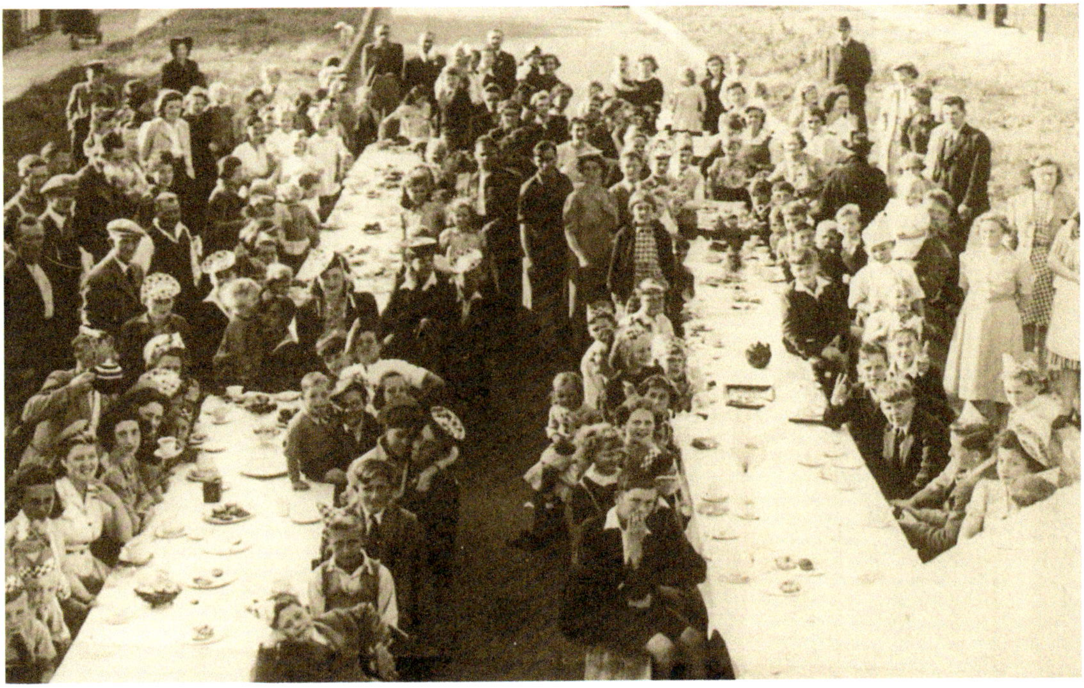

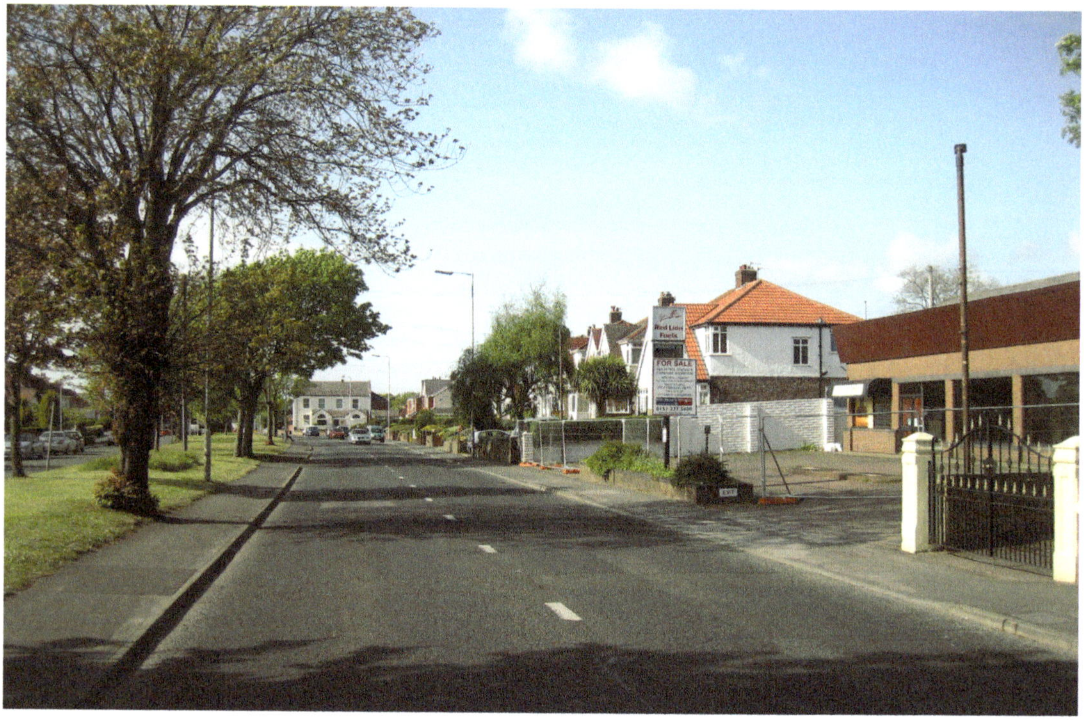

Liverpool Road North Looking North

The view looking towards Lydiate is still dominated by the building known as High Pastures, a doctors' surgery, and while the trees in front of the modern houses have been cut down, those on the left have flourished. The business on the site of the garage has closed down.

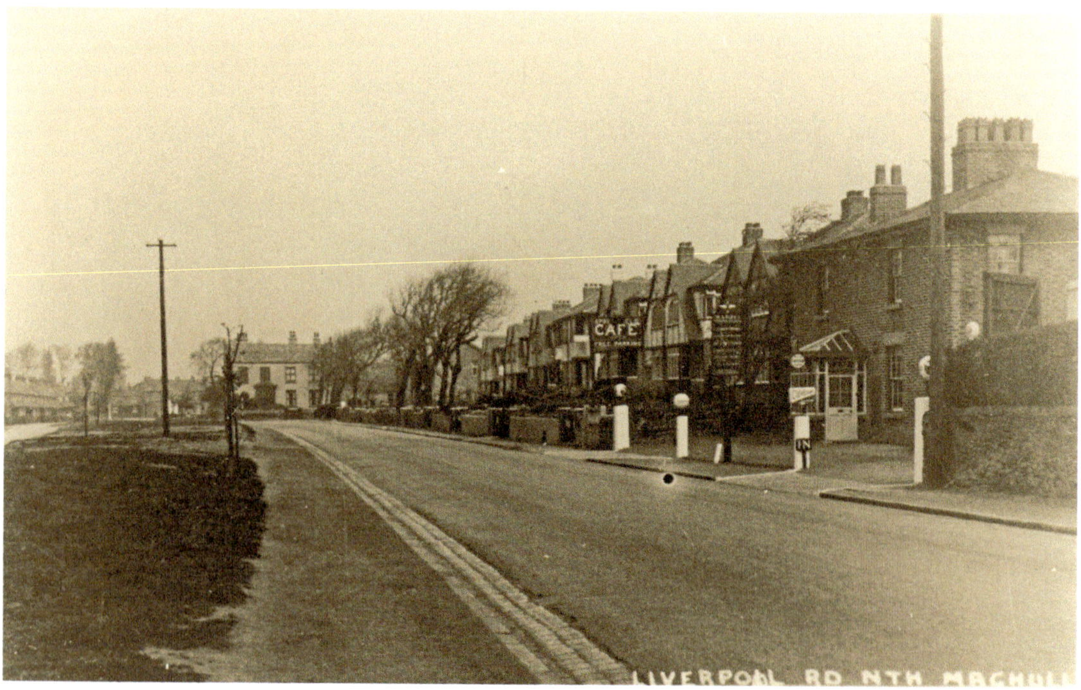

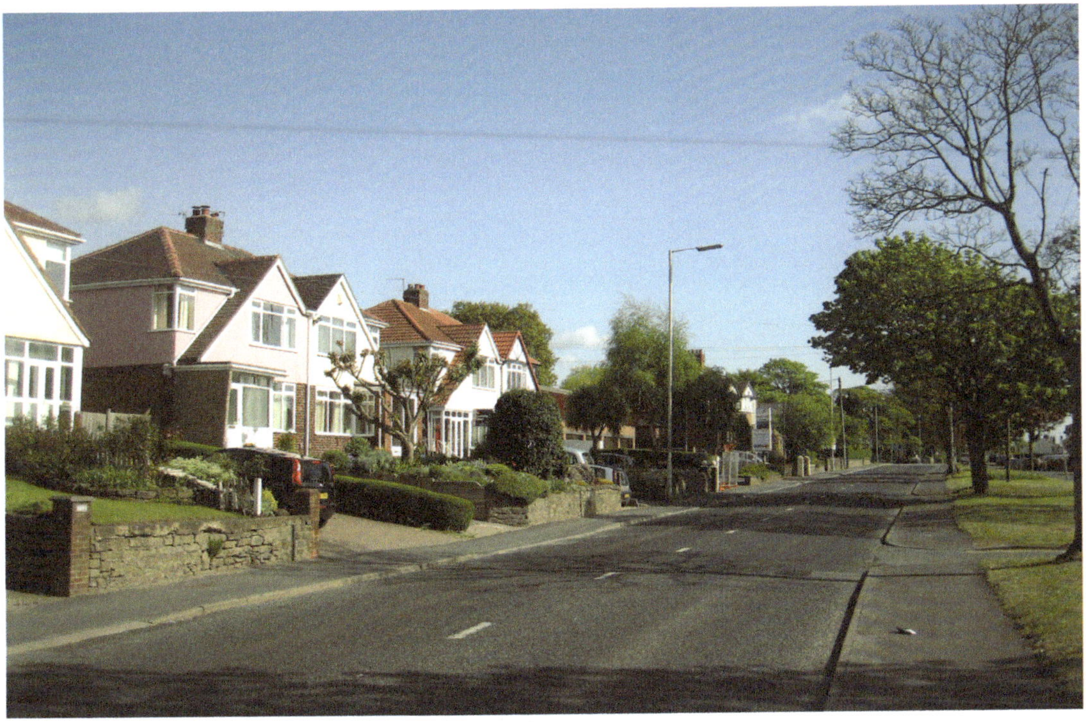

Liverpool Road North Looking South

Over sixty years seems to have brought about little change, apart from some modernisation of the houses. Despite the opening of Northway it remains a major route for traffic passing through Maghull.

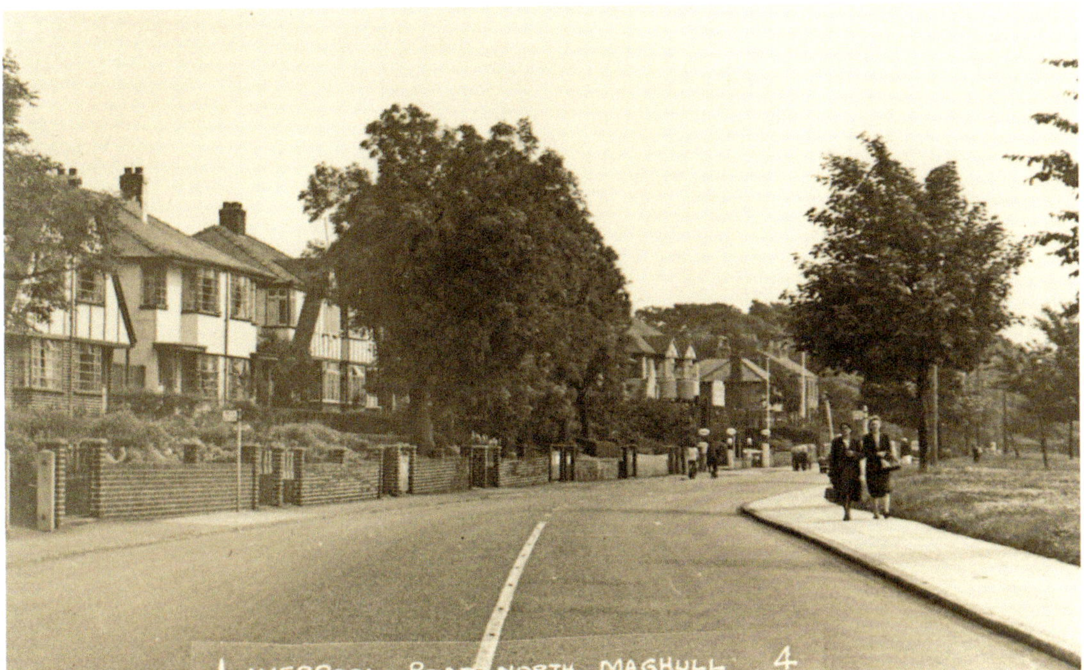

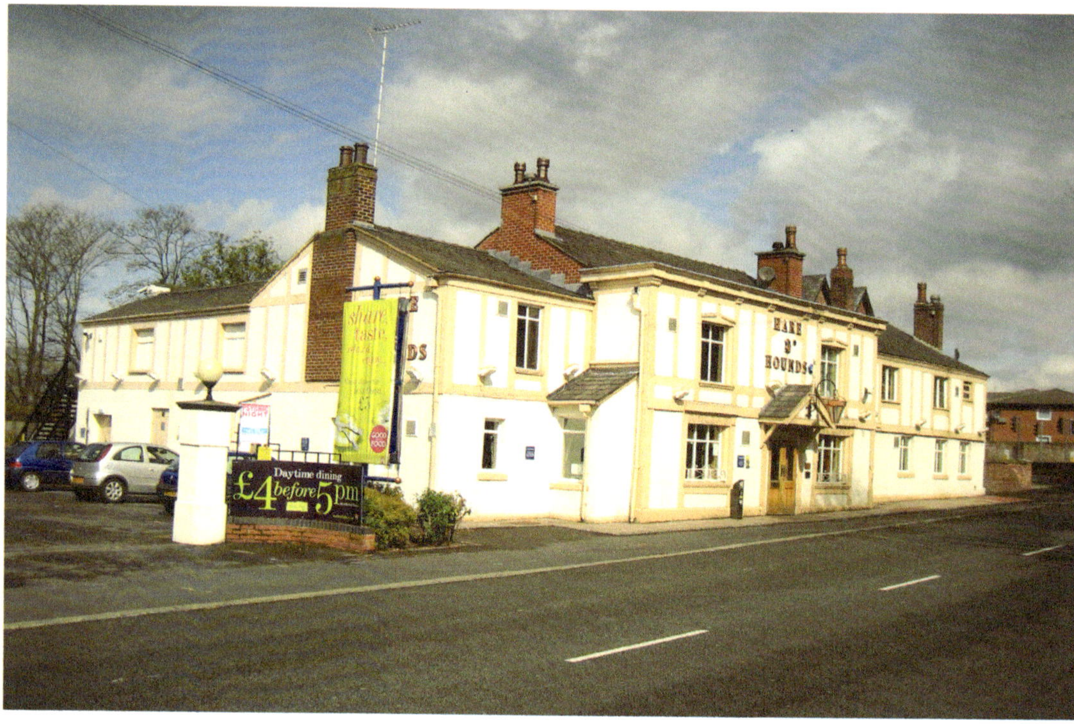

The Hare and Hounds Hotel

This view from 1909 seems to show a busy market day. The hotel was built with stables at the rear, on the Liverpool Road, as a staging post for the coaching trade. Apart from the timber facing and advertising signs, the building appears little changed.

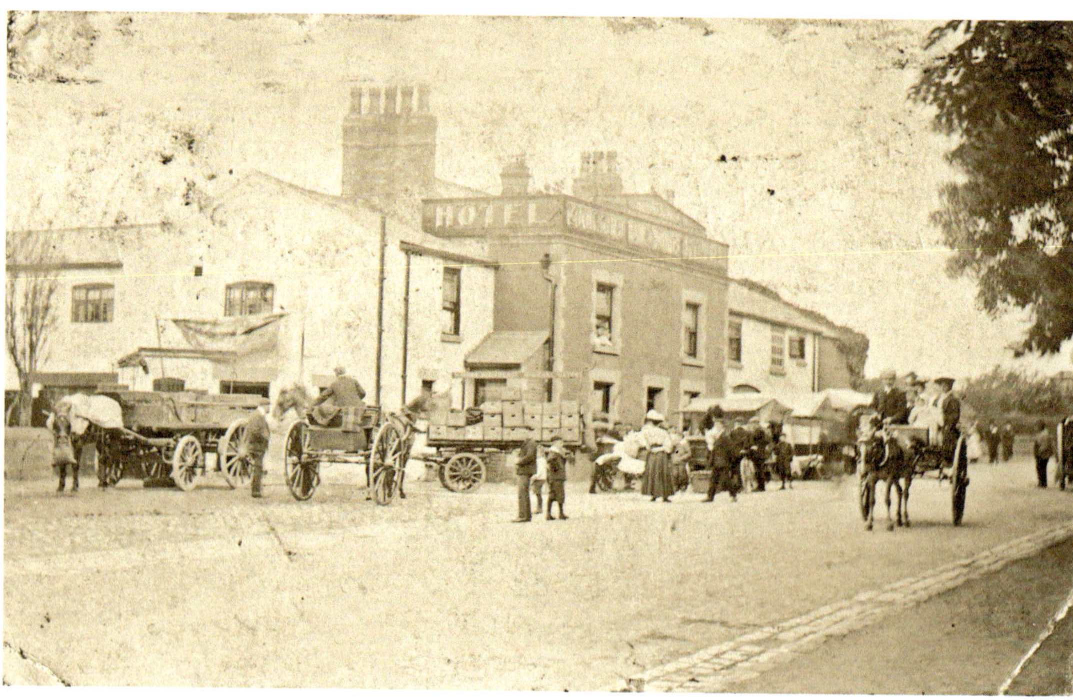

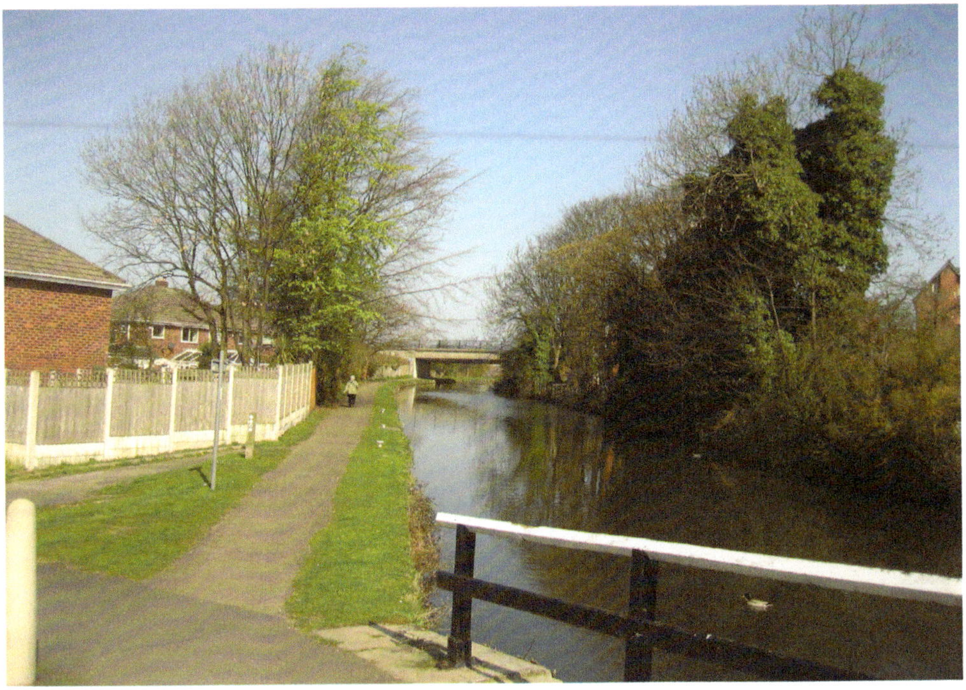

The View from the Shaw's Turn Bridge

Standing at the end of Shop Lane, this is a scene seemingly not changed for over 100 years, and still makes a pleasant walk along the towpath with the magnificent trees on the opposite bank. An estate has been built on the open fields, and the Westway crosses the canal over the bridge in the distance.

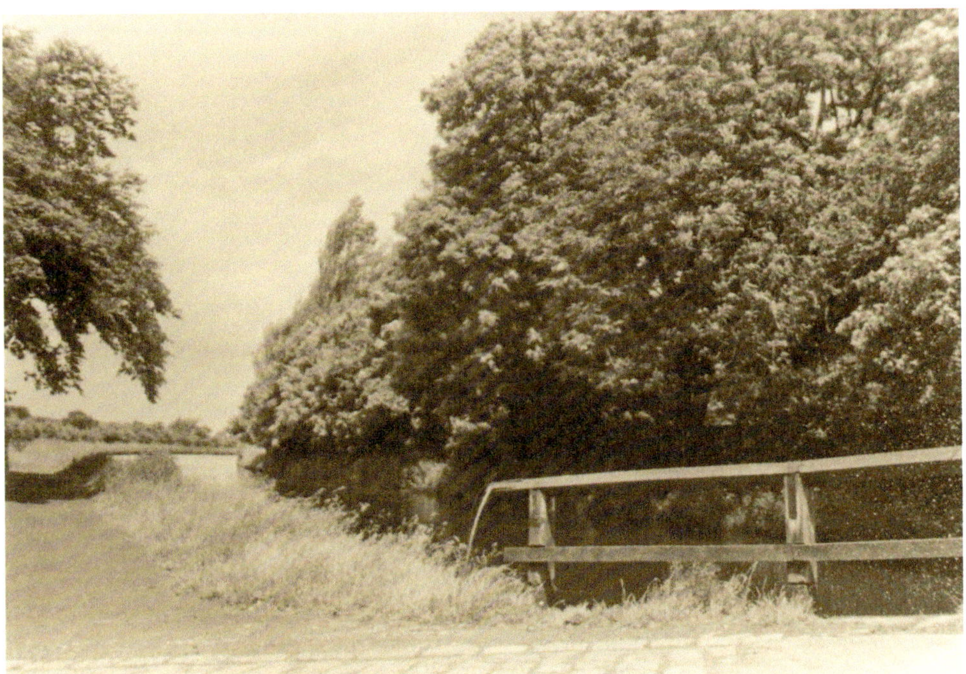

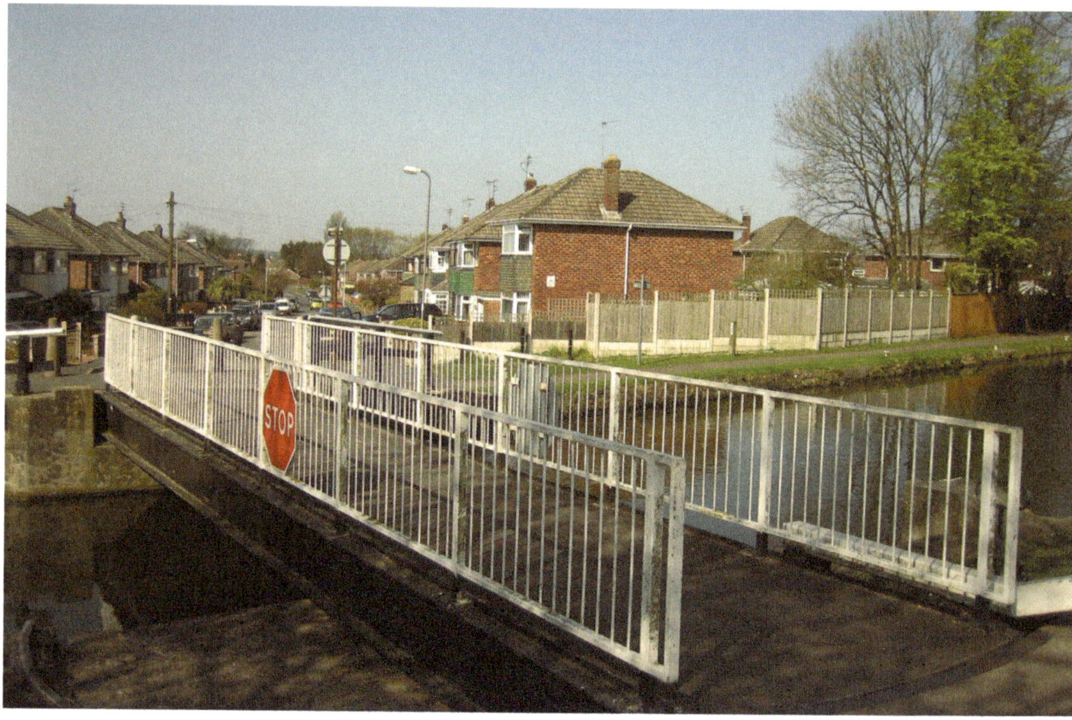

The Shaw's Turn Bridge

The modern bridge has replaced the wooden bridge, but is still placed at an acute angle to the canal. Spring Cottage, just visible through the trees to the right, has been demolished and houses built on the land at both sides of Shop Lane as far as Green Lane.

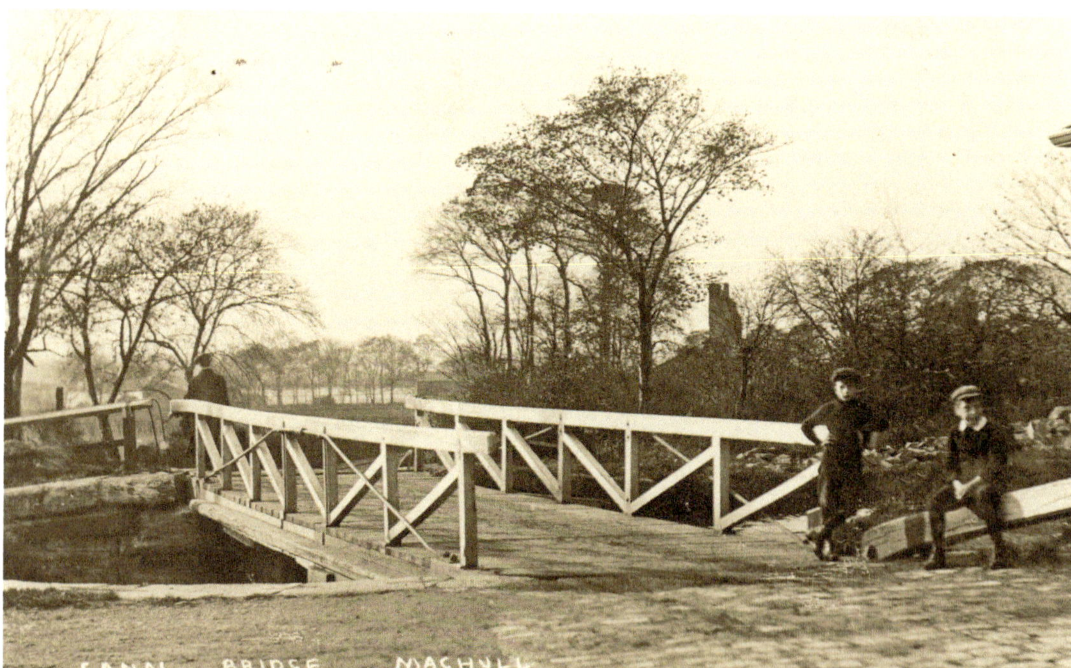

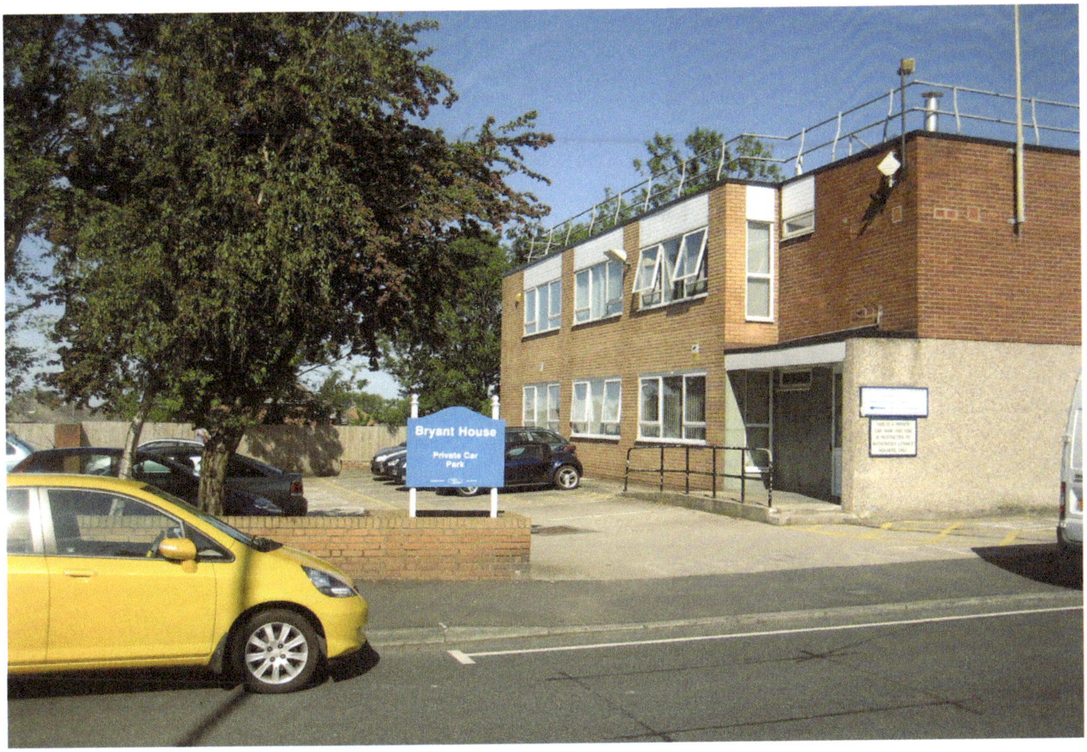

The Junction of Liverpool Road North with Shop Lane

The thriving, long-established butchers' shop fell victim to the opening of the shops in Maghull Square, and was replaced by this example of modern architecture, Bryant House, the offices of Sefton Youth Services.

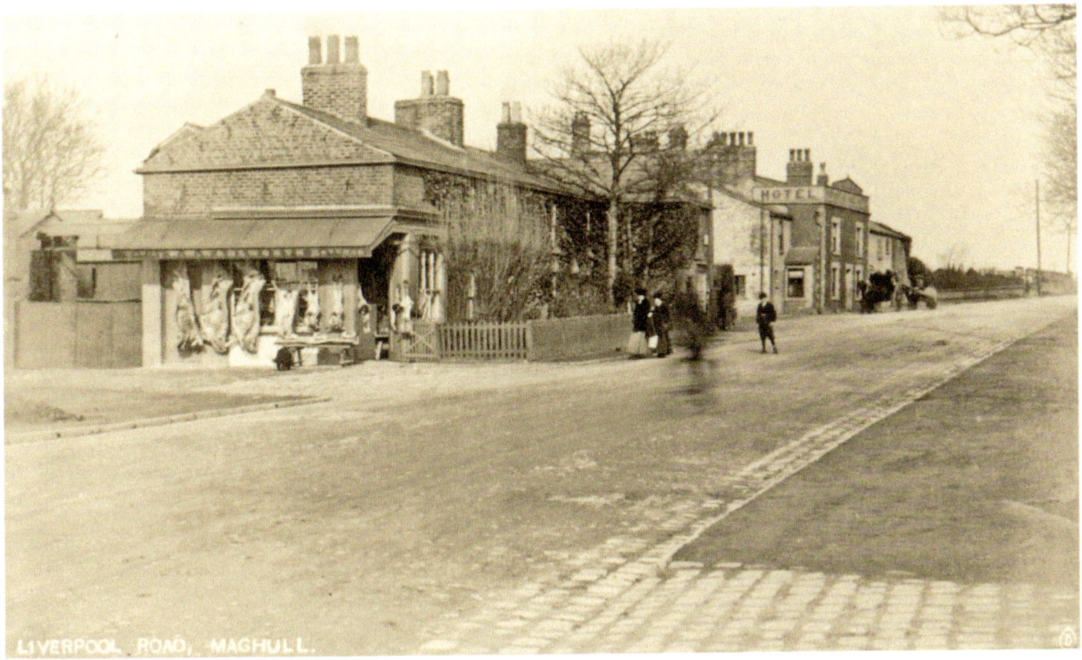

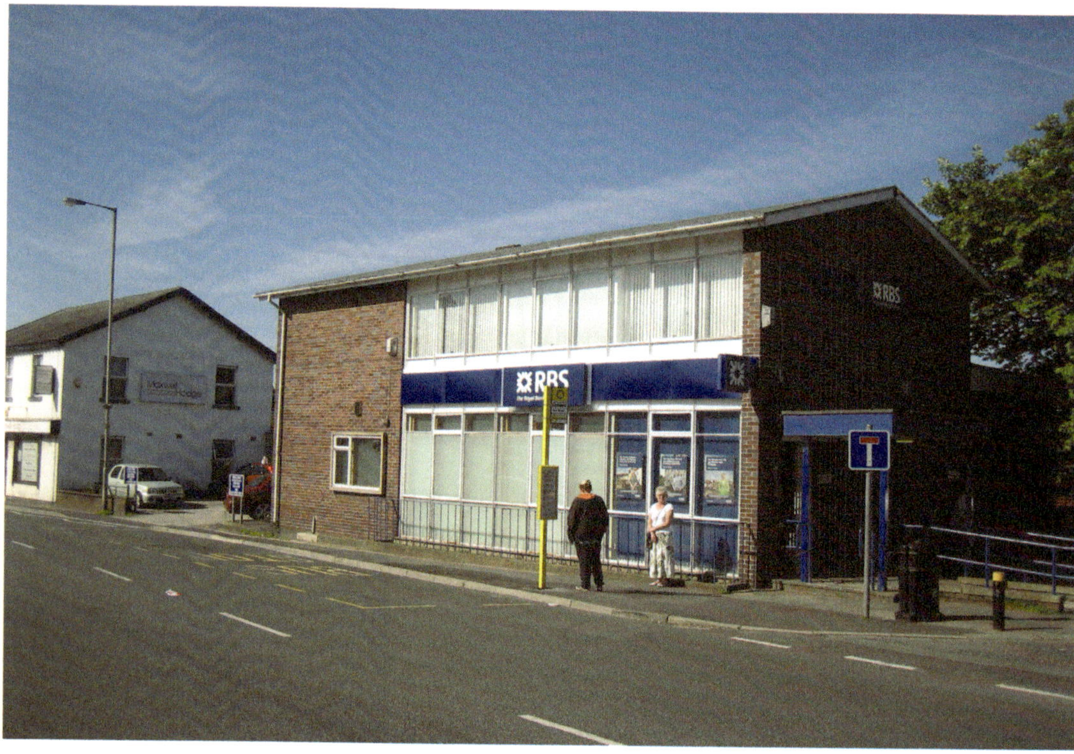

The Shop Lane Junction

This view is taken looking from the position of the photograph below. The land on which this impressive line up of cars stands has been replaced by the Royal Bank of Scotland office, and the Old Cocoa Rooms in the background is now a solicitors' business.

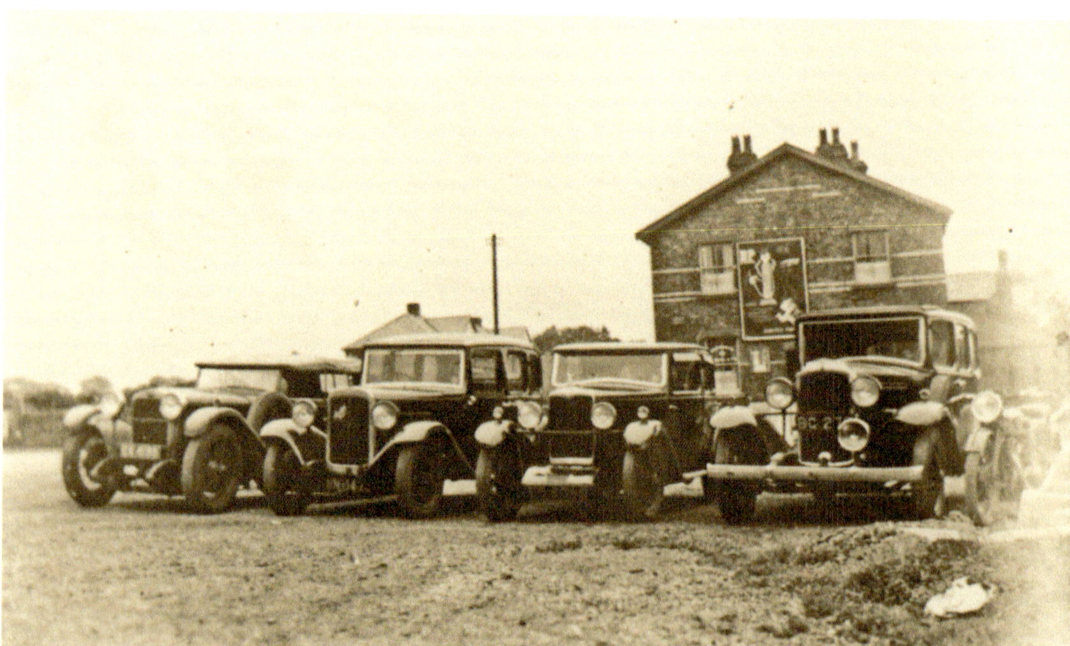

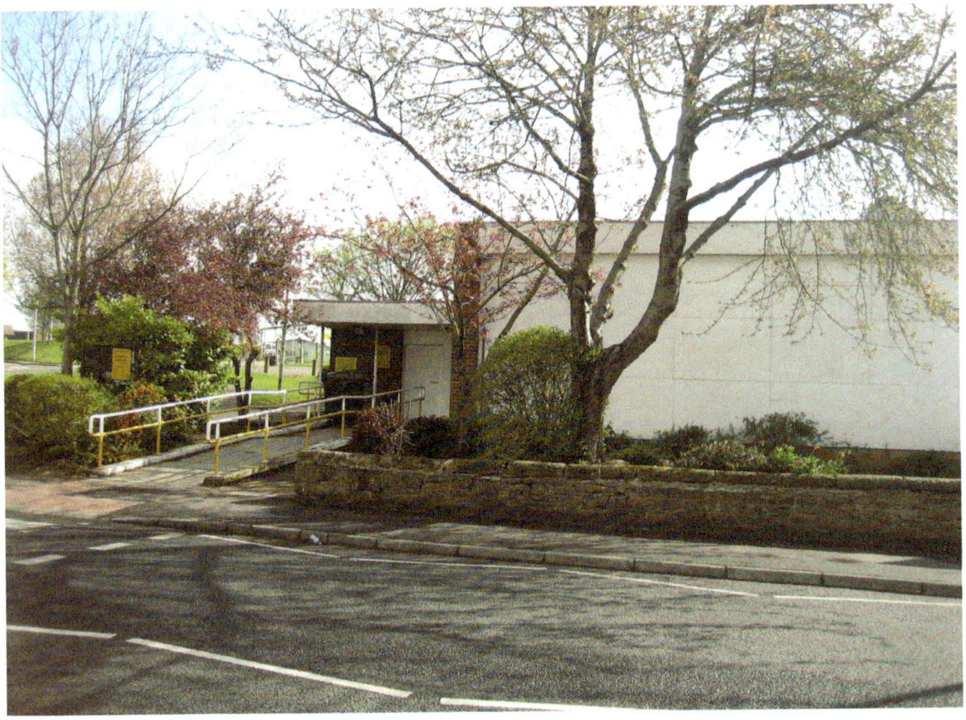

The Maghull Library

The library opened in Liverpool Road North in June 1940 with a mere 6,500 books, and was extended some years later. However, in 2010 a new library was opened on the Meadows site on Hall Lane, and there are proposals that a small housing estate be built on the old site.

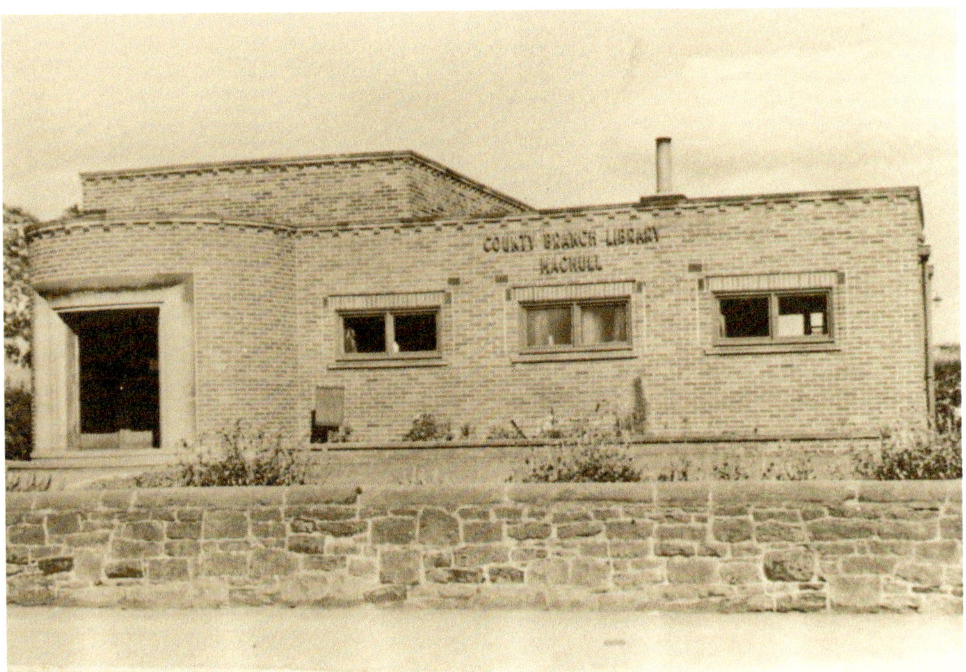

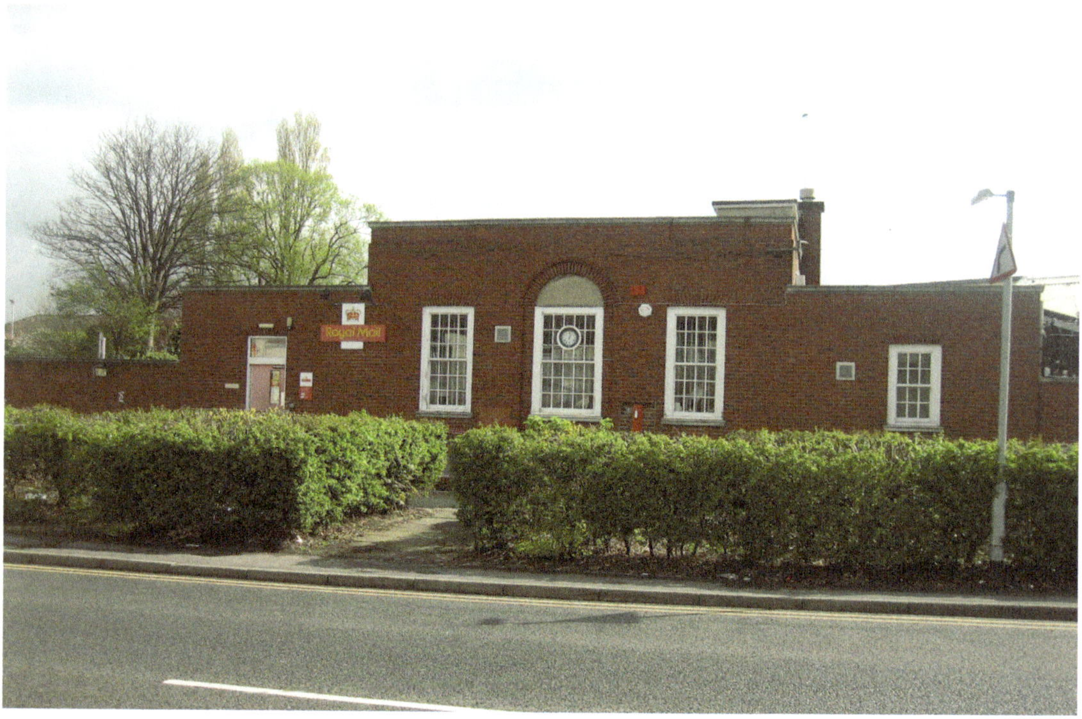

The Postmen

This group of postmen from 1954 are seen outside of the pre-war General Post Office sorting office, which was built on land close to the library. The sorting office, although now part of the Royal Mail, is still in use.

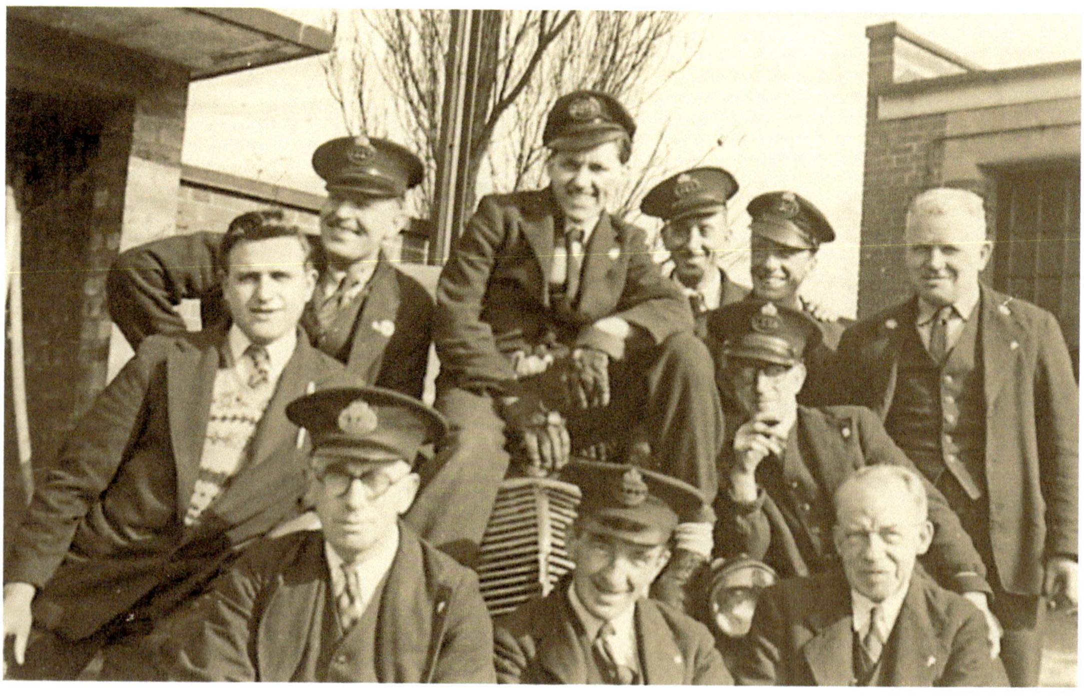

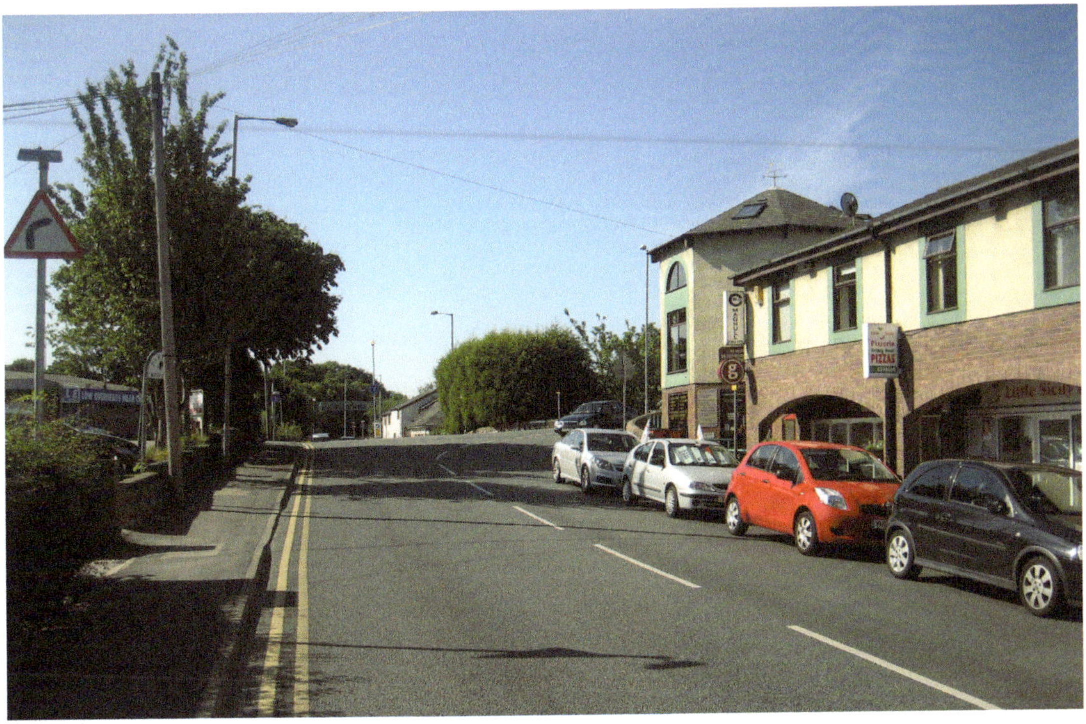

The Approach to Red Lion Bridge from the North

This classic scene of the sloping approach to the Red Lion Bridge has not changed since this Victorian photograph was taken. The Red Lion Inn and its outbuildings have disappeared, as have the warehouses on the right, which were replaced by canal workers' homes.

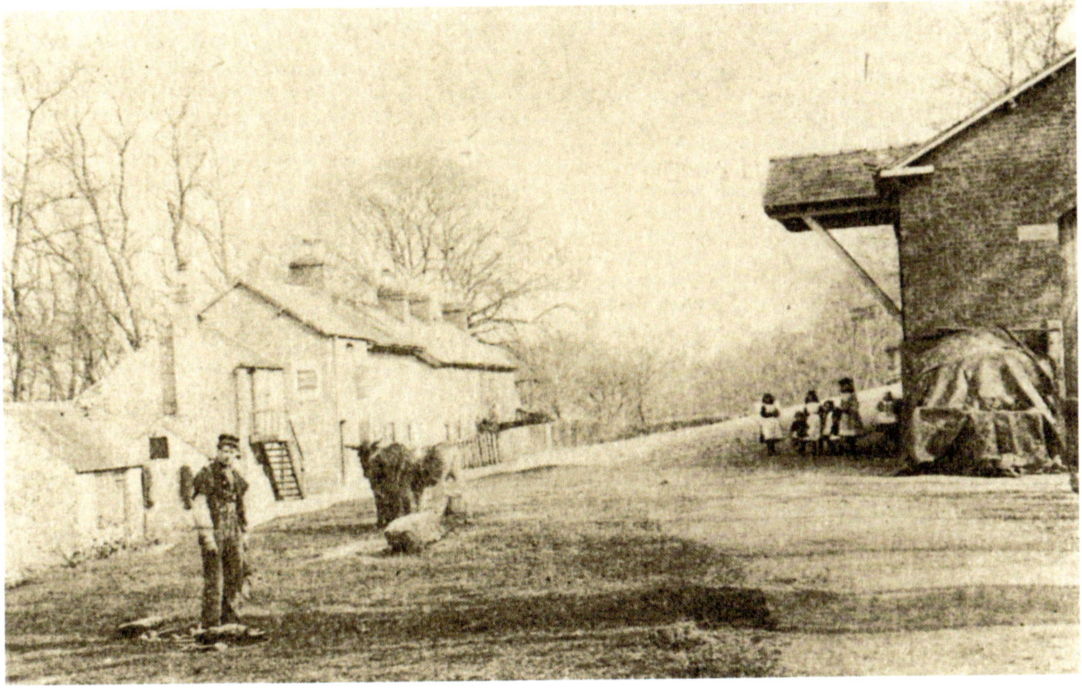

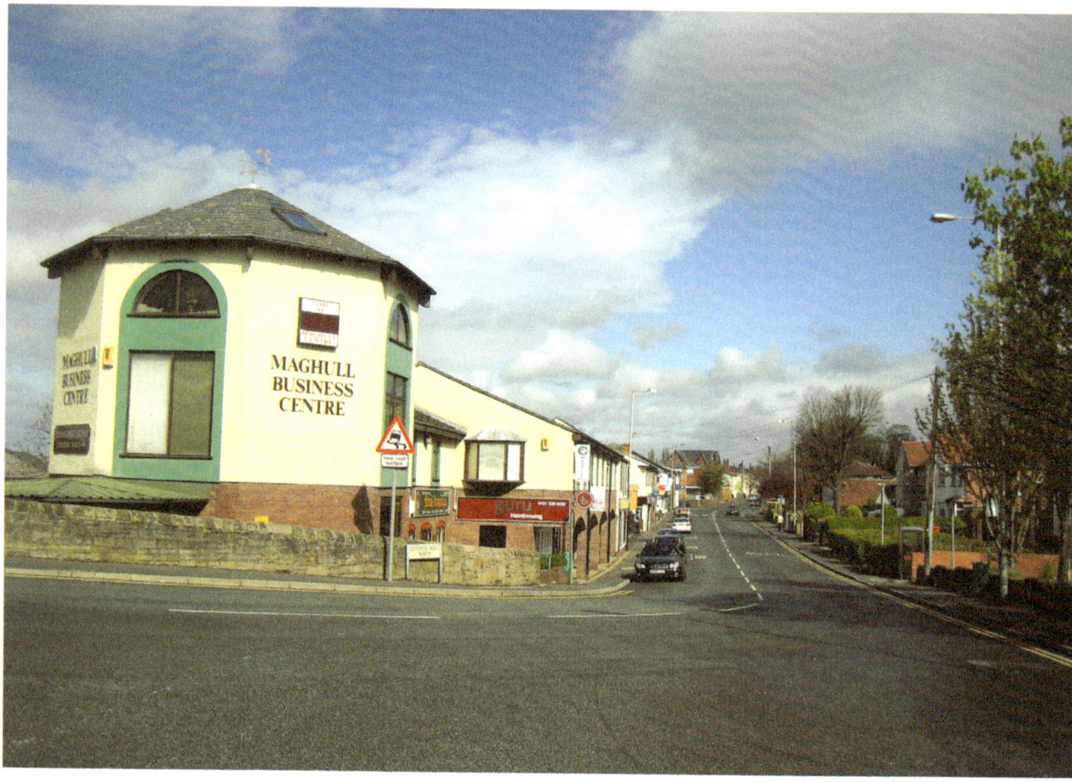

The Junction of Damfield Lane with Liverpool Road North

The unusually shaped buildings on the left, known as 'on the slope,' which could only be reached by a small footbridge, have been replaced by offices, while houses and the Royal Mail sorting office occupy the field on the right.

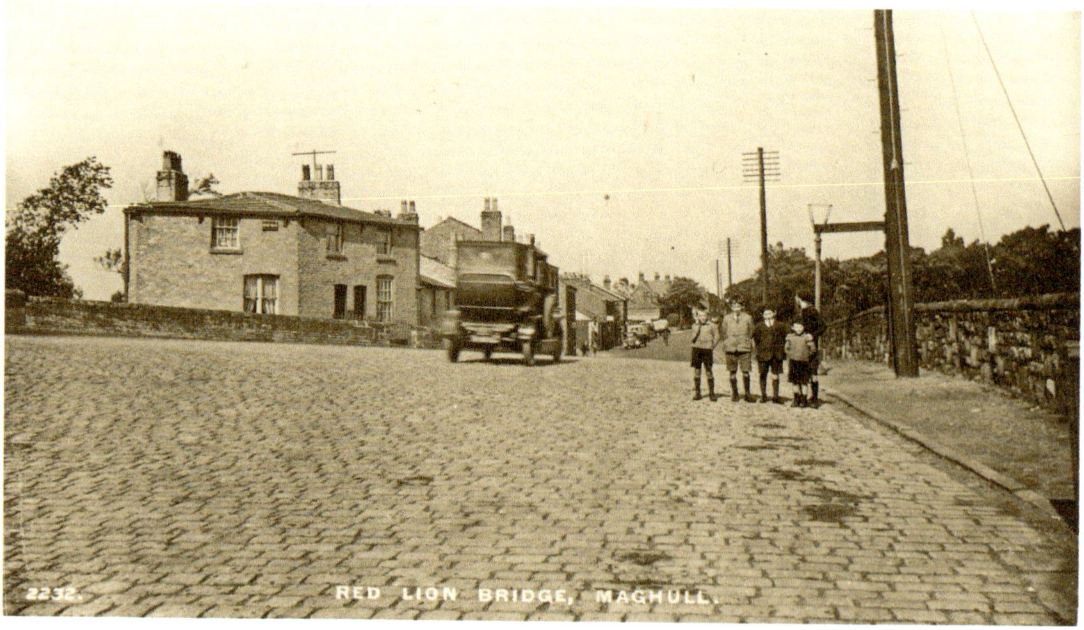

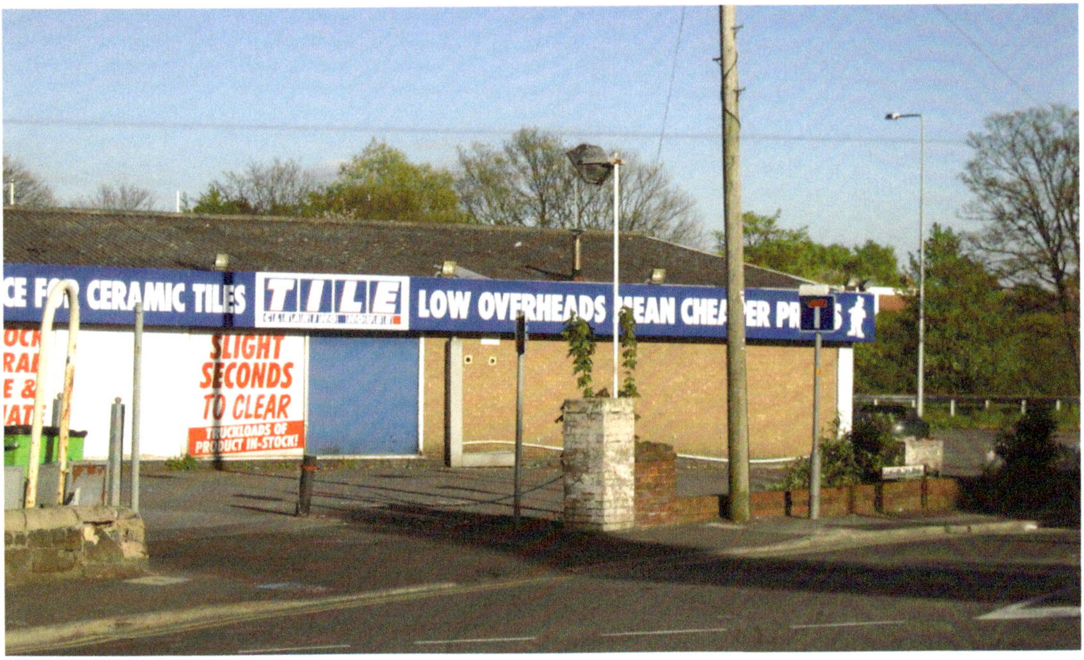

Damfield Lane

The Red Lion Inn was once the centre of life in Maghull, and although the name lives on for the nearby canal bridge, the building is long gone. All that remains is the wall at the entrance to the group of businesses. The inn closed and became a general store in 1910, before being demolished after the Second World War.

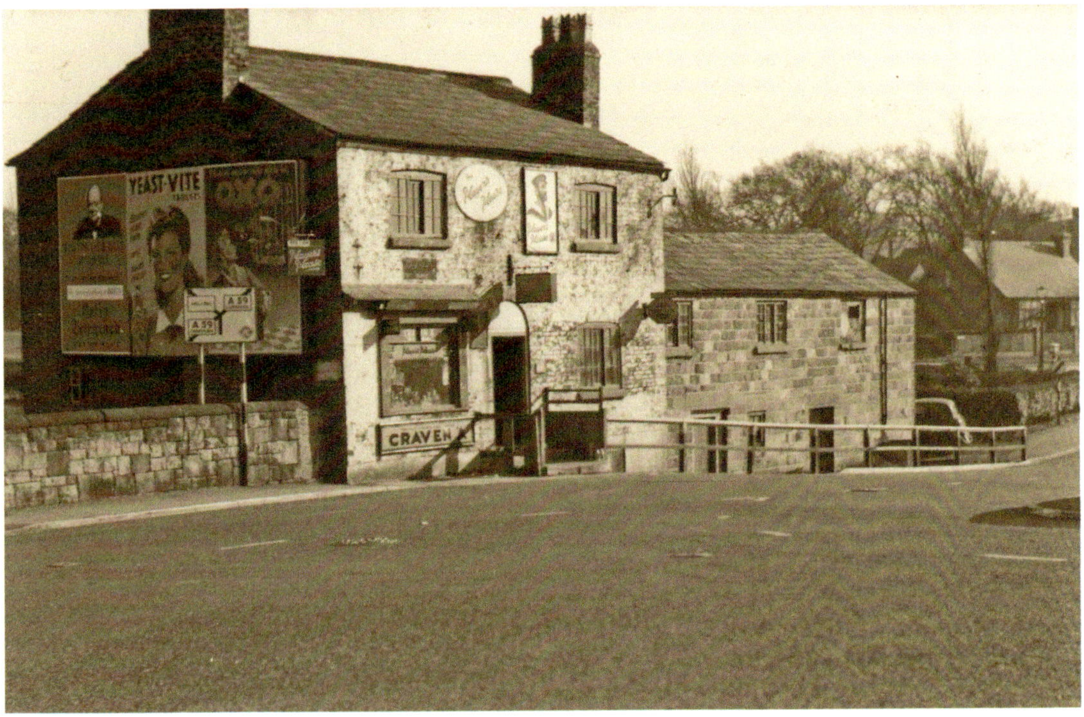

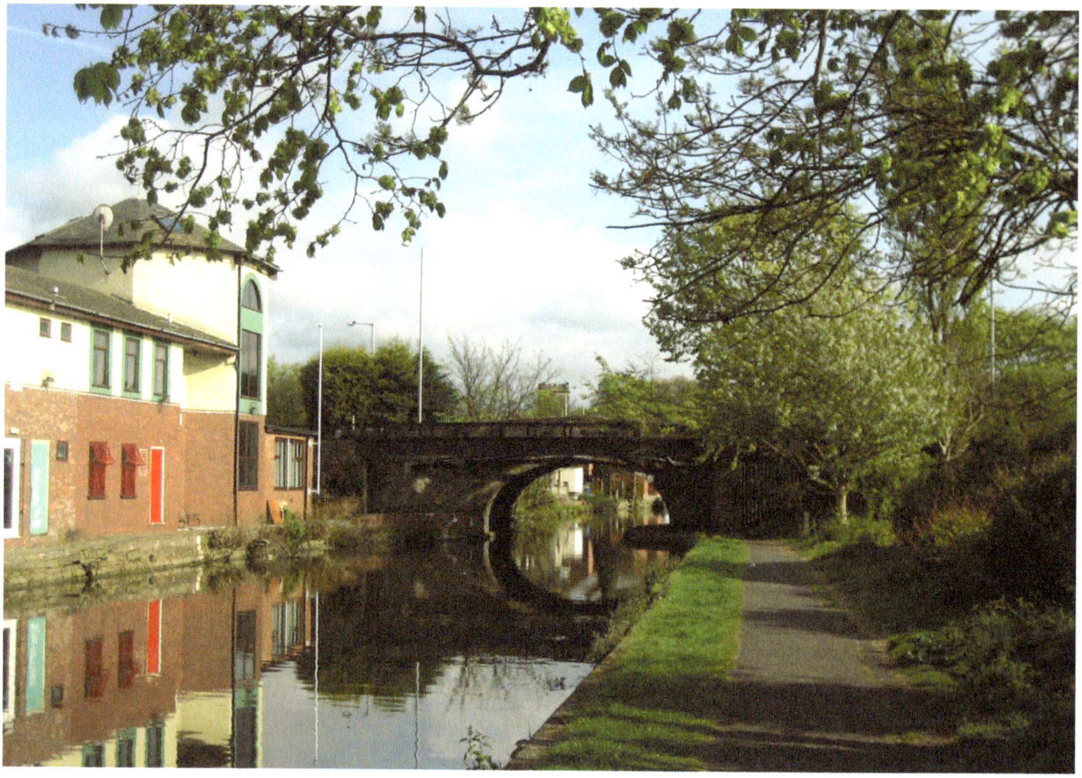

Approaching the Red Lion Bridge Along the Canal

A timeless view from the canal of St Andrew's Church from among the trees above the ancient bridge, which now has pedestrian walkways at the sides of the bridge walls. The houses on the bank before the bridge have been replaced.

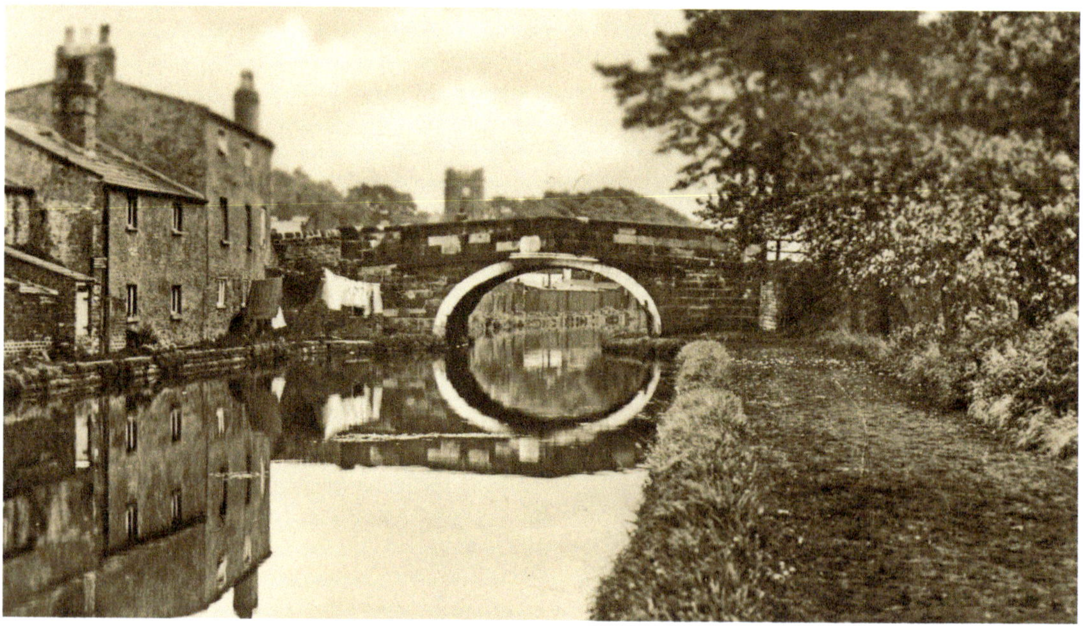

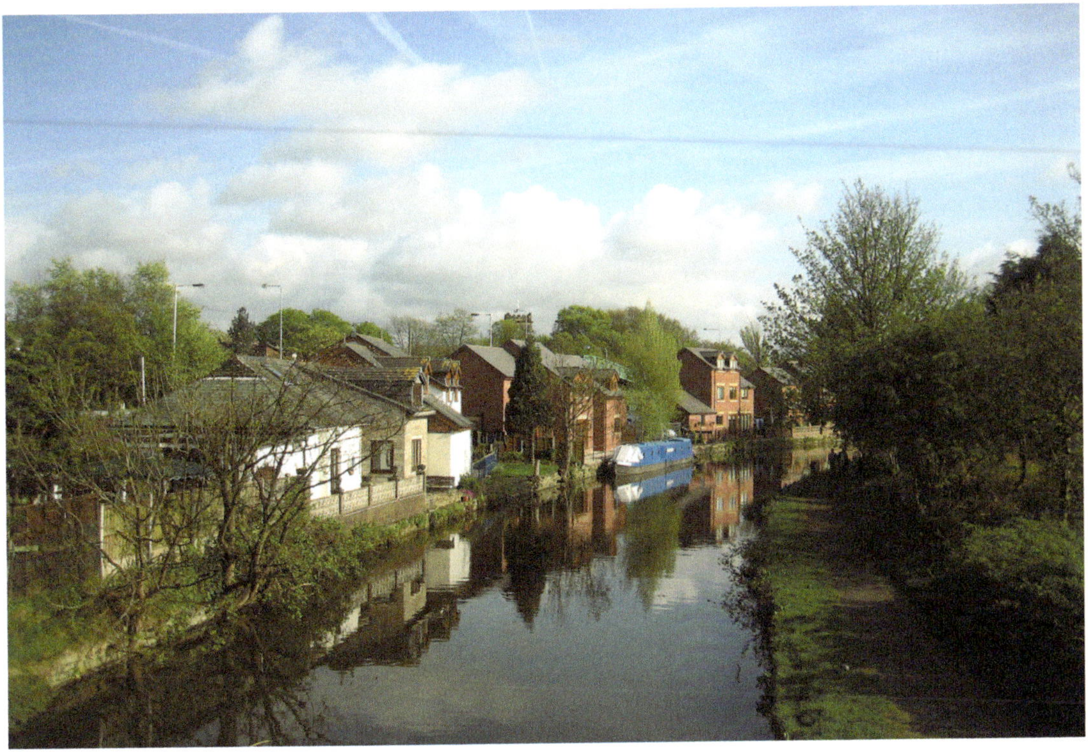

The Canal from Red Lion Bridge Looking South

In recent years the land on the canal bank opposite the towpath has been developed, with private residences replacing the work buildings. The trees add to a charming scene on a spring day.

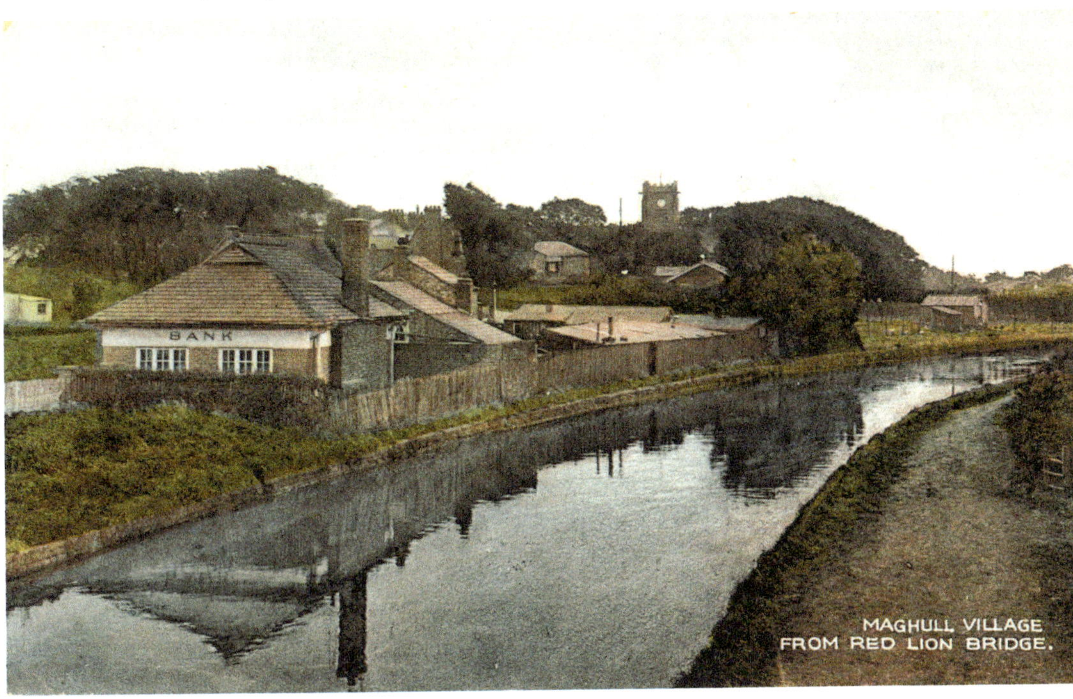

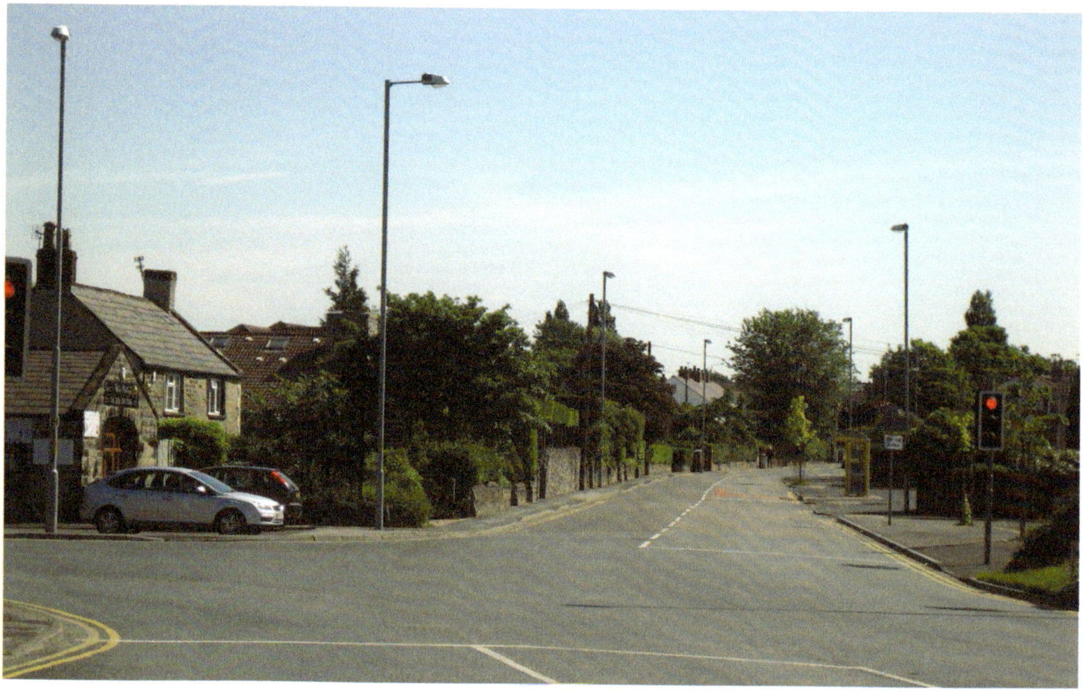

The Junction of Liverpool Road South with Green Lane

The opening to the original Green Lane on the left has been blocked, and the wall demolished when the new road was made. West House in the distant right has been replaced by a block of flats, and a slip road has replaced the hedge. The old building on the corner of Green Lane, where coffins were made, still exists and is now a photography business.

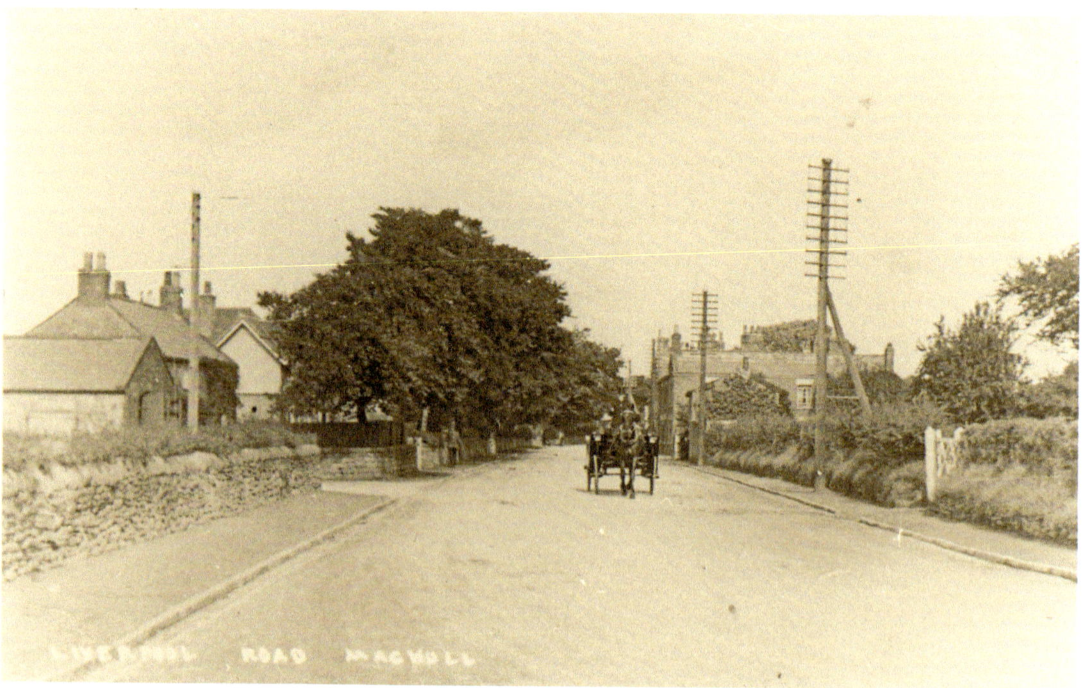

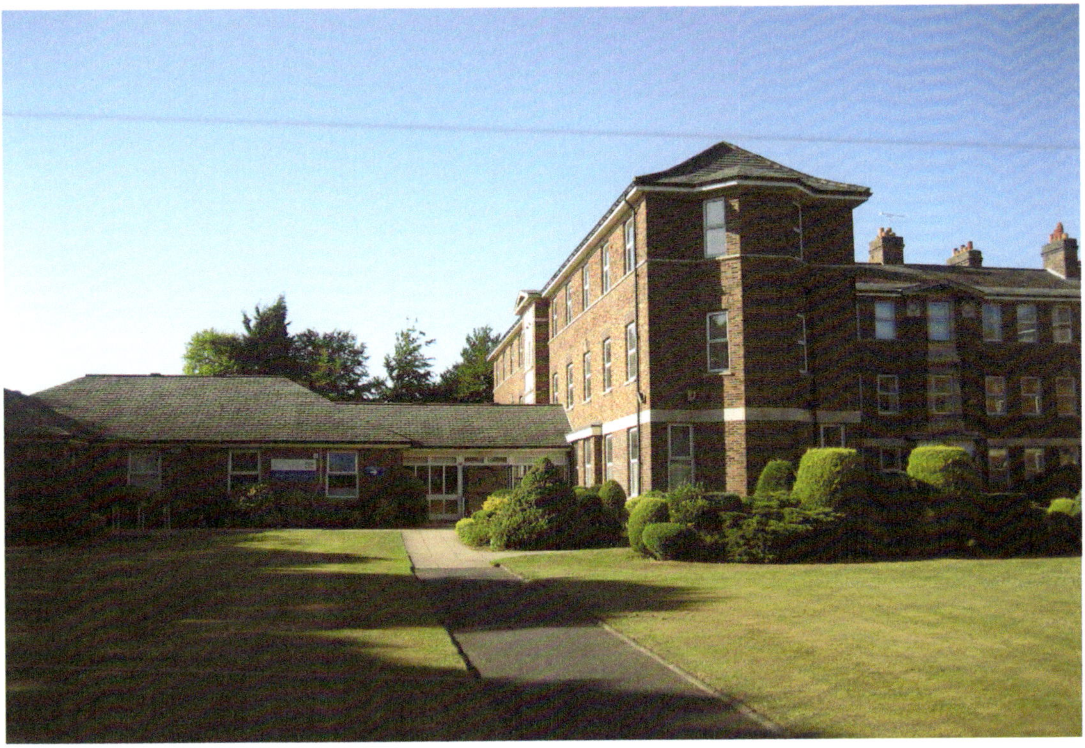

The Parkhaven Trust Estate

The Bartlett Home, which cared for male patients only, was opened in 1922 as one of the Maghull Homes for Epileptics. Some of the chimneys have been removed, and the gardens at the front have matured and are immaculately kept. The new extension is the Maghull Primary Care Trust general practice surgery.

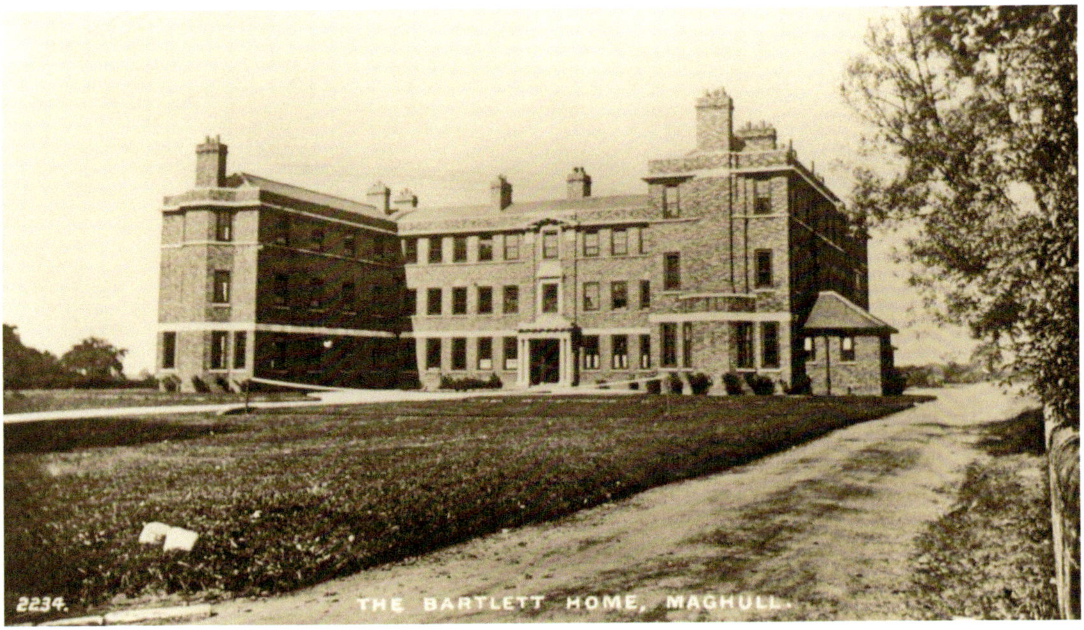

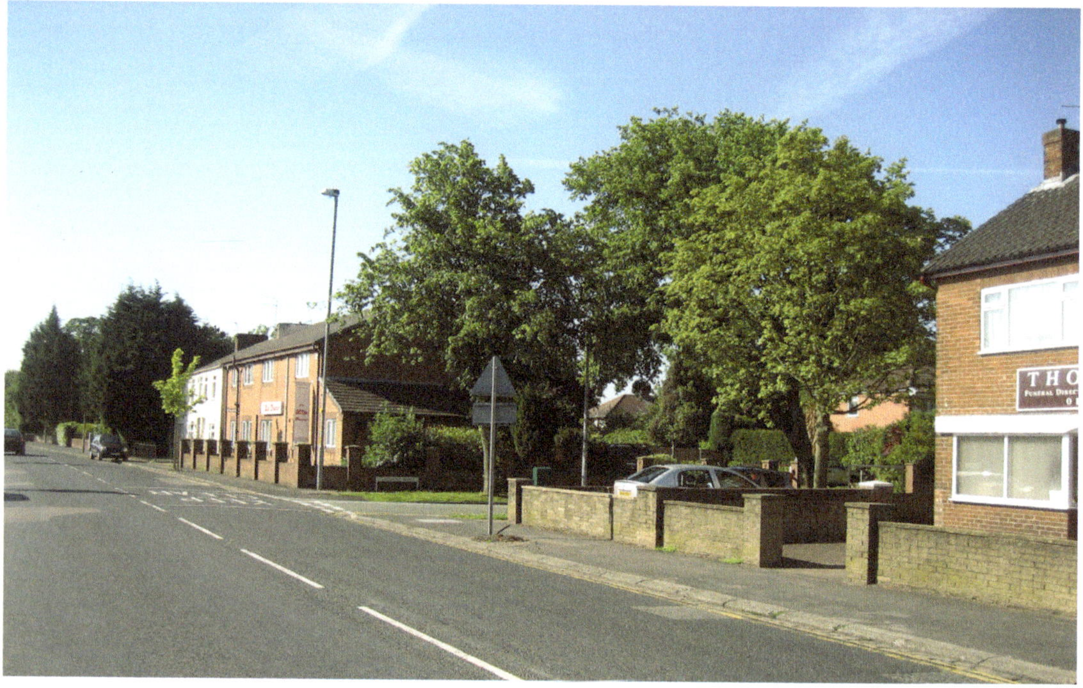

Liverpool Road South Looking South

The white houses have been demolished and replaced with a doctor's surgery. Beyond the parked cars is the site of the white cottage, which extended into the road and was known as 'Granny Foster's cottage'. She is seen with her family in the small photograph.

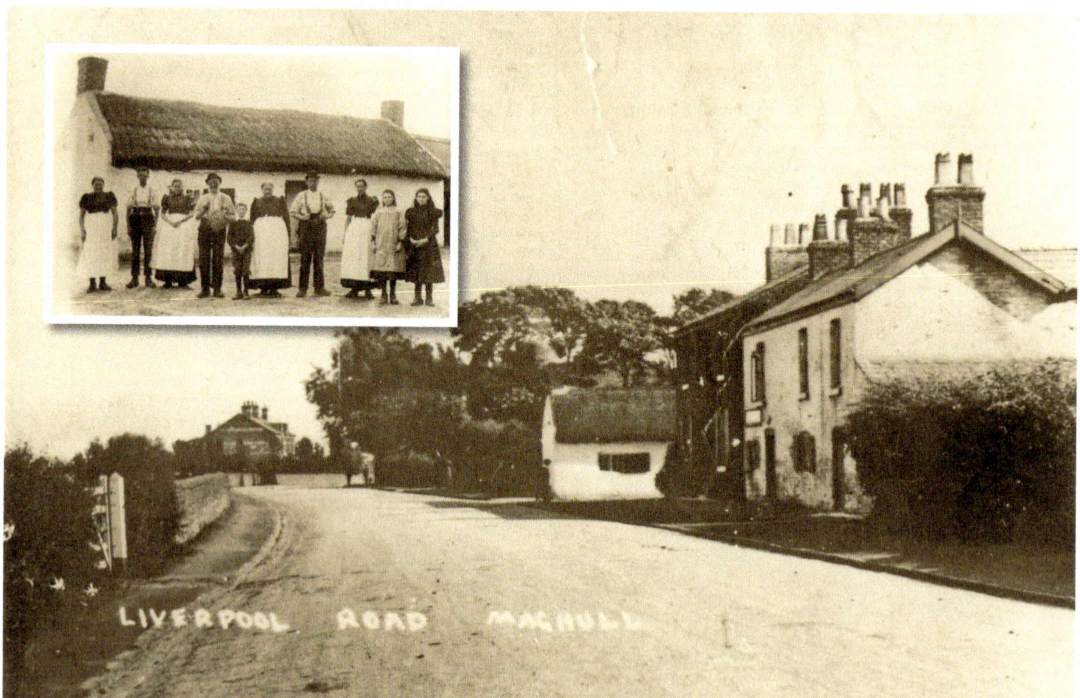

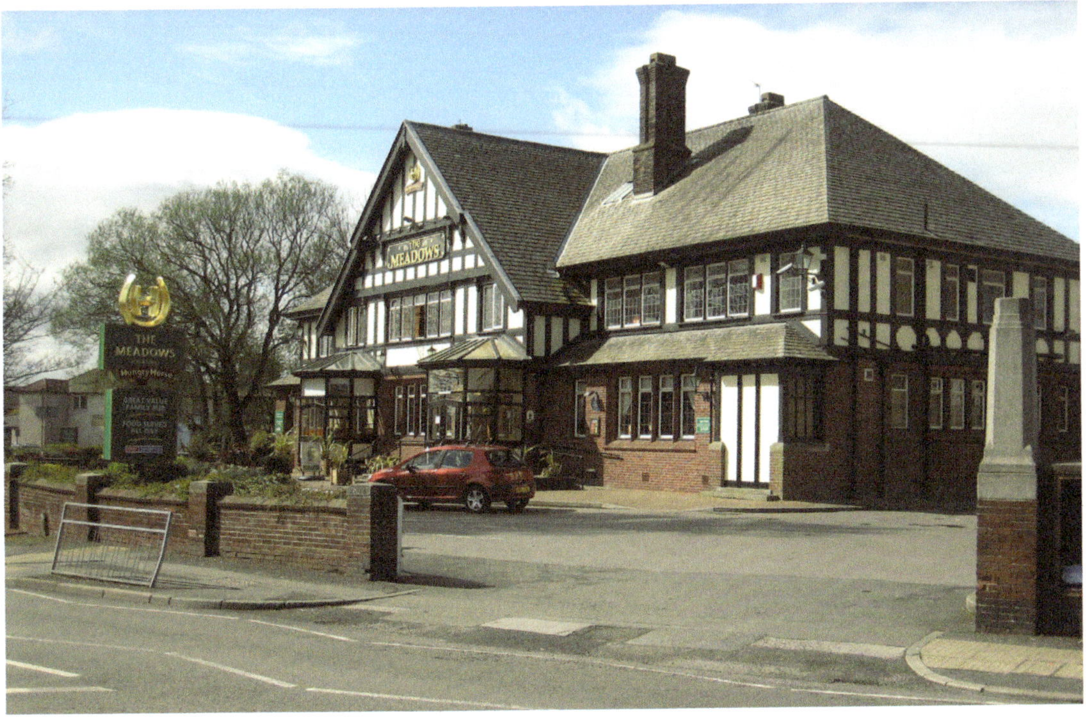

The Meadows Hotel

A prominent feature in the town since before the war, The Meadows seems to have changed very little since this photograph was taken sixty years ago. There are two new glazed entrances, and outdoor benches and tables.

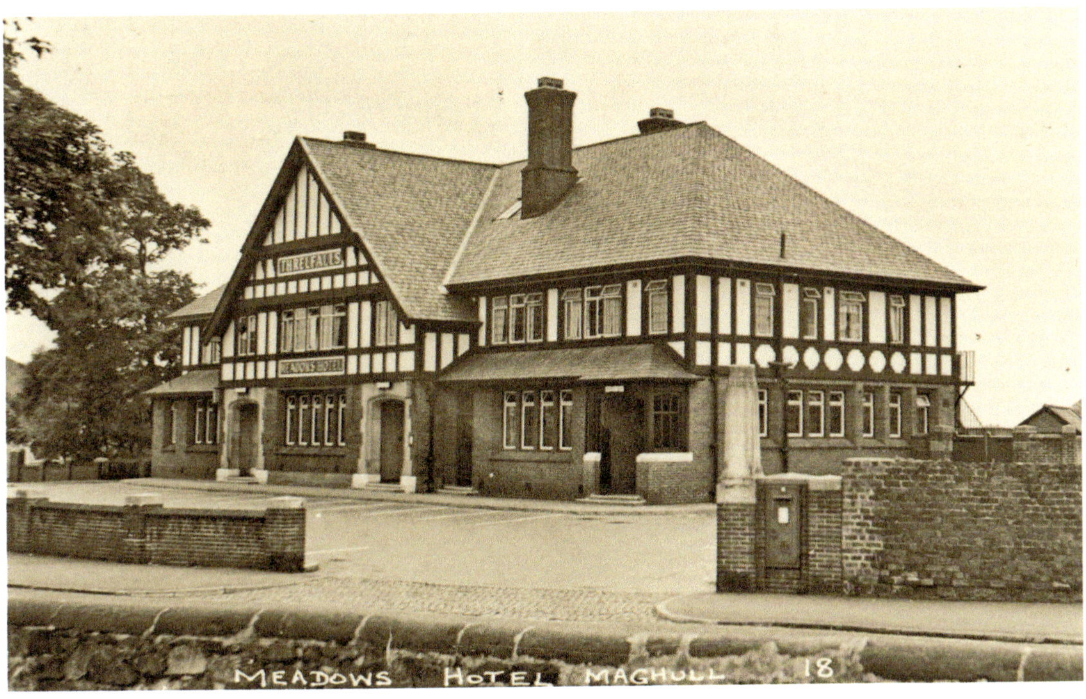

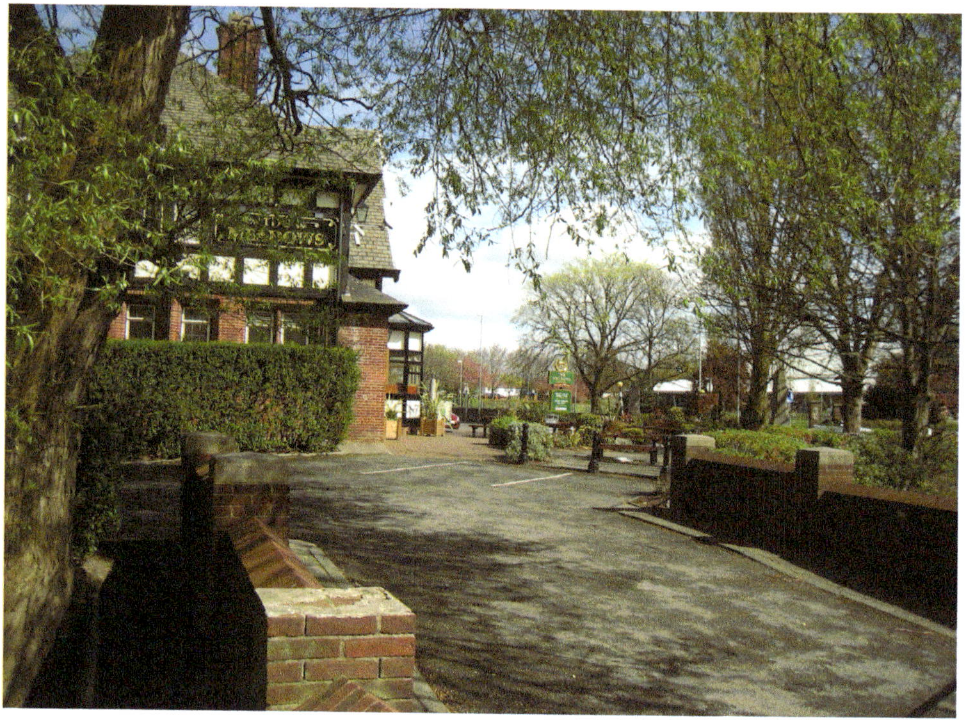

Old Racecourse Farm

Apart from the line of trees, nothing remains of the Old Racecourse Farm, named after the famous racecourse on its land. The site of the farm is occupied by the Meadows Hotel and the car park at the rear. There is a plaque on the outside wall of the hotel commemorating the racecourse and the Grand National race.

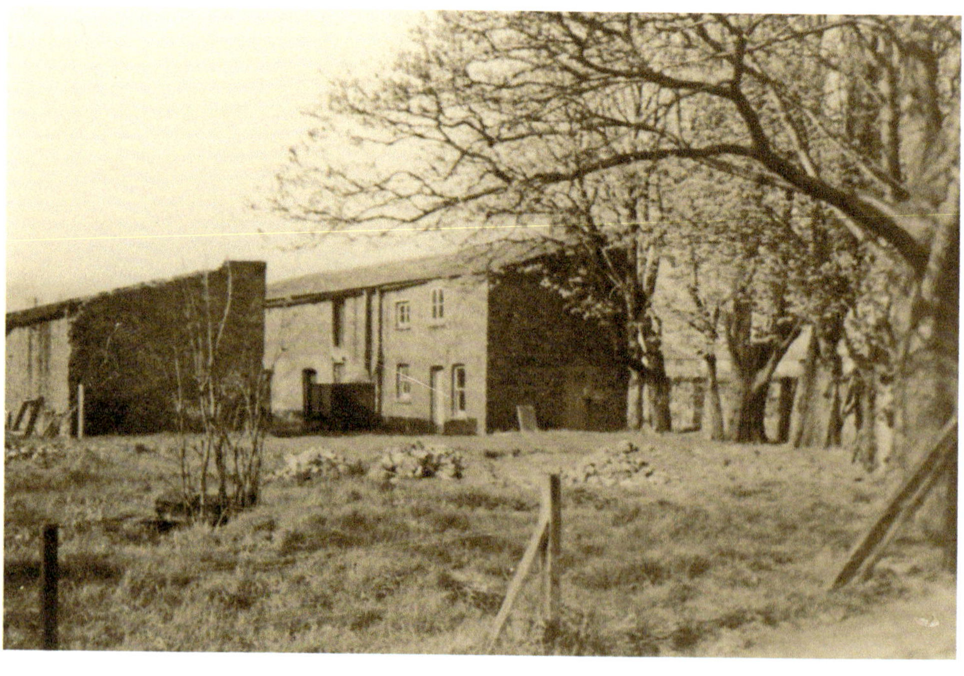

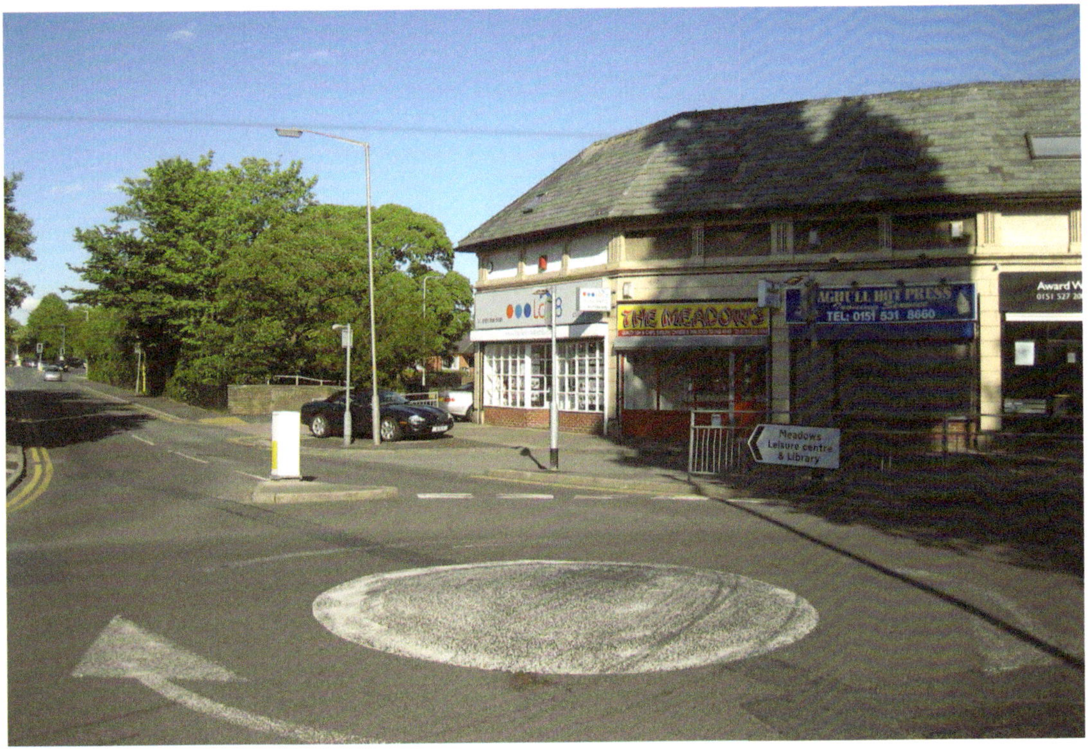

The Junction of Hall Lane and Liverpool Road South

Rankin's Cottages have been replaced by the group of shops, and the peaceful country lane is now a busy route into Maghull. The farm that was among the trees has been replaced by the bungalows in Bailey Way.

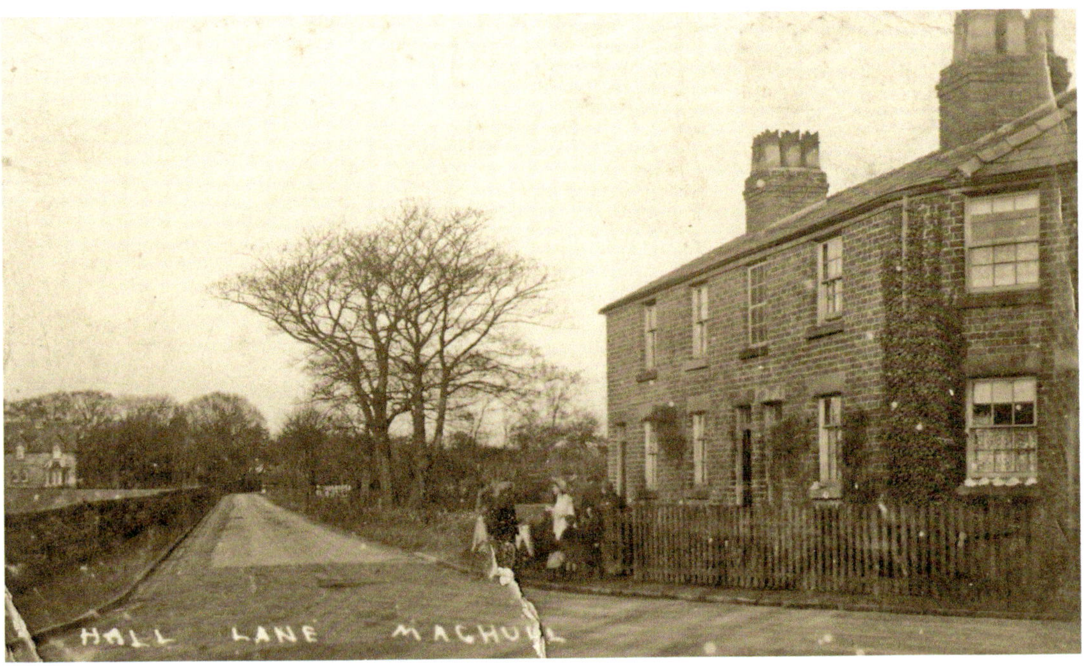

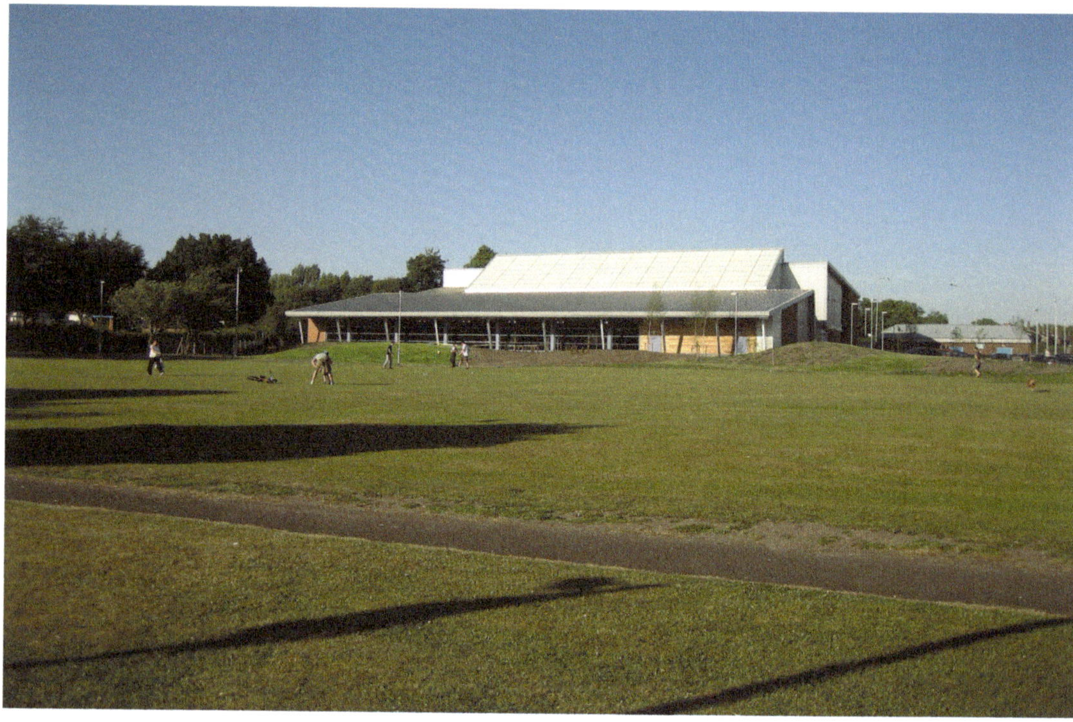

King George V Playing Fields

The field was originally used by a local farmer to entertain parties from Liverpool, and was also the natural venue for the town's events. After the war, the farm buildings were demolished and Maghull Town Hall and, more recently, the Meadows Centre were built on the field. The trees have obscured the church and Northway.

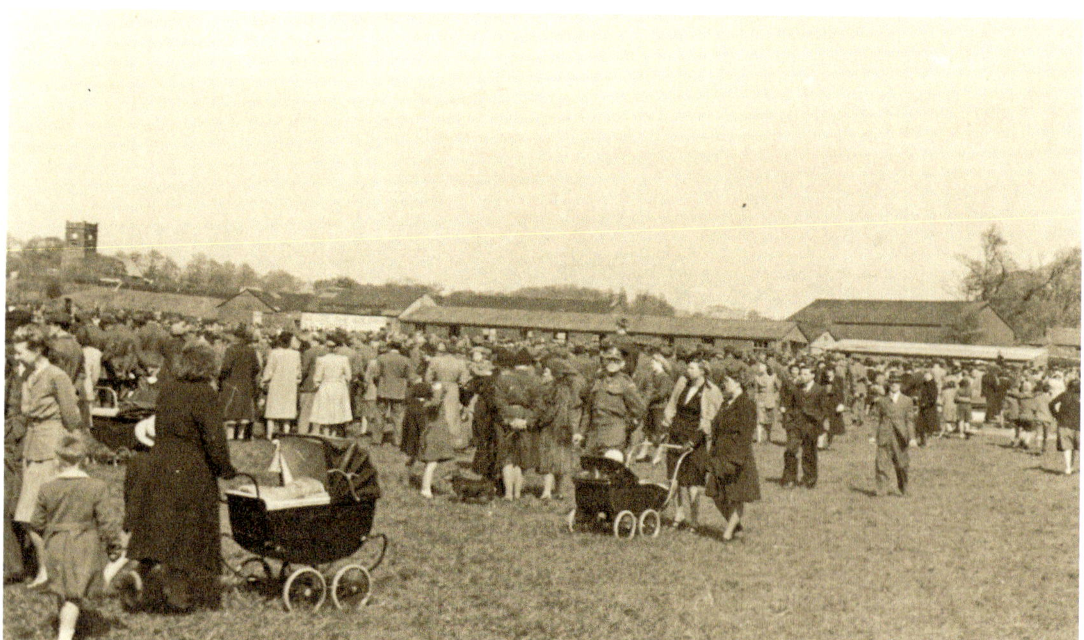

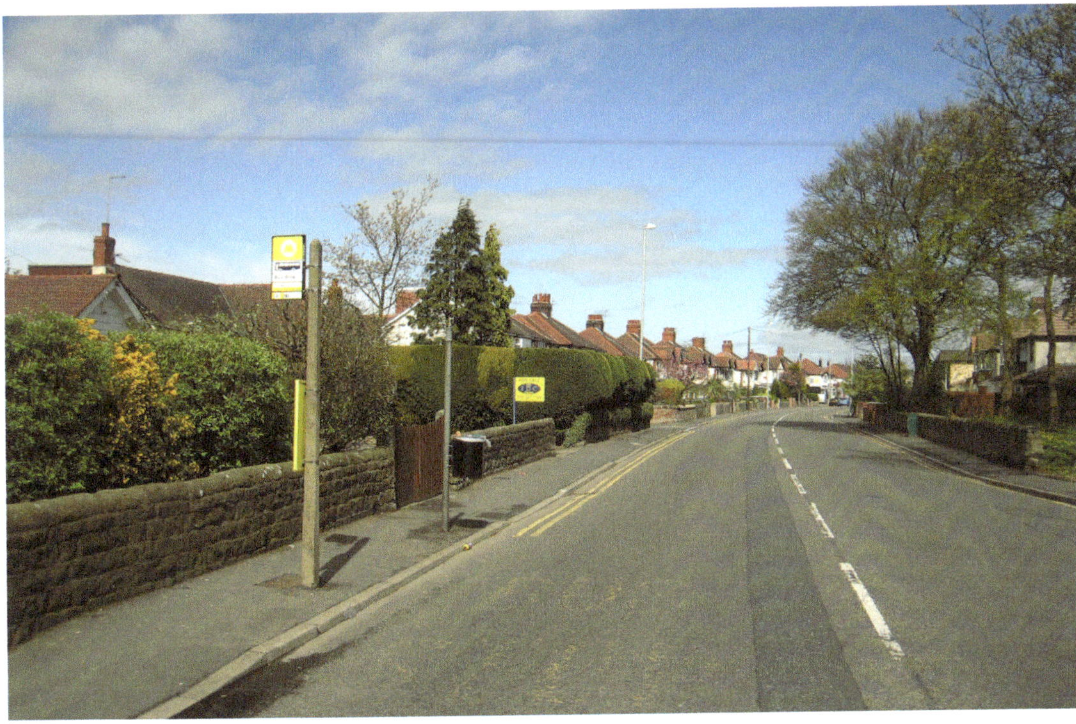

The Approach to Maghull from the South

The typical pre-war bungalows up to Woodend Avenue are now obscured by the trees and hedges, while the gap between the houses in the distance has been built upon. The road appears to be wider, but the wall is still present in front of houses on the right.

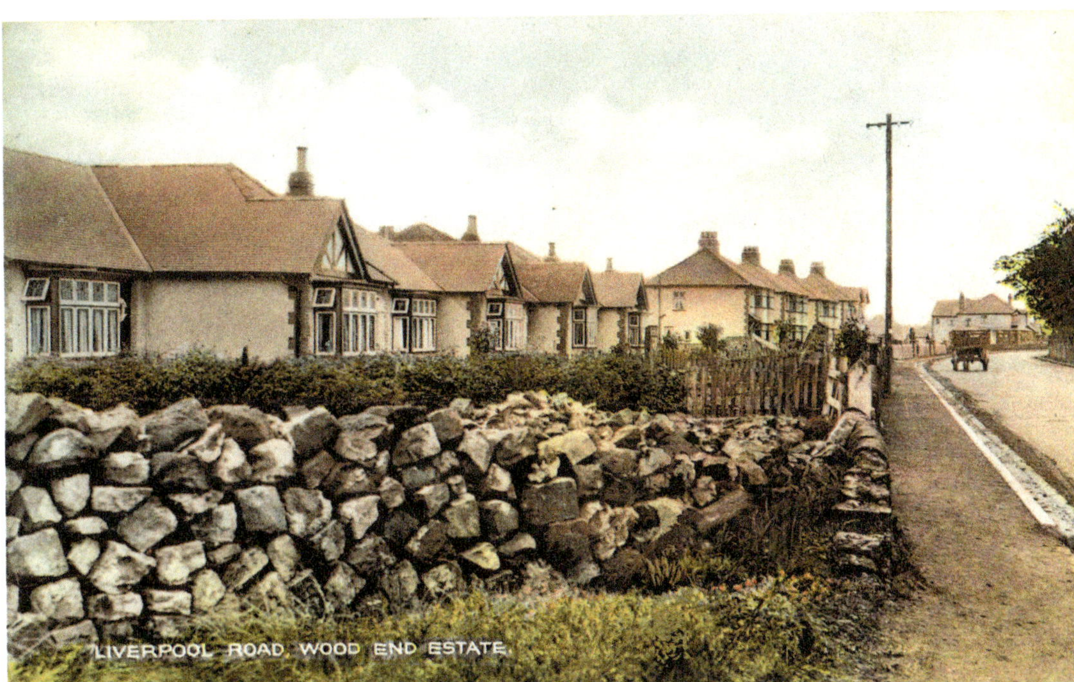

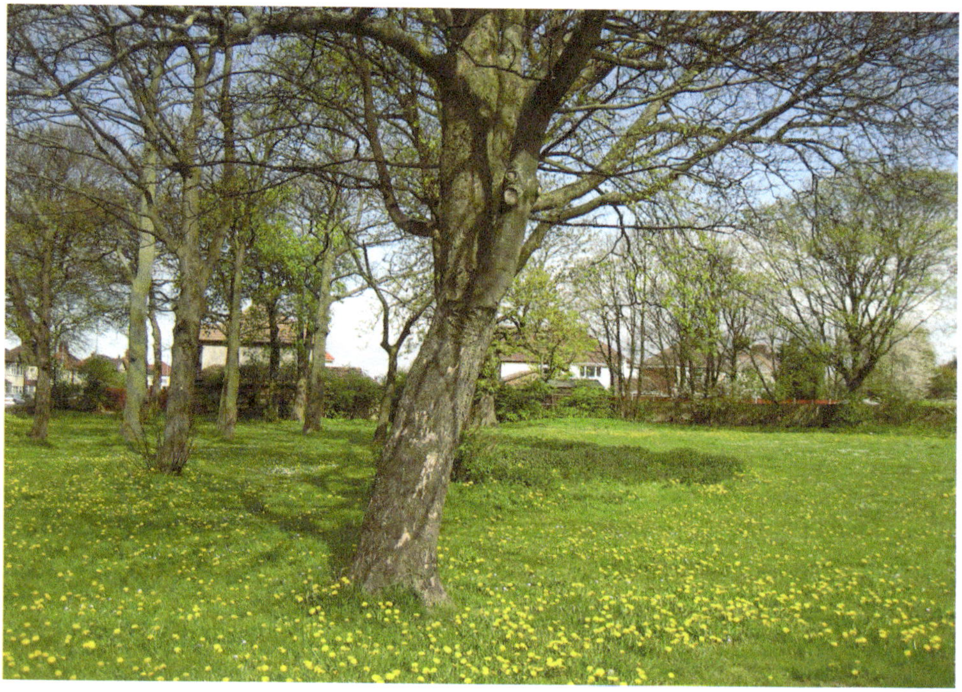

The Junction of Liverpool Road South with Northway

Broadwood House was a gentlemen's residence and, later, a Roman Catholic boys' boarding school before it was demolished in the 1930s to make way for Northway. The small wood in the grounds still exists, and the name lives on in the doctors' surgery situated on the land, and a road.

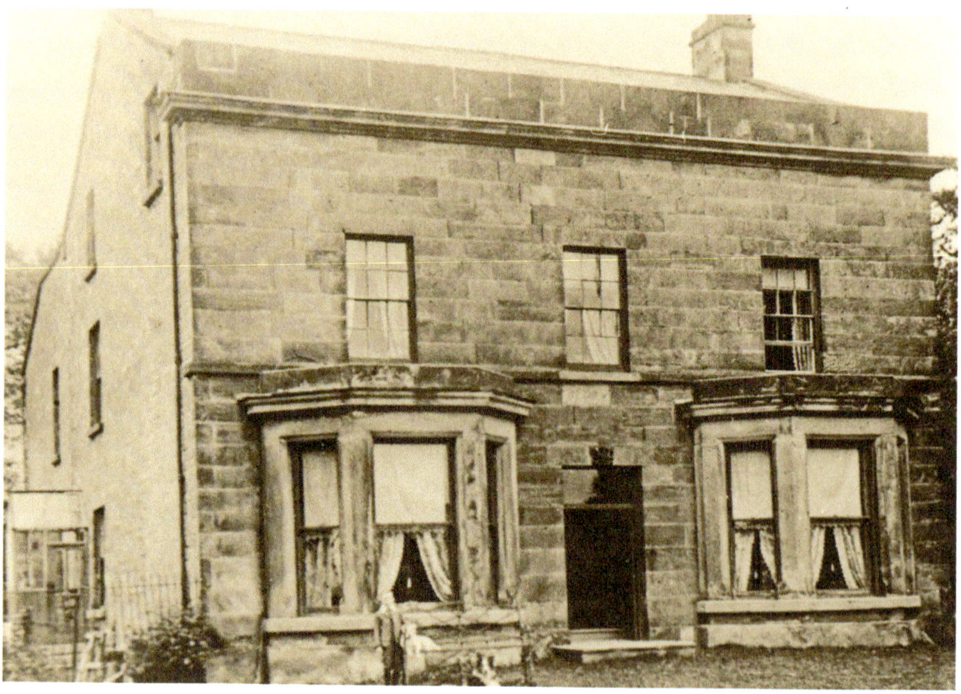

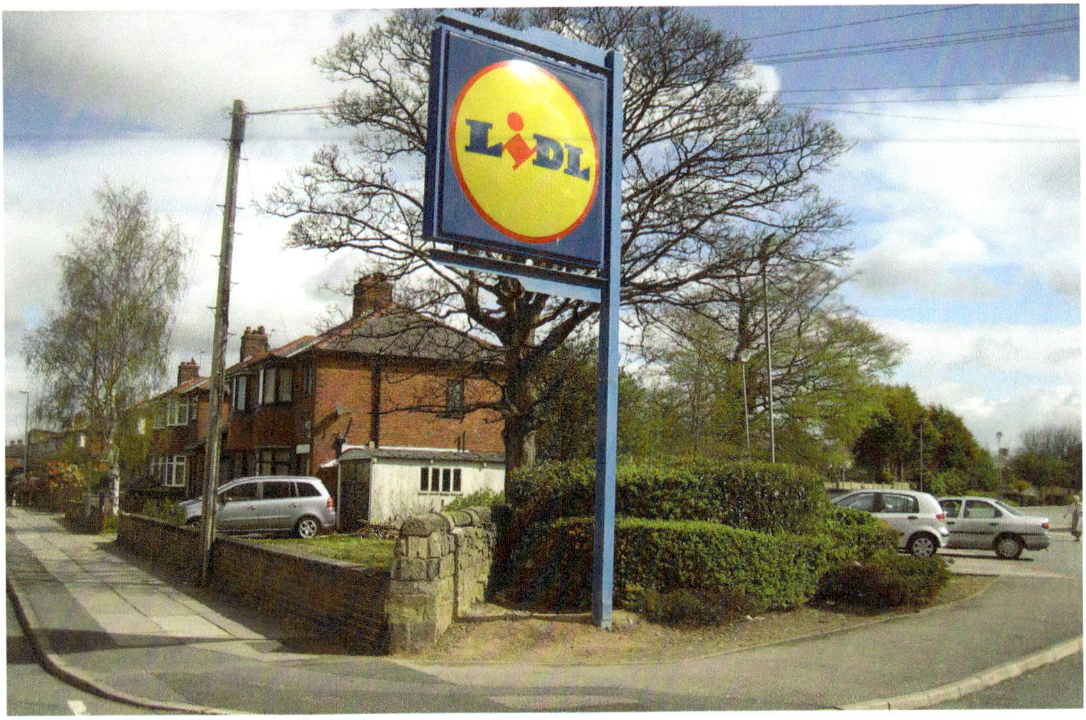

The Maghull Wood

The former Woodend Farm is a reminder of the ancient wood which covered a large area of the south part of Maghull. Only a small part of the garden wall edging onto Northway remains, with two lonely trees.

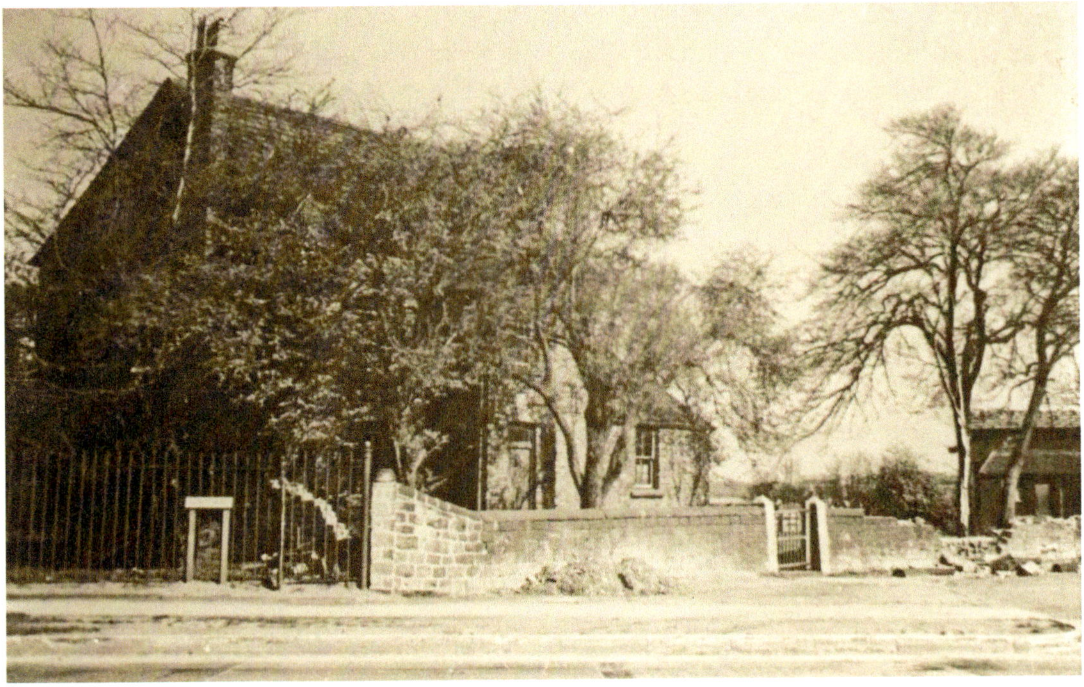

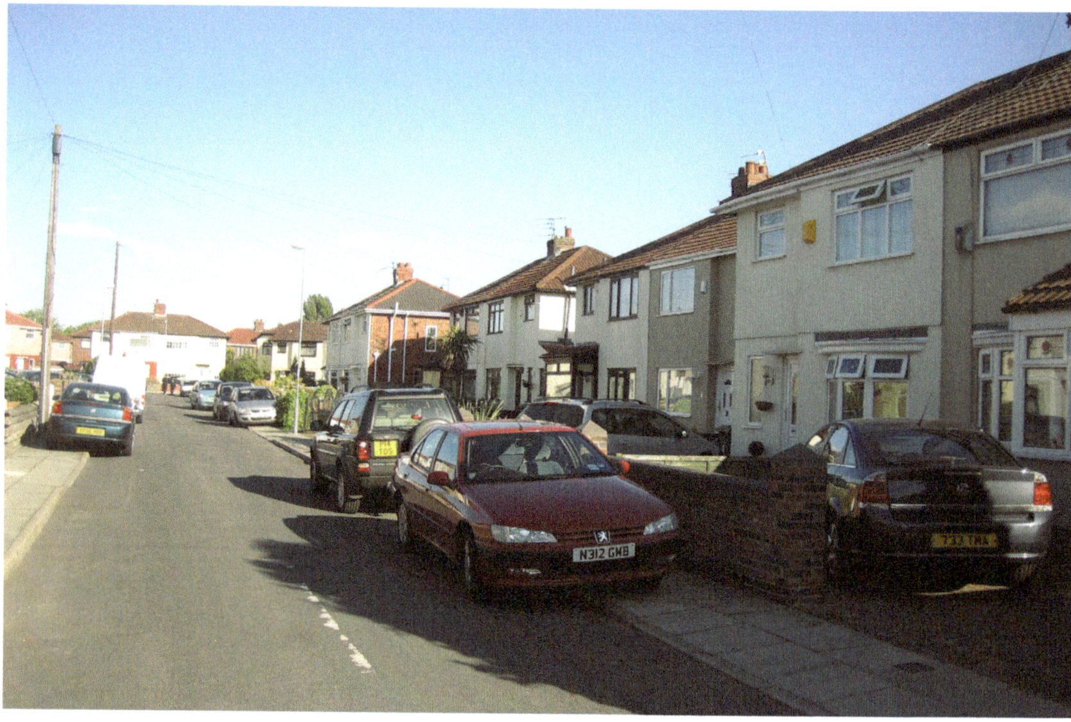

A New Queen

Typical of the houses built in the Alt Park Estate during the extensive pre-war building in Maghull, the houses in Norton Grove, here pictured at the 1953 party to celebrate the coronation of Queen Elizabeth, are easily recognisable today.

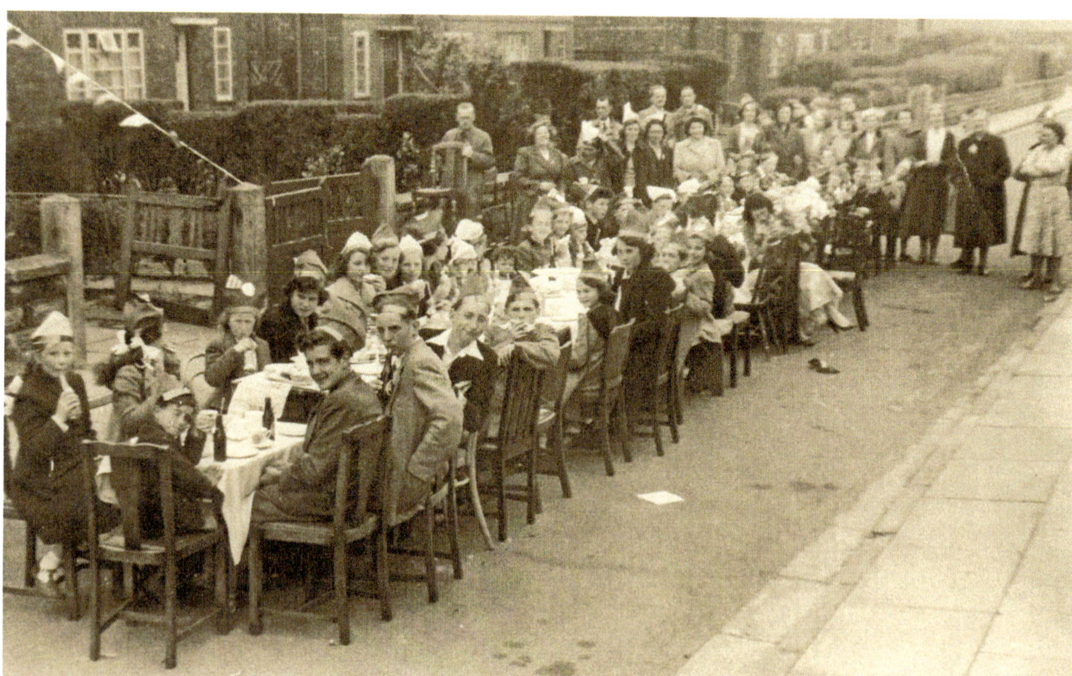

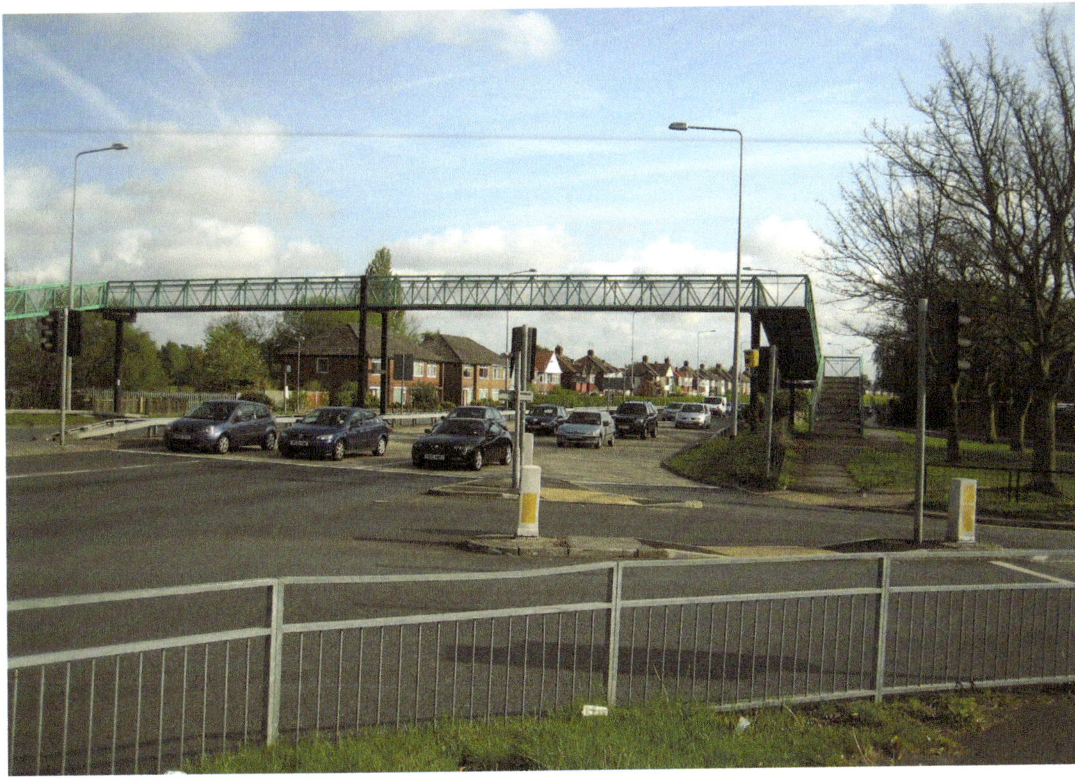

'Gentlemen, Start Your Engines'

The typical rush hour scene at the Northway and Hall Lane junction is such that the two lonely Belisha Beacons in this 1950s view appear pathetically inadequate.

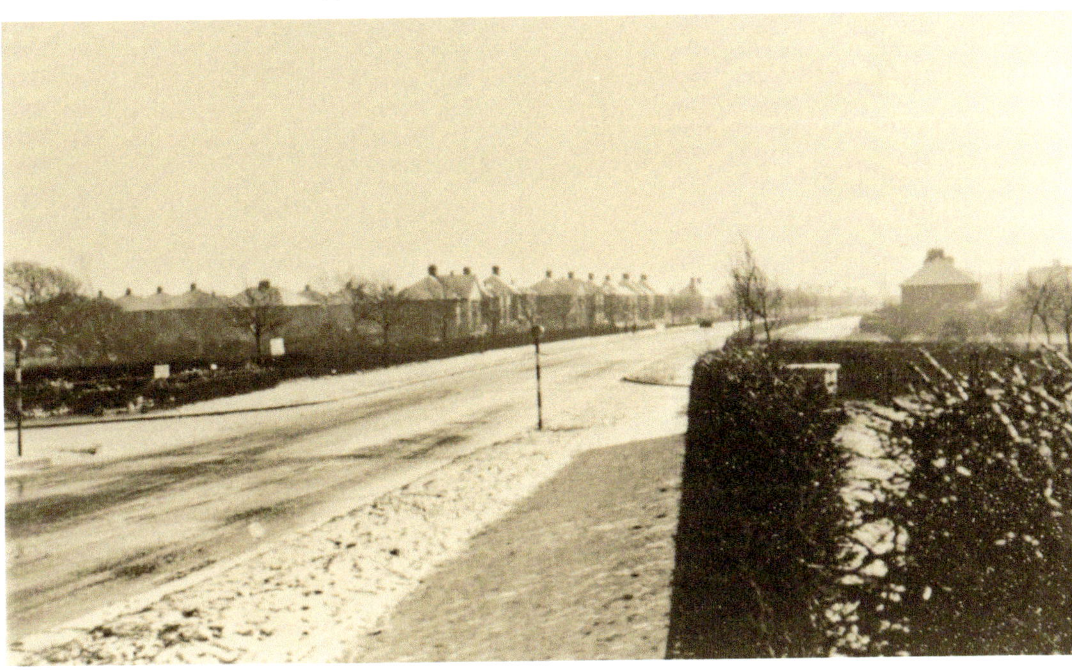

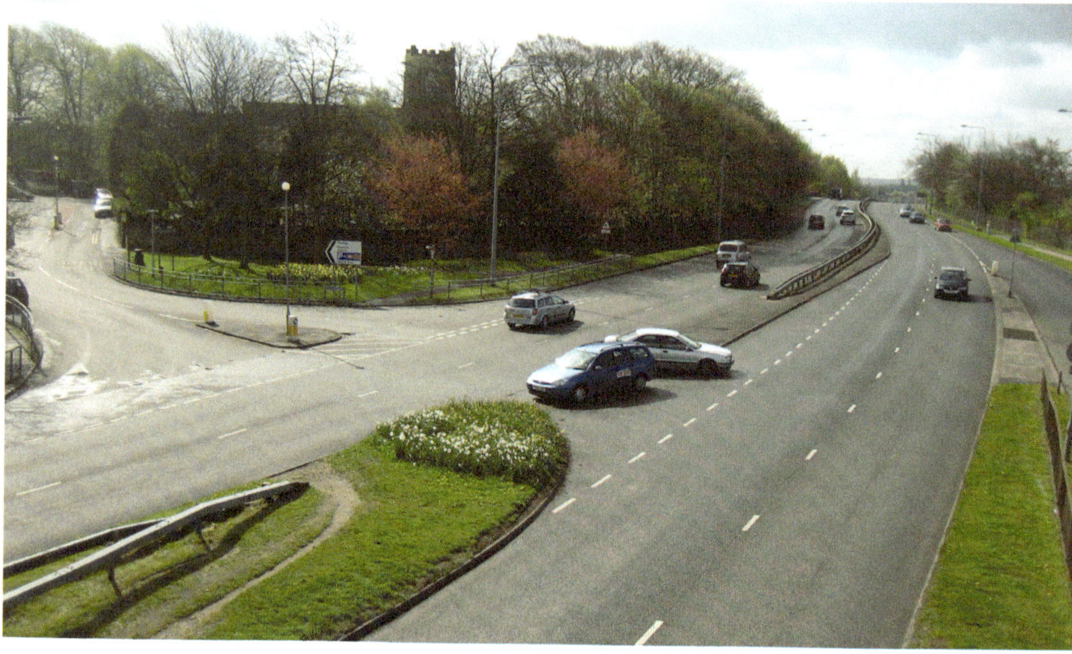

A Bird's Eye View

The single track road proved inadequate, and when the dual carriageway on the left was built in 1963, it required the removal of the Coronation Gardens adjacent to the church grounds, planted to celebrate the coronation ten years previously.

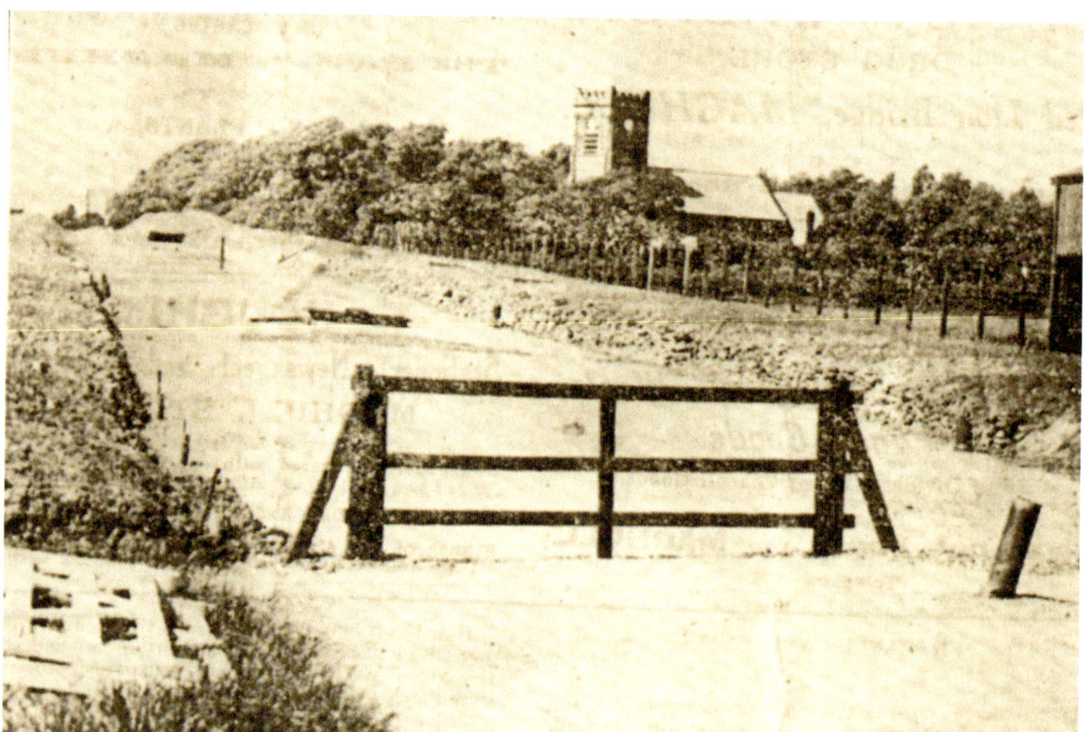

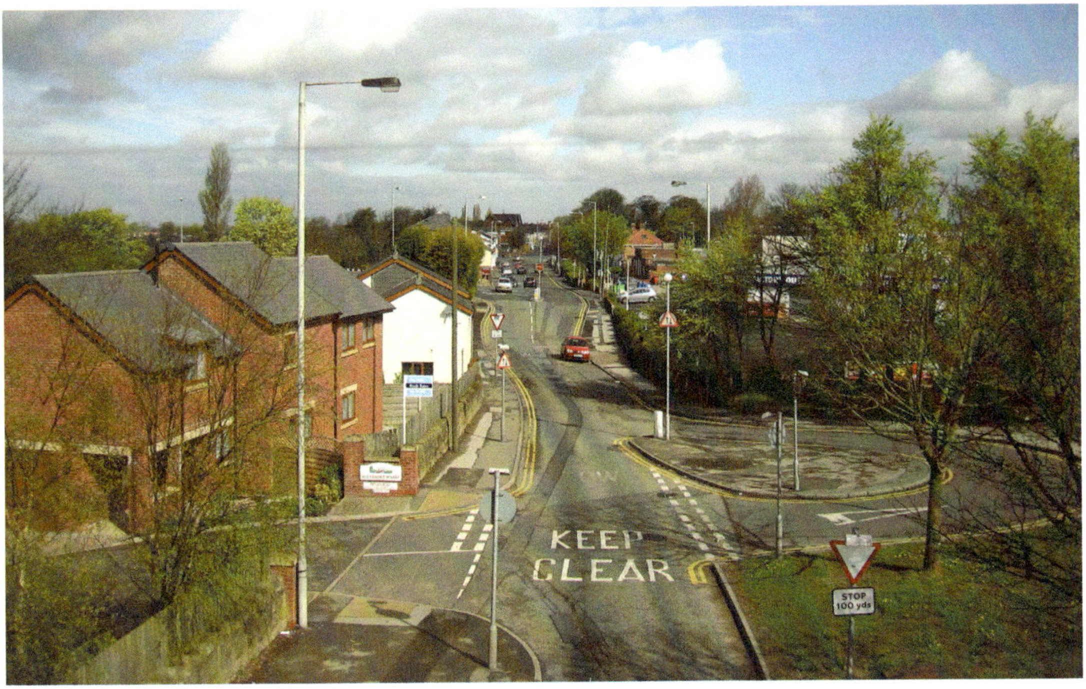

The View from the Northway Road Bridge

In this 1950s view, the Damfield Lane traffic passes the site of the former Red Lion Inn into the busy Liverpool Road North. The main changes are the building of new houses, Alexander Wharf, in the land at the left foreground and, although the site is obscured by trees, the garage to the right has closed. The working barge on the canal would be a very rare site today.

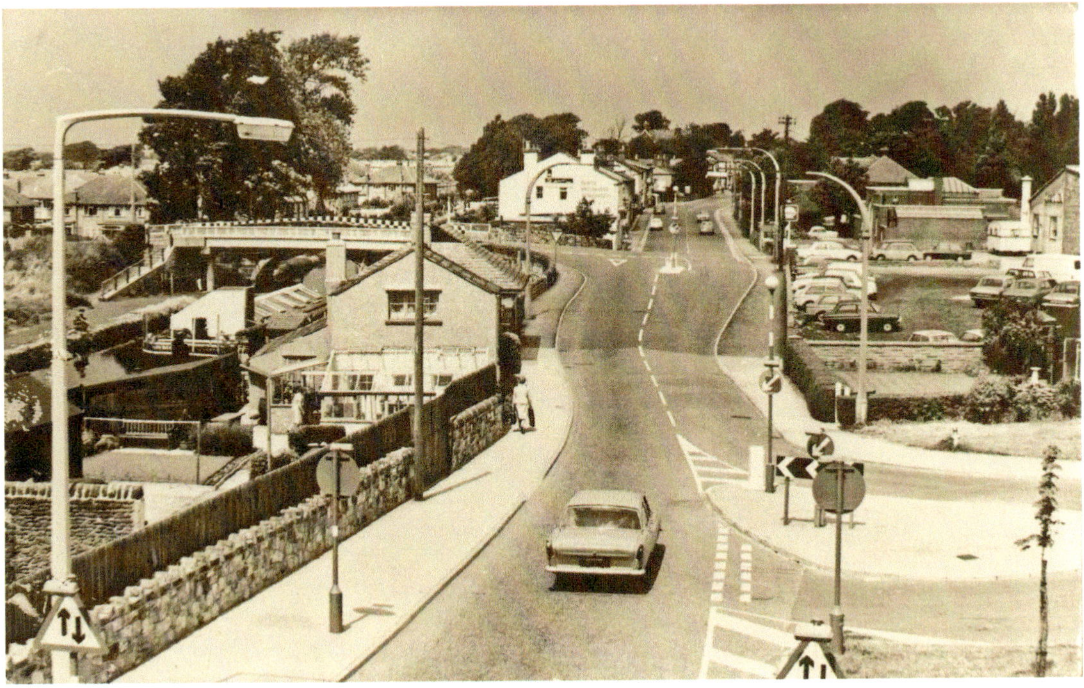

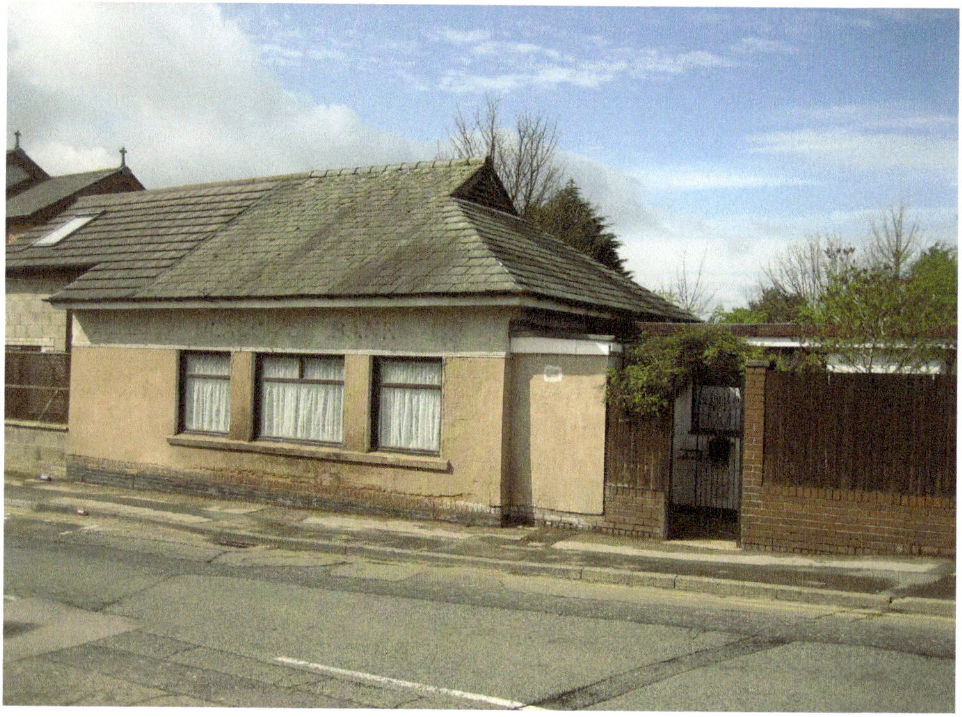

Damfield Lane

Originally built as a branch of the William Deacon Bank, the name of which is still just visible above the windows, it became the Maghull Parish Council offices in 1961 before being converted into a private residence when the new Town Hall was opened in 1984.

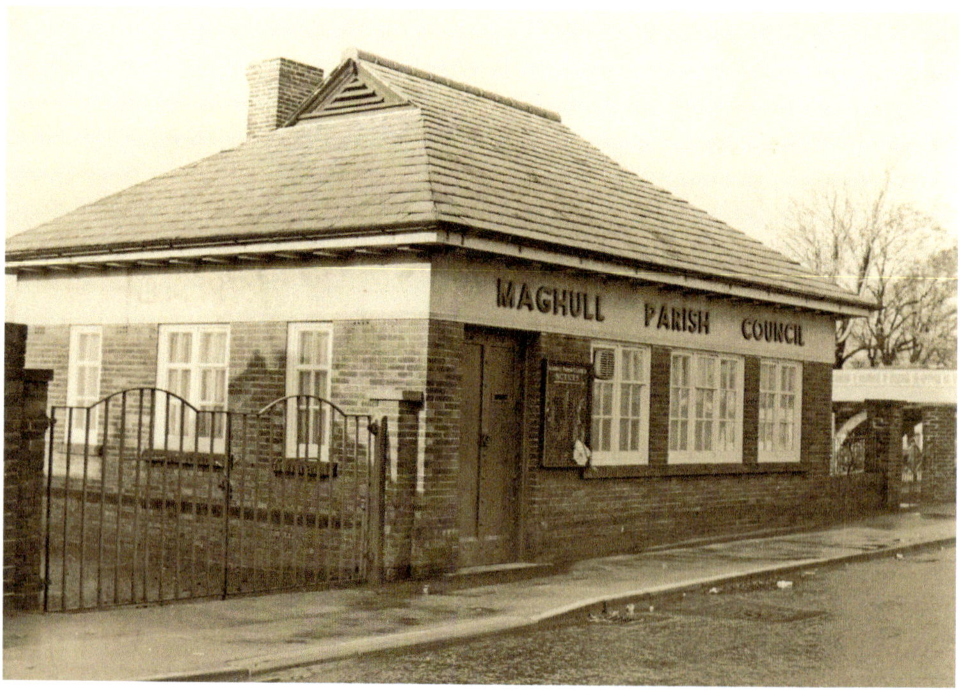

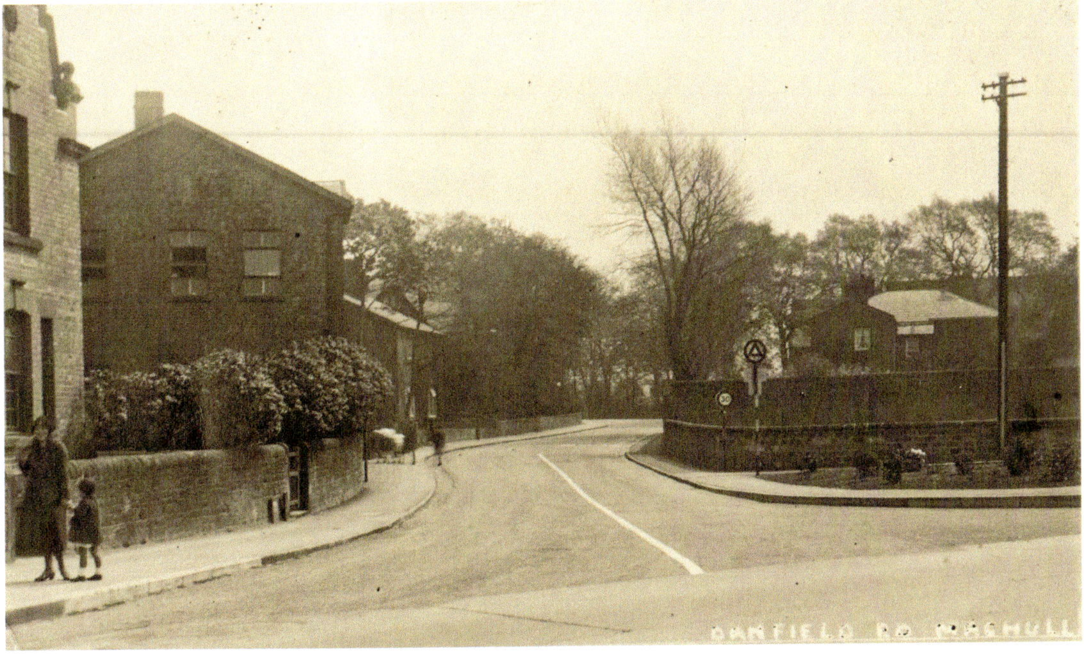

The Junction of Damfield Lane with Northway

The building on the right, below, with its recognisable design, was the Maghull Police Station, and was demolished to make way for the dual carriageway of Northway. The top picture is the view from the police station as it must have appeared for generations. The school, headmaster's house and vicarage are all in the distance. Northway has not yet been constructed.

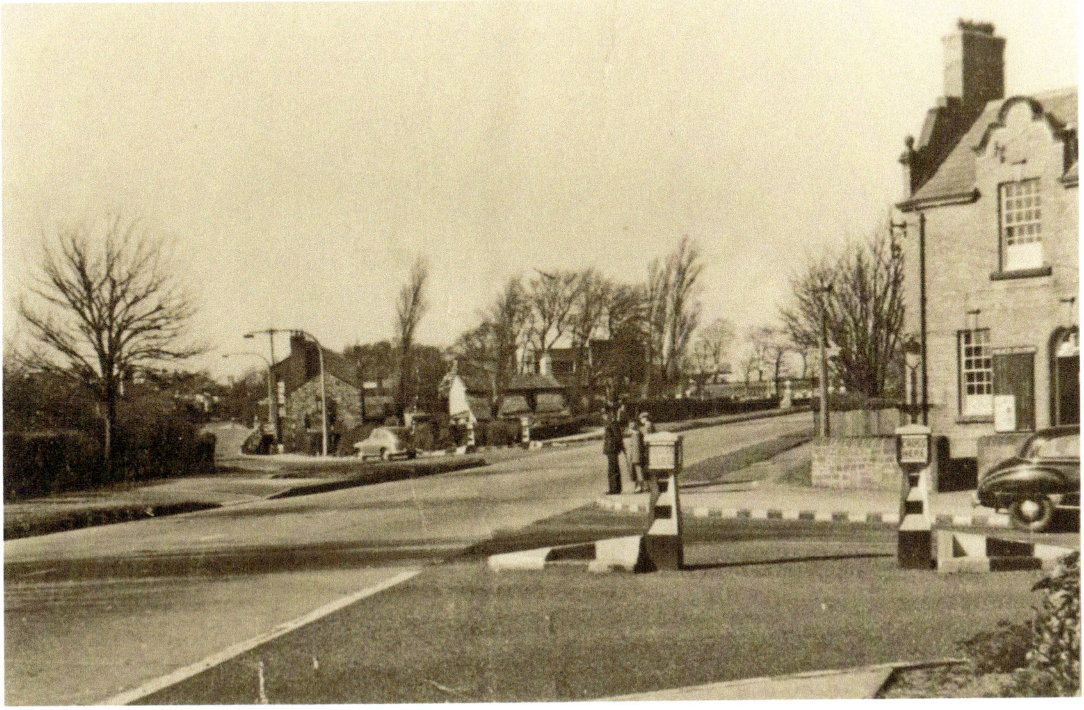

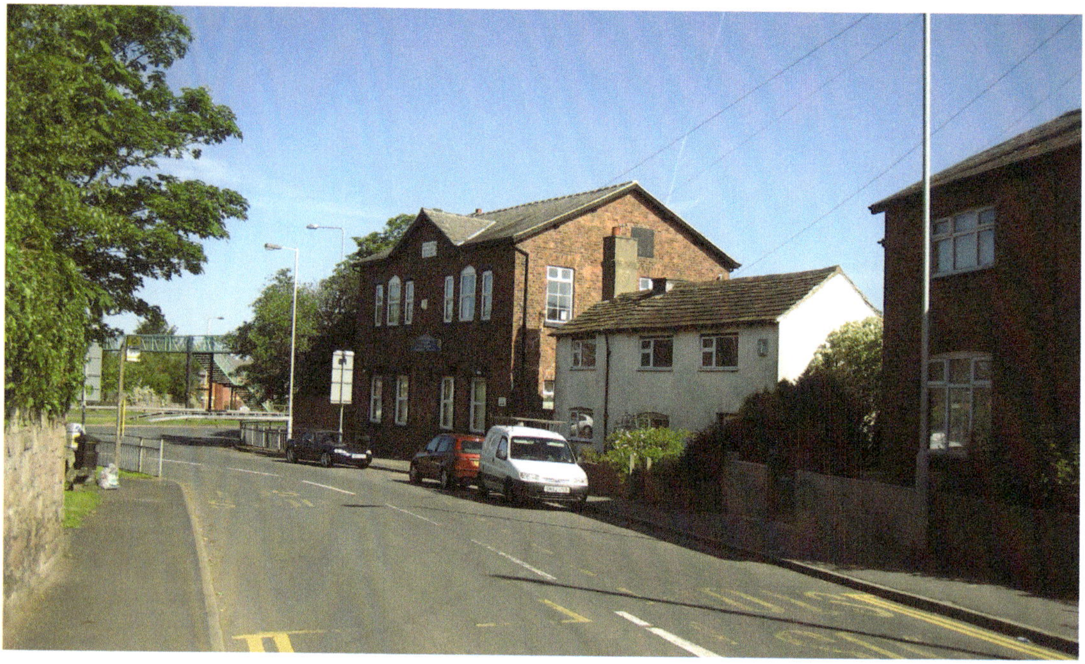

St Andrew's School in Damfield Lane

Although not the first school in Maghull, St Andrew's School started in what became the headmaster's house, the light-coloured building, in 1830, and the Maghull National School was built next door nine years later. A further storey was added in 1873, and the building has changed very little since then. However, the present-day main school building is to the rear of the early school.

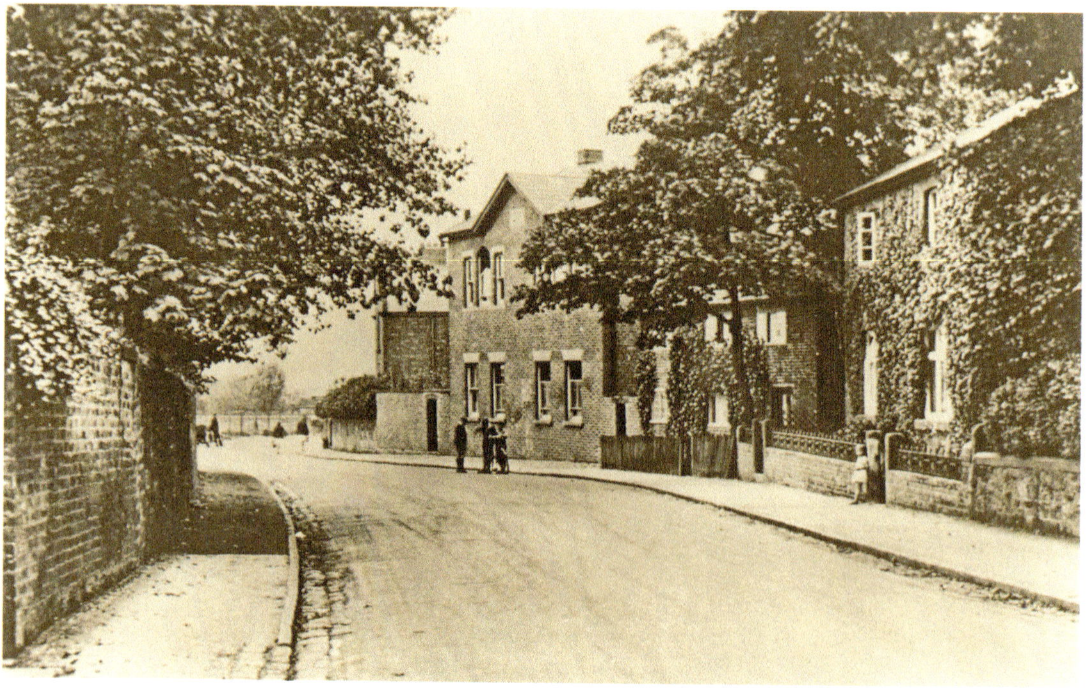

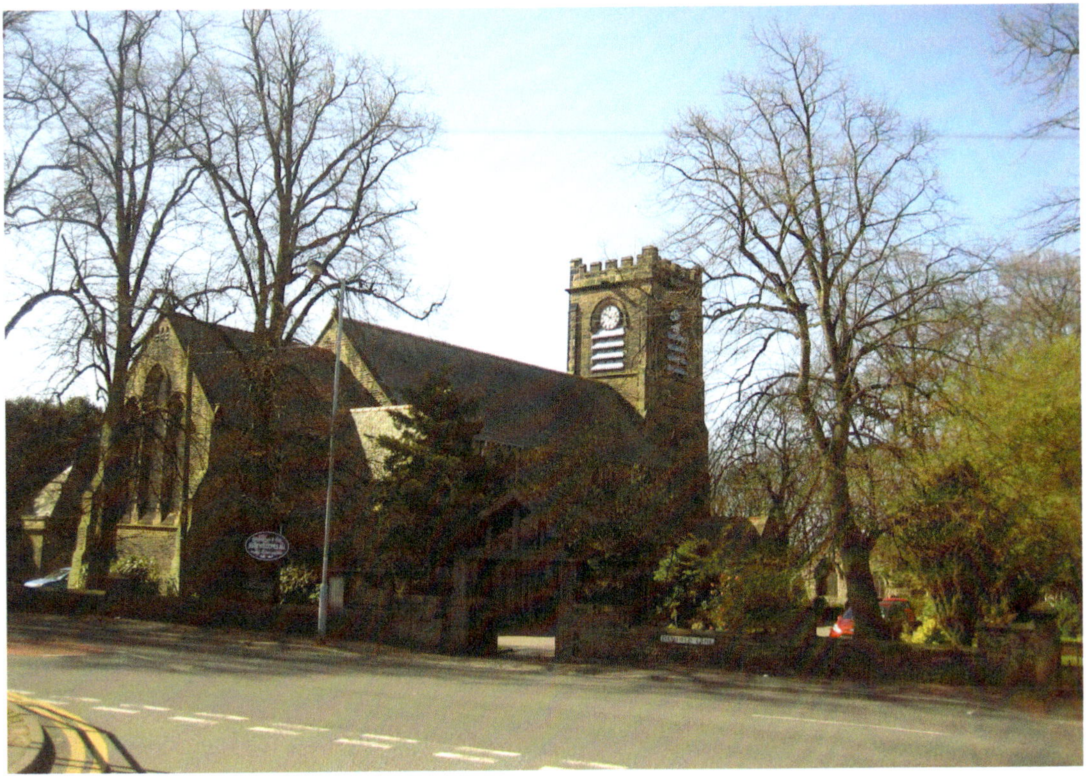

St Andrew's Church

Building work started in 1878, and the church has changed very little since completion. The tower clocks have been added and the simple gate replaced by the lychgate memorial commemorating members of the town who died in the Second World War, which was dedicated in 1952.

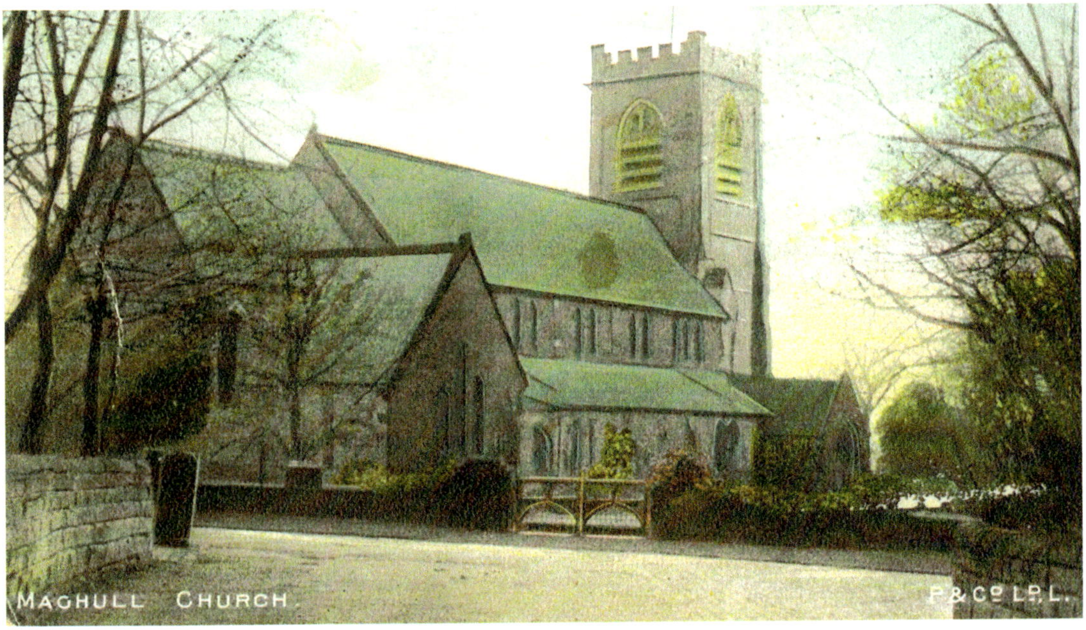

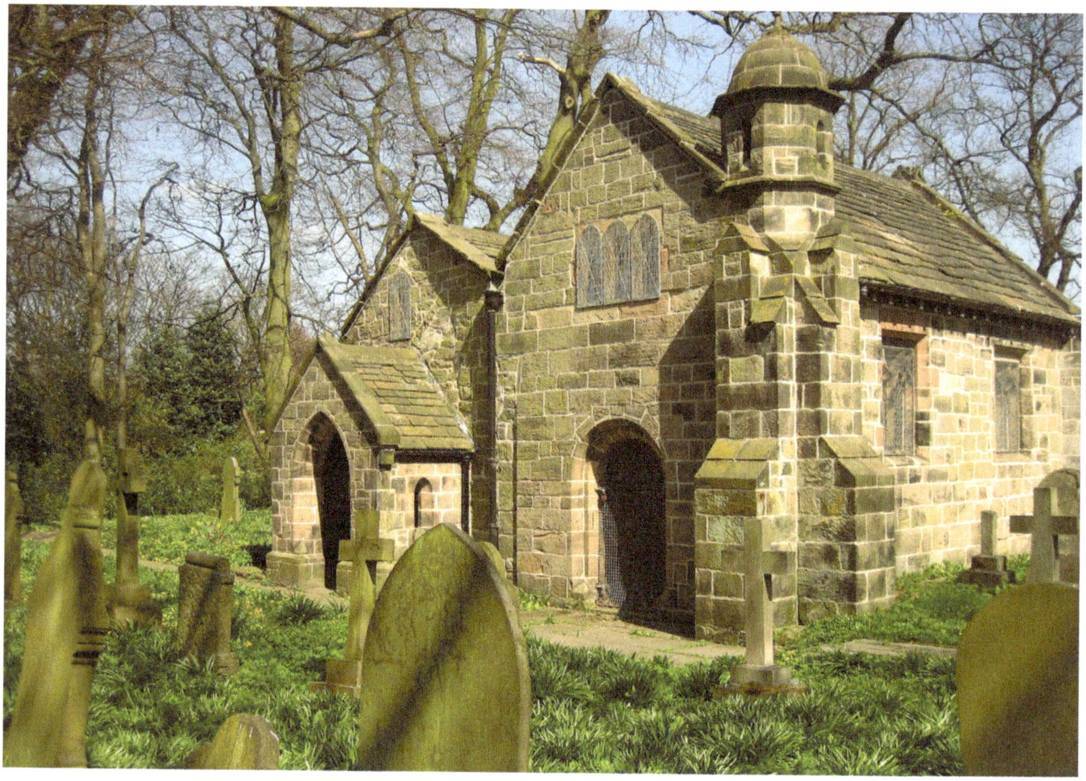

The Treasure in the Grounds of St Andrew's Church

Tucked away in the graveyard of St Andrew's is the Unsworth Chapel. Built between the twelfth and thirteenth centuries, it is one of the oldest buildings in Merseyside. Apart from protective mesh on the windows, there is little change over the century between the photographs. Today the chapel is used for occasional services.

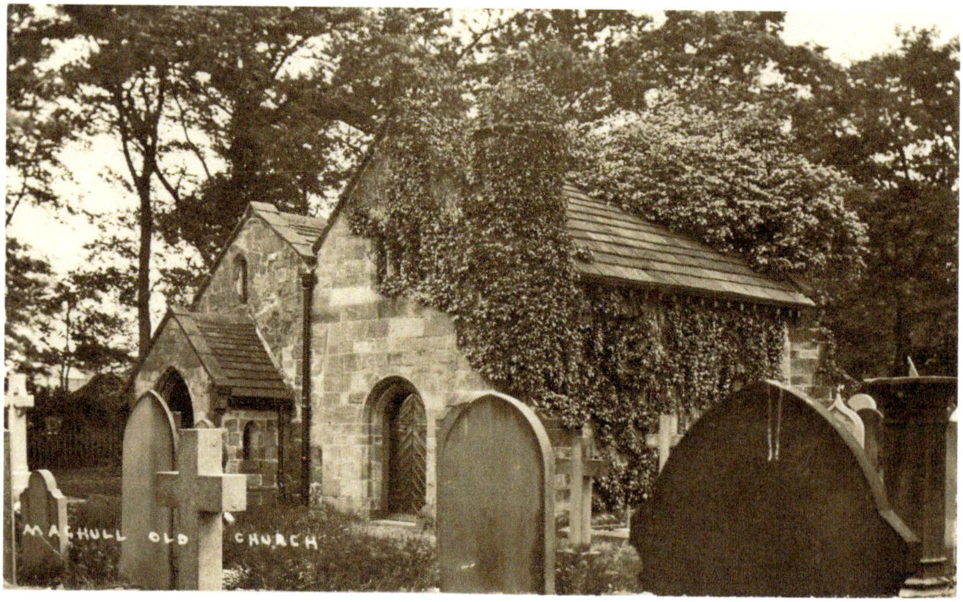

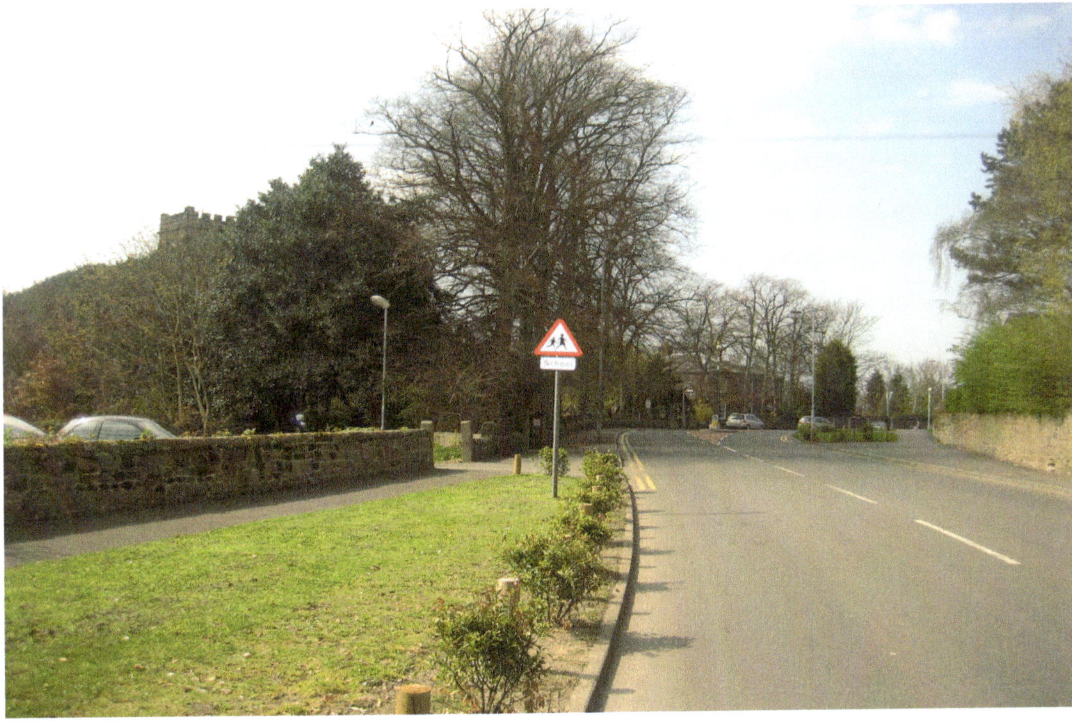

Damfield Lane

The view of St Andrew's and the vicarage is today hidden by the trees, as is the farm building behind the wall, which has been converted into a residence. The wall has been moved back and traffic restrictions confirm how busy the area is, especially at school times.

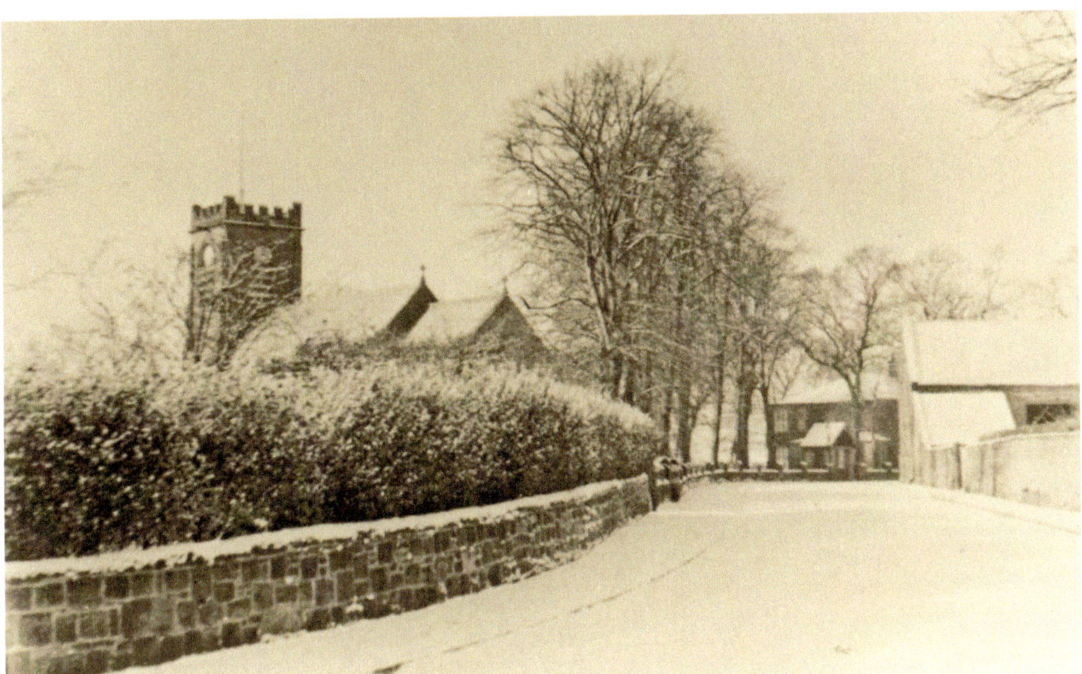

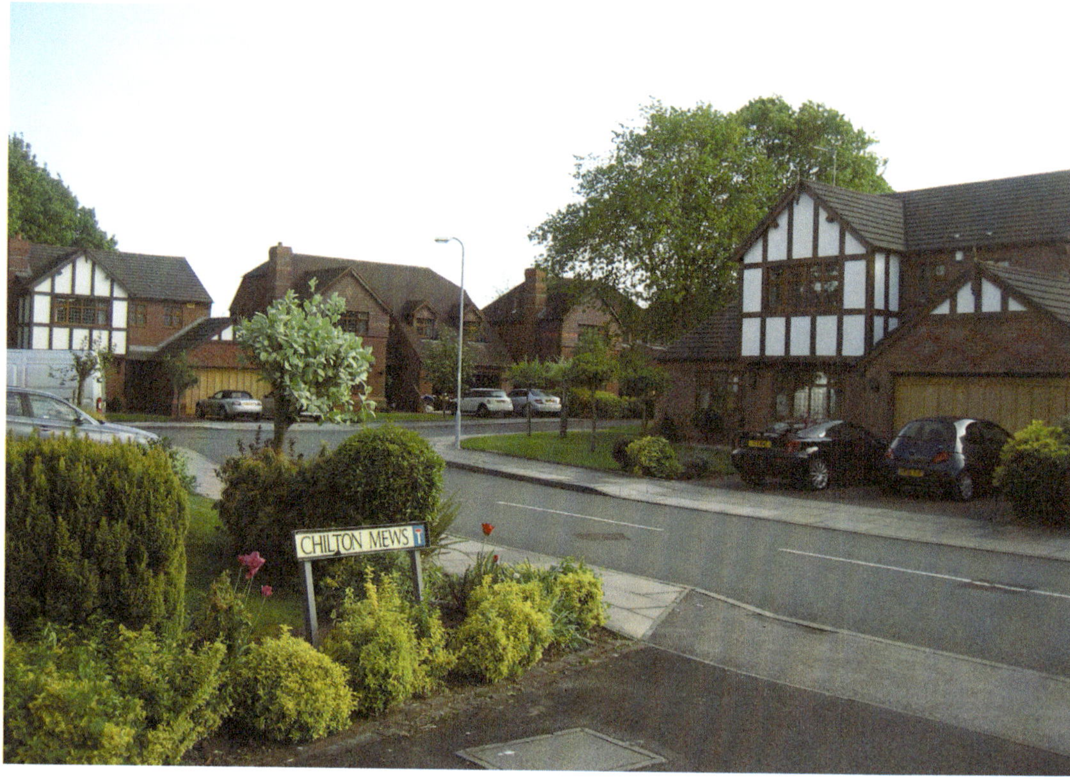

Deyes Lane

Situated on Deyes Lane, the Chilton Home was opened in 1908 for the treatment of children, as part of Maghull Homes. It has been demolished in recent years and replaced by a housing estate, and only the name Chilton lives on.

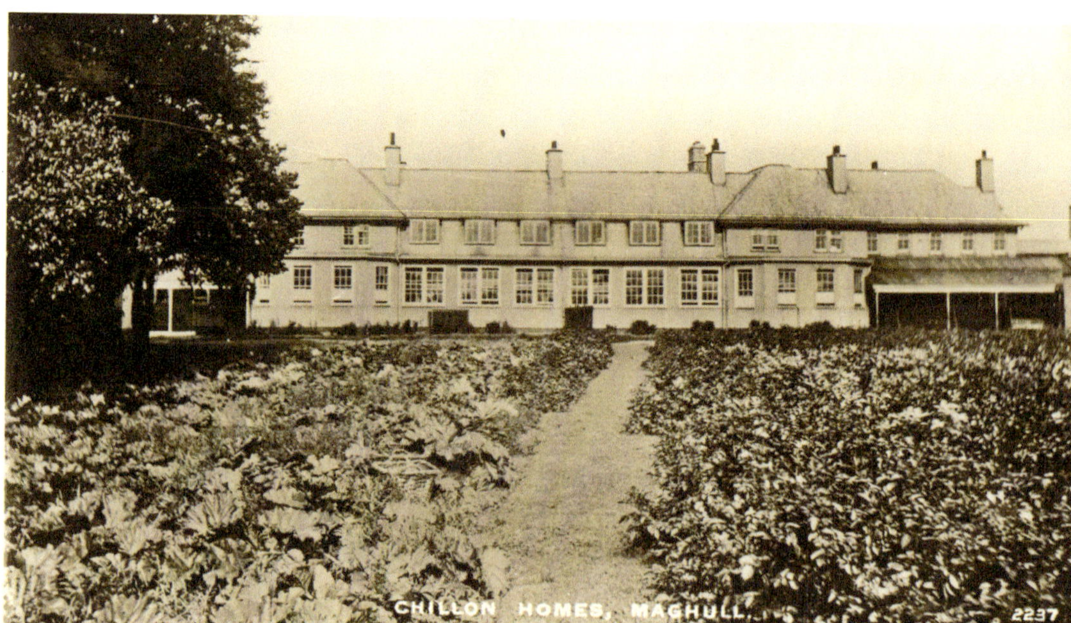

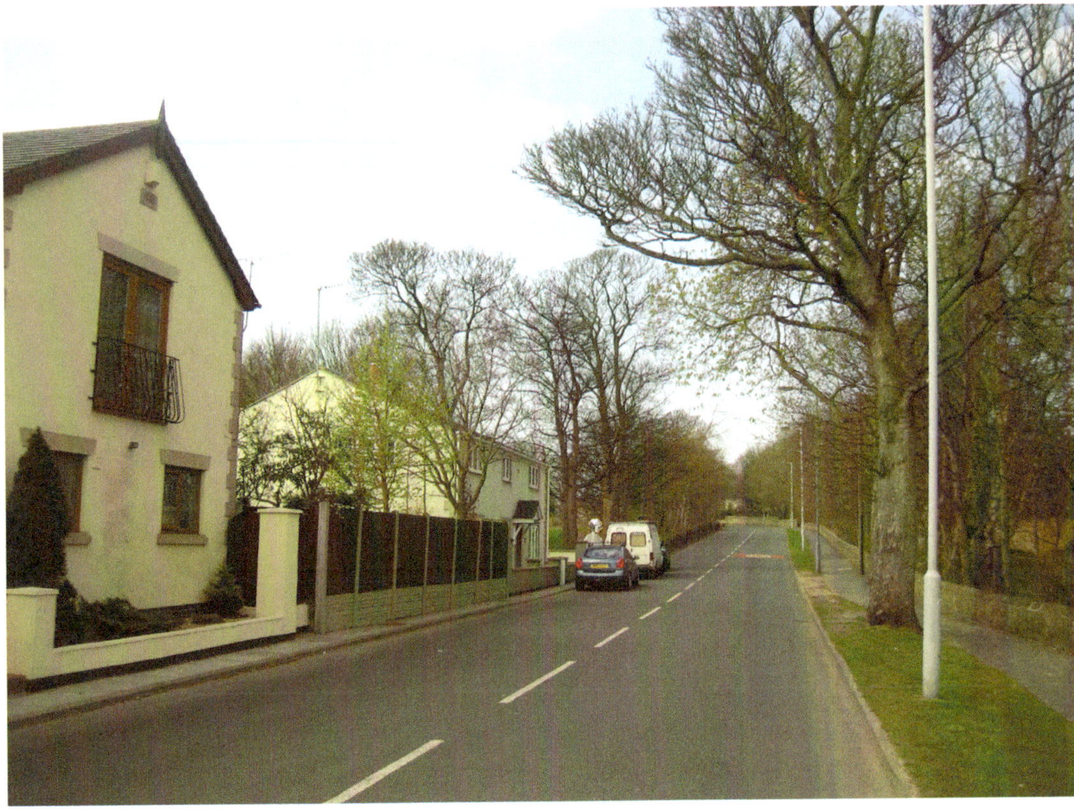

The Workmen's Cottages in 1908

The three cottages in Damfield Lane have been converted into one building: Damfield Cottage. The road has been widened and has lost some of its rural charm.

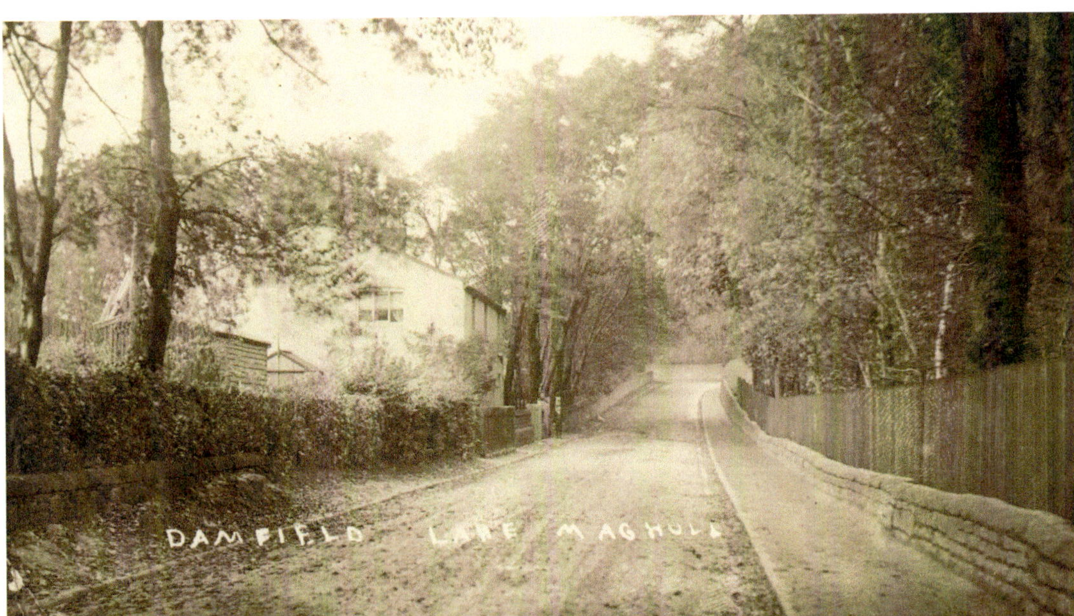

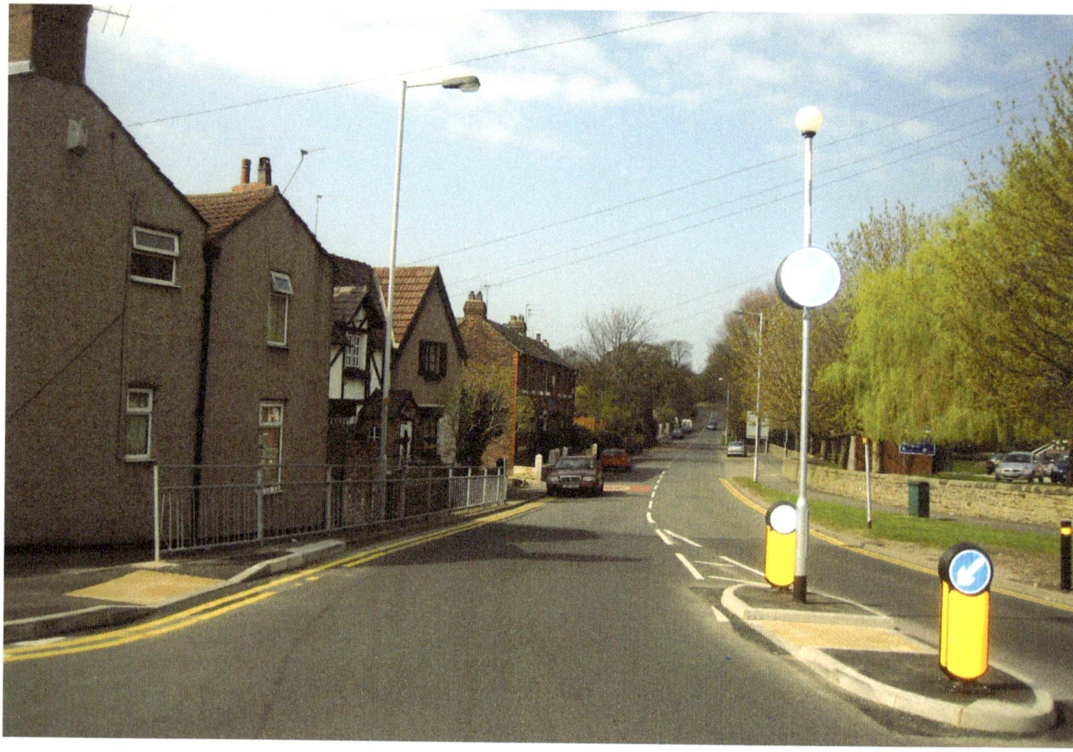

The Junction of Damfield Lane and Hall Lane

The furthest group of buildings, known as Coronation Cottages, were built in 1902, and a new building has been squeezed in beside them. The wall has been moved and Maricourt Catholic High School occupies the land behind it.

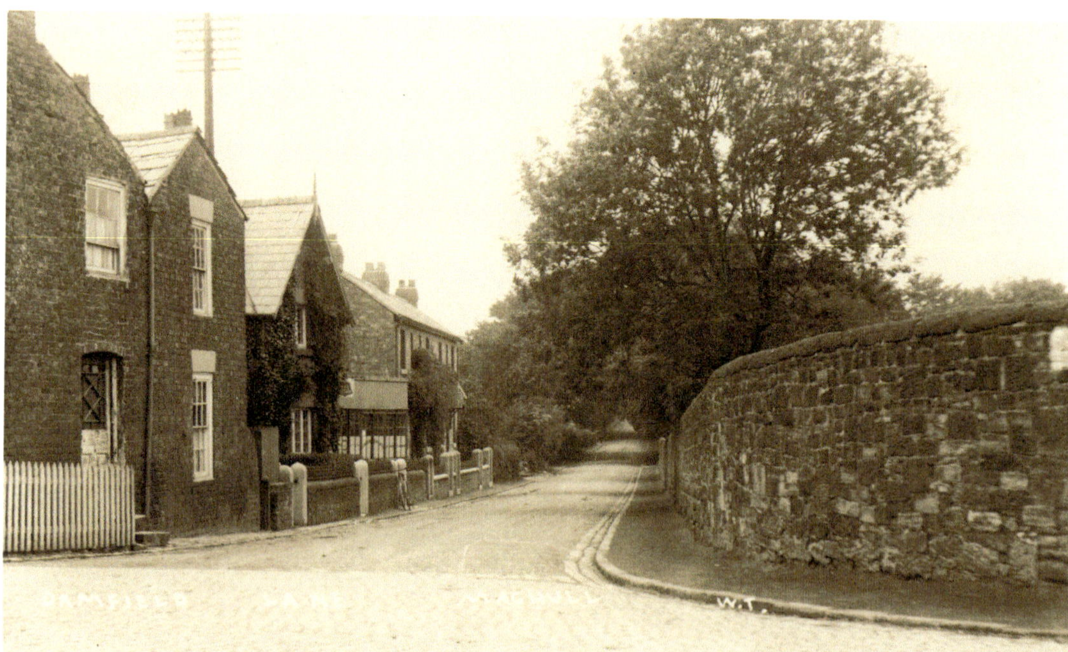

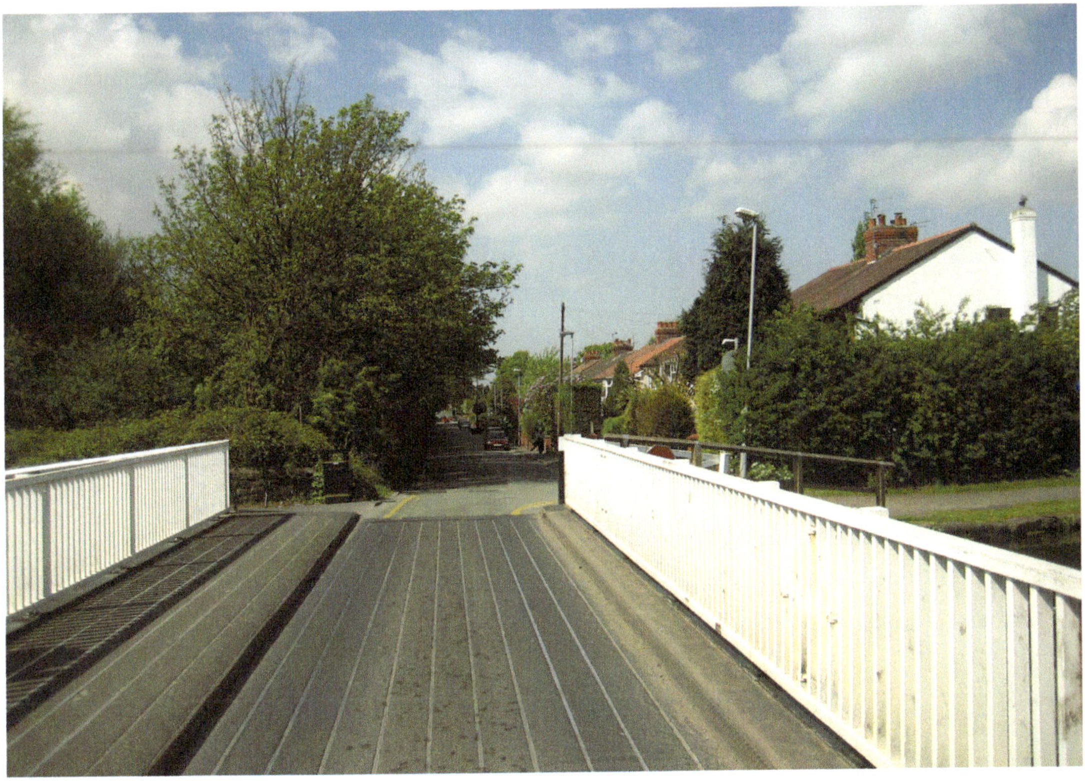

Hall Lane Looking West

Hall Lane is still a narrow road, due to the presence of the Whinny Brook passing through the channel beside the trees and the row of houses along the whole length on the right.

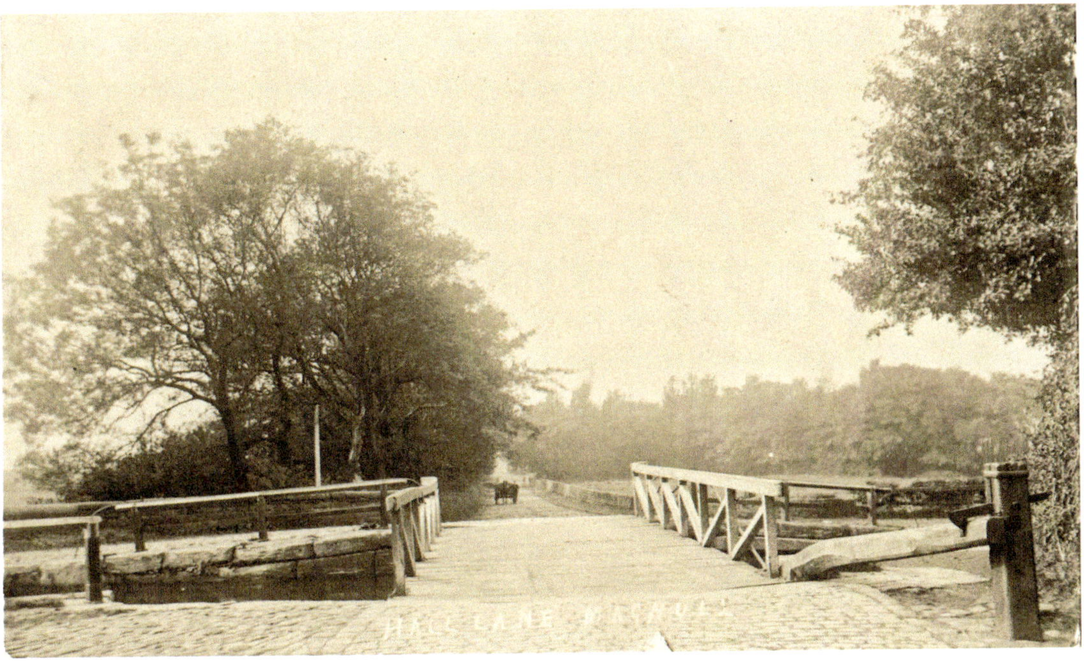

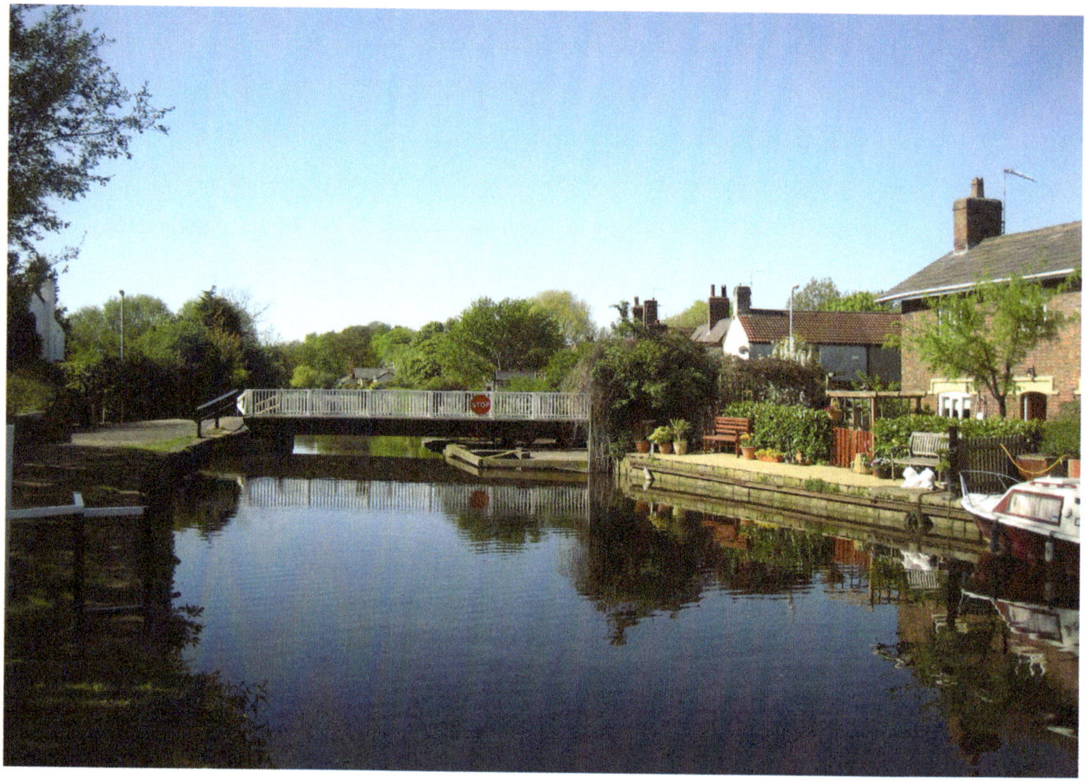

The Maghull Hall Canal Bridge

The building in the older photograph is the former Horse and Jockey Inn, but is now private houses. There has been little change, but the swing bridge has been modernised like all of those in the district.

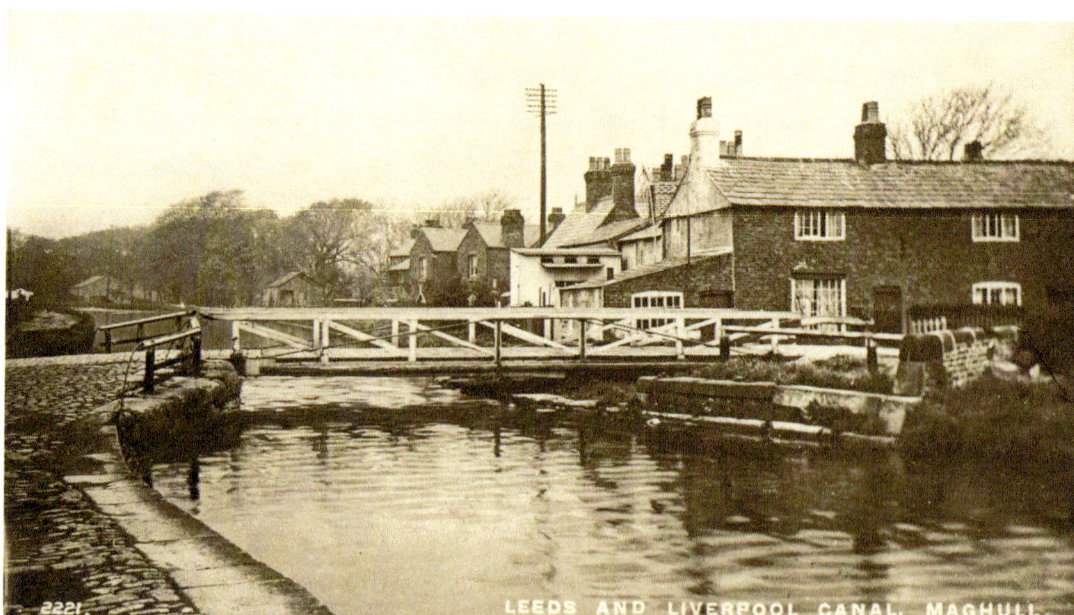

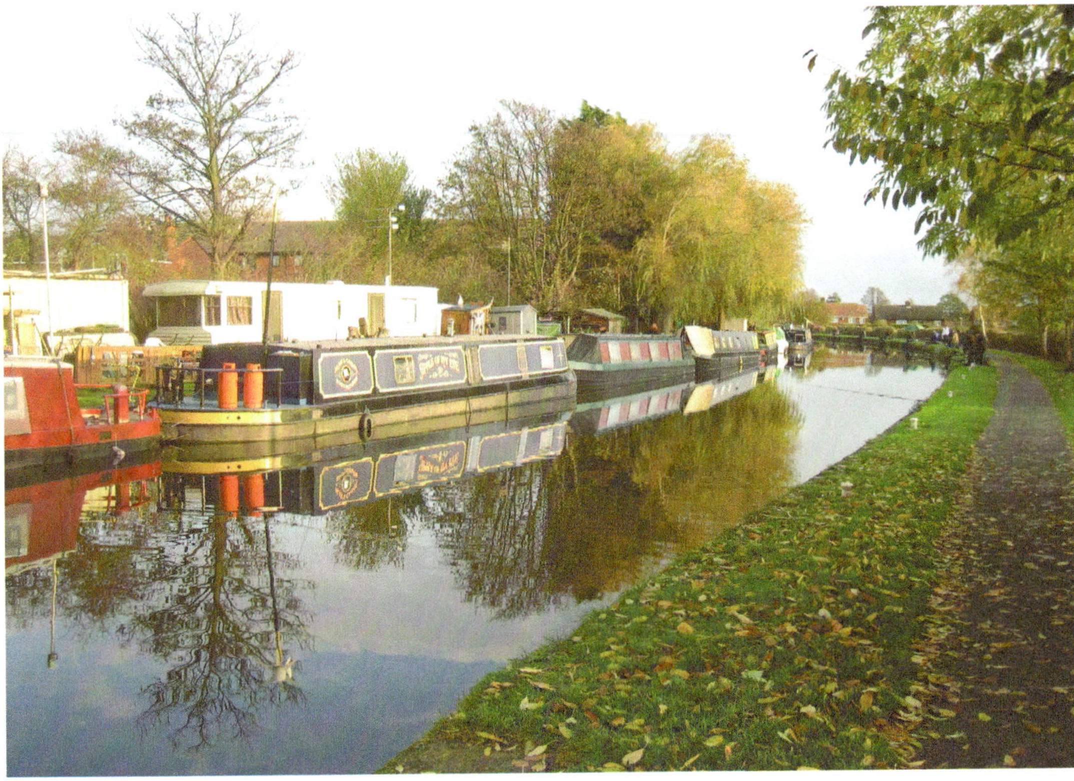

The Canal Near Hall Lane

For many years the canal bank was lined by boats that rarely seem to move, but today the canal has come to life and private boats are familiar sights cruising along the canal.

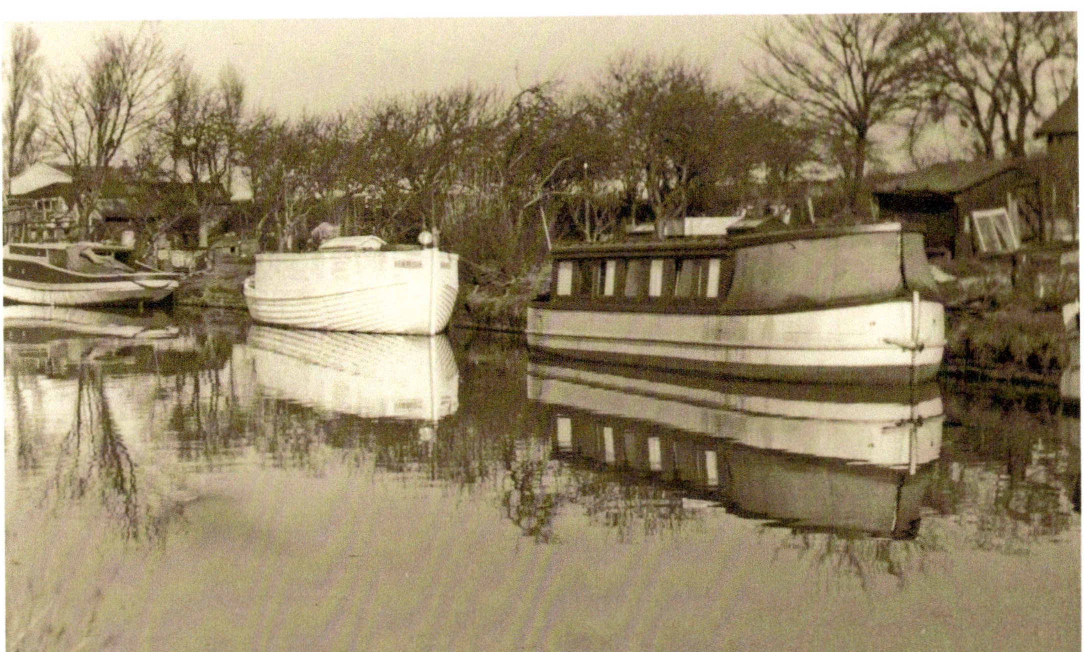

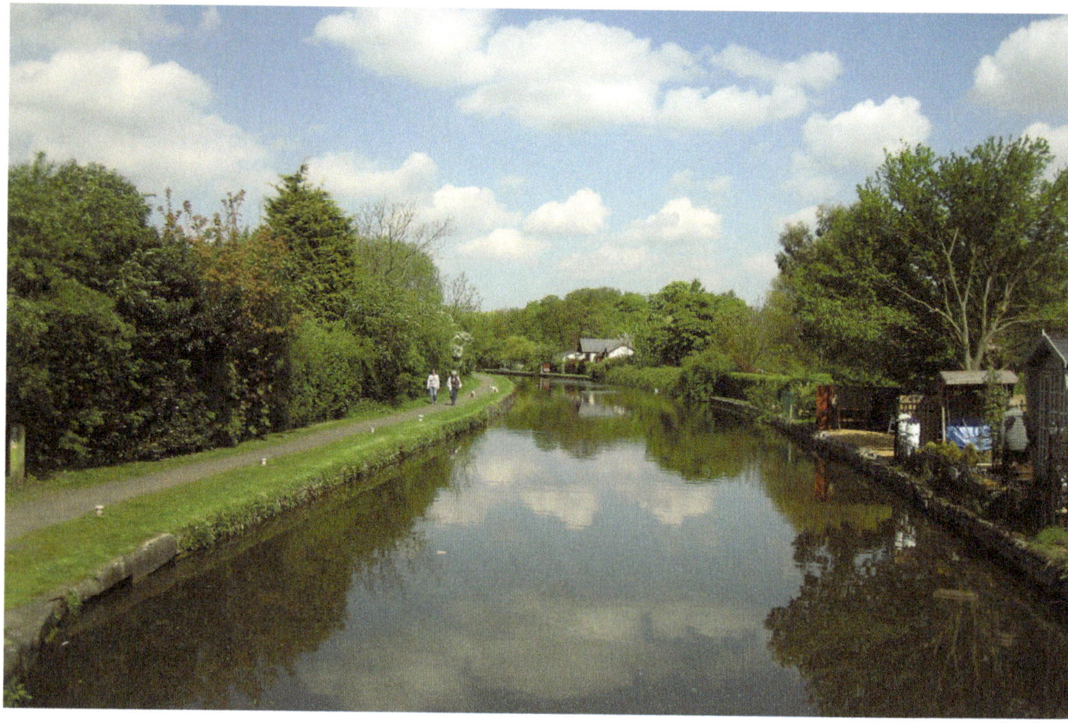

A Peacetime Scene

This view from Maghull Hall Bridge looking towards St Andrew's Church shows Maghull at its best on a lovely spring evening. It is hard to imagine the existence on the bank of the camouflaged pillbox from the last war.

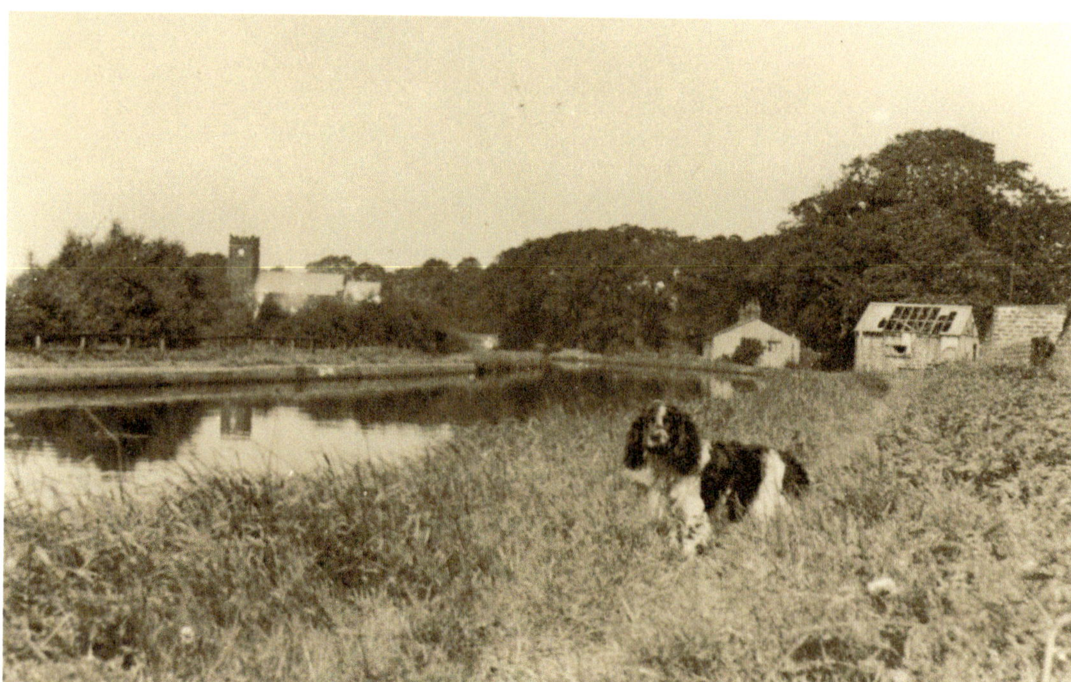

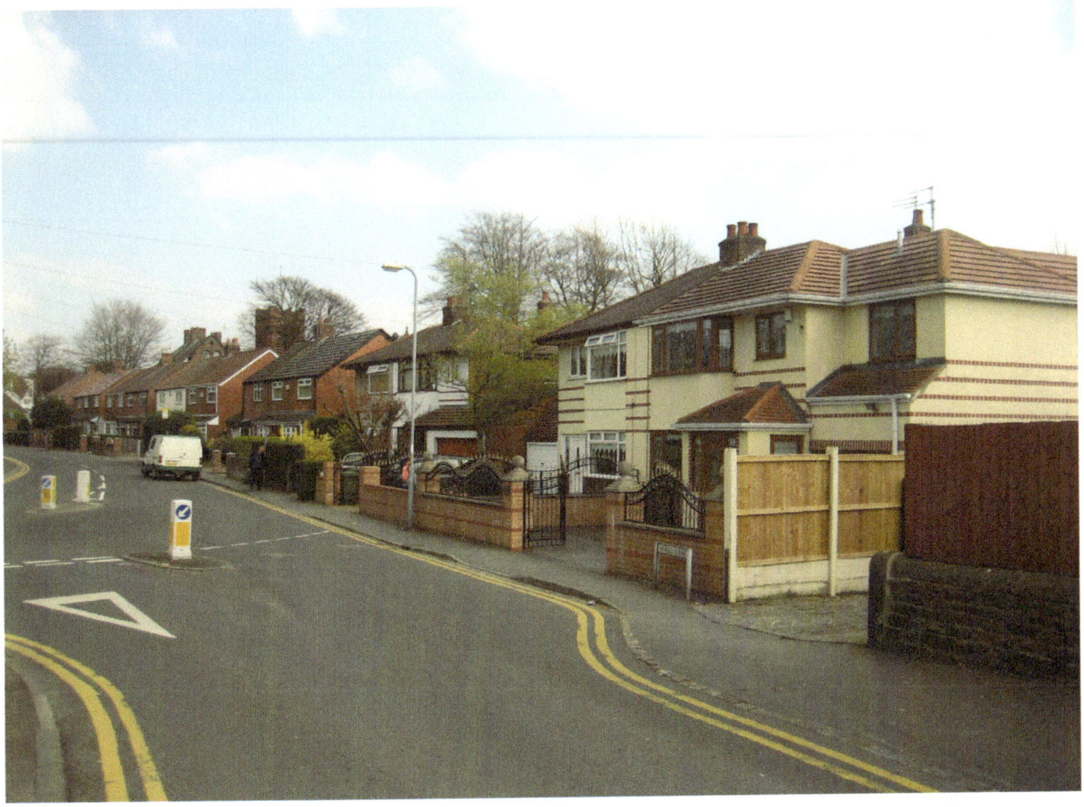

Hall Lane Looking Towards the Station

The Travellers' Rest Inn, built for the canal trade, was demolished in 1936 and houses were built upon the site and adjacent open land.

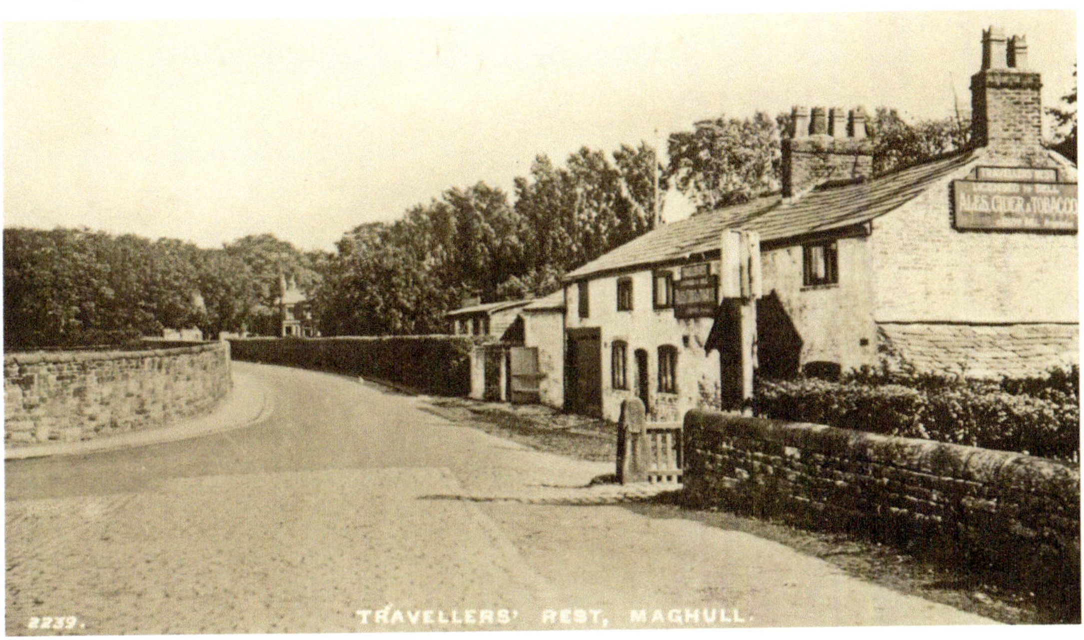

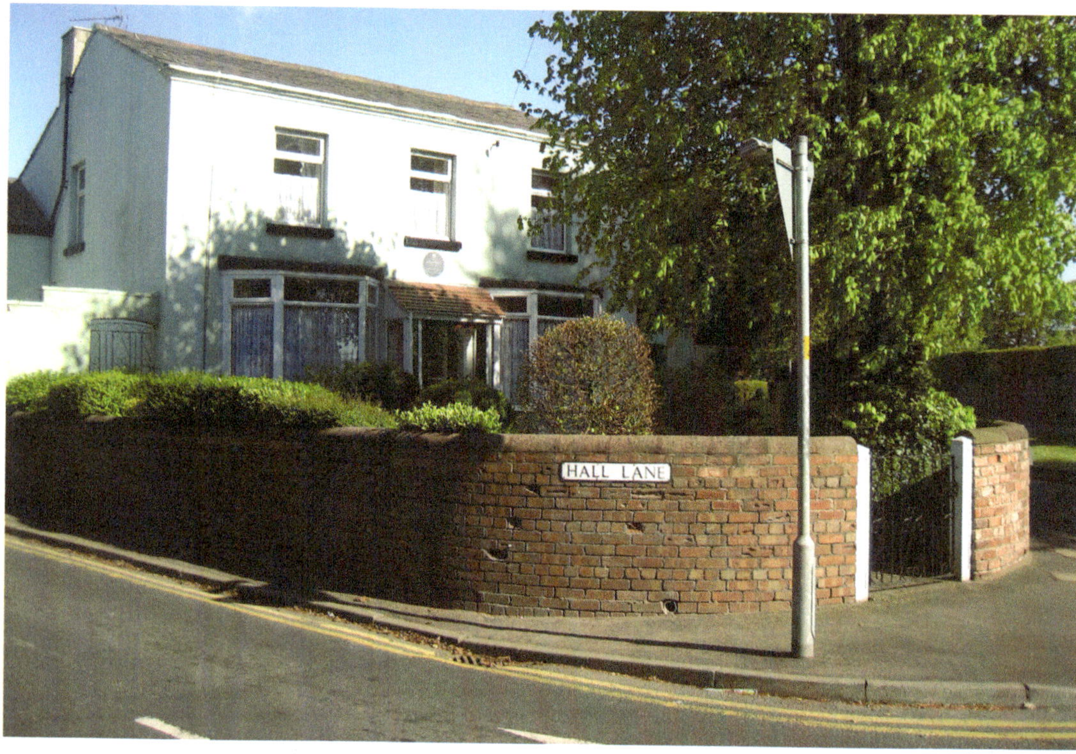

The Junction of Hall Lane with Station Road

Still shielded by the trees, the house made famous as the boyhood home of the eminent author Rafael Sabatini stands proudly on the corner. There is a plaque on the front of the house commemorating its nineteenth-century resident.

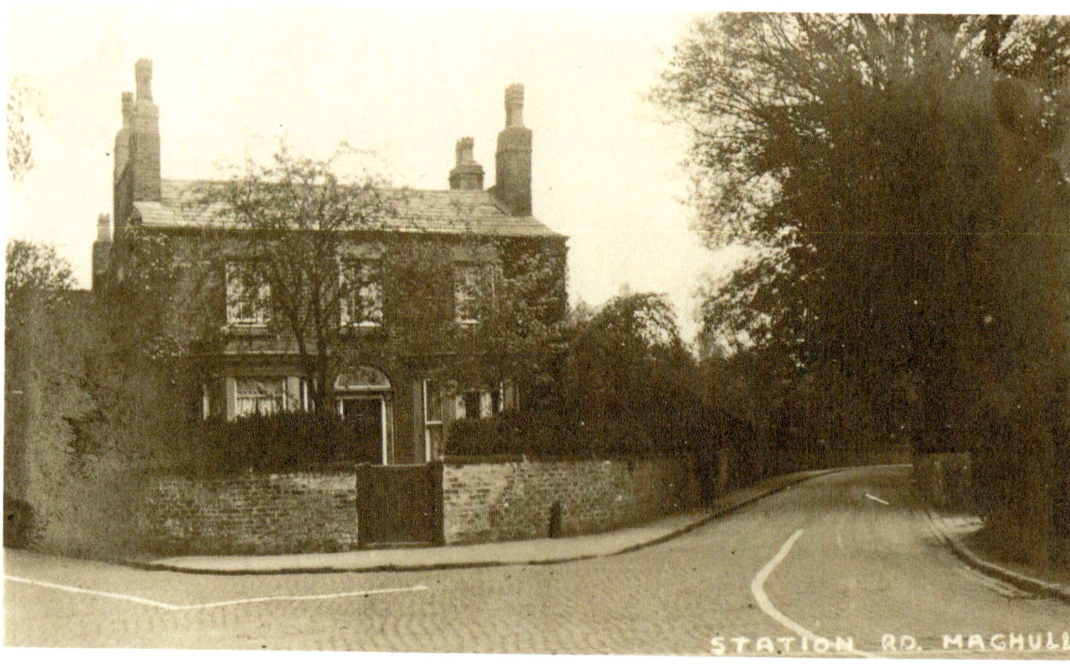

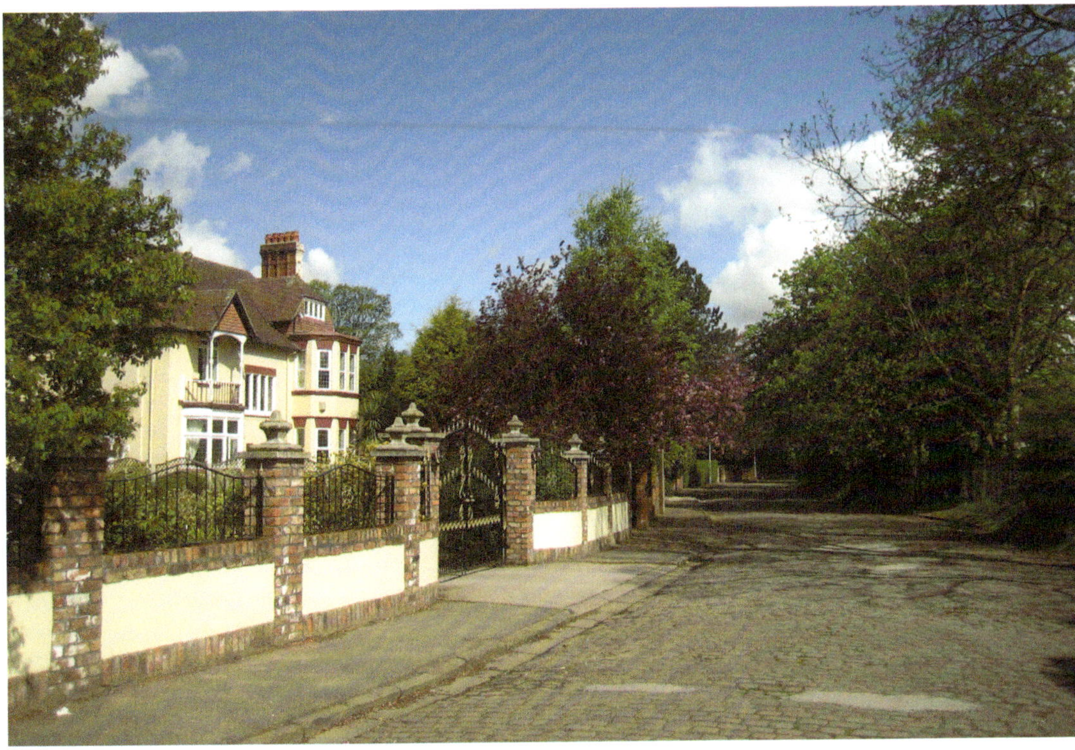

Brook Road

Building of what was possibly the most exclusive road in Maghull started at the turn of the century. The trees have matured but the house can still be recognised. The hedge and row of trees have been replaced by a brick wall.

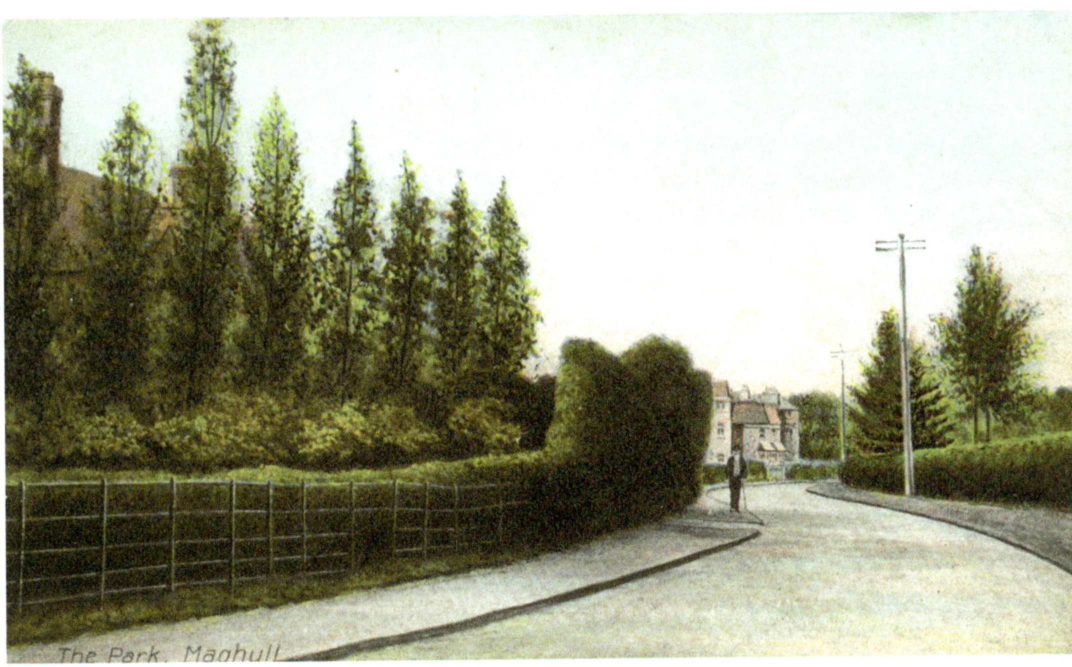

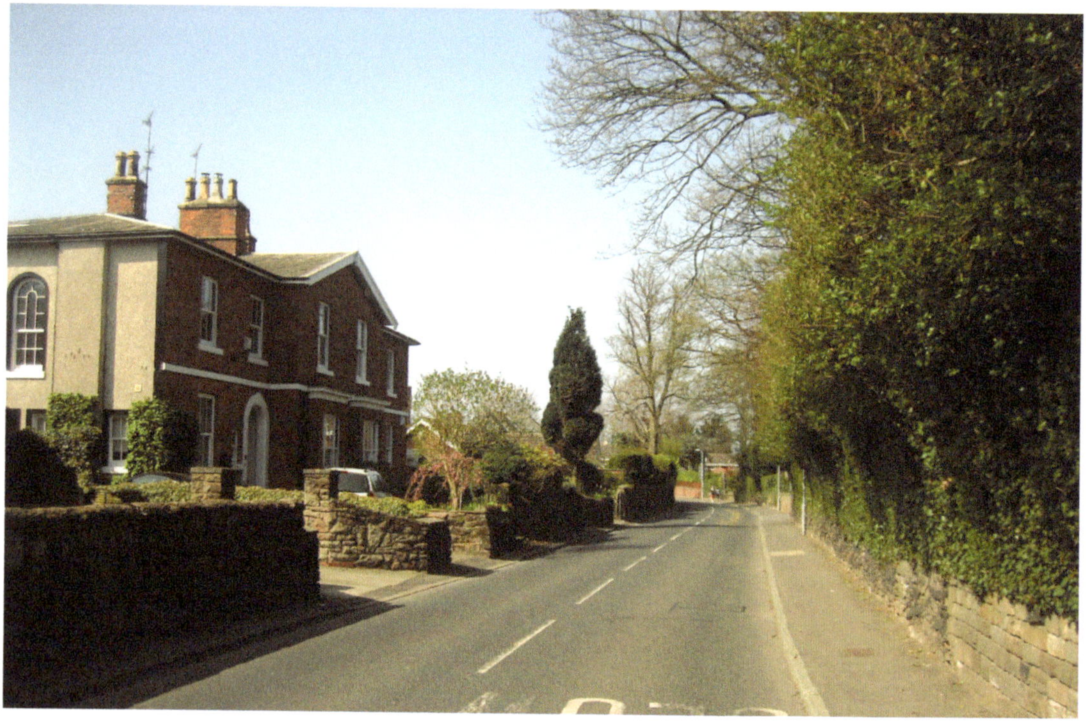

Old House Lane

The trees and hedges have been cut down to reveal the lovely Victorian villas situated in one of the prettiest and oldest parts of Maghull, known as Kennessee Green.

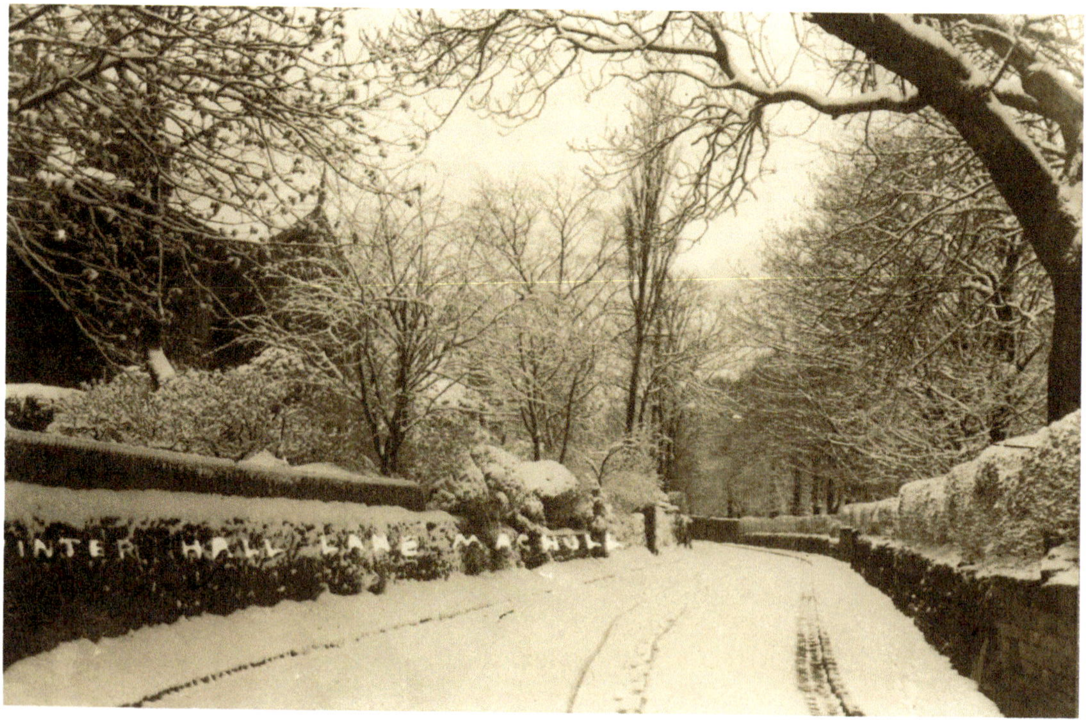

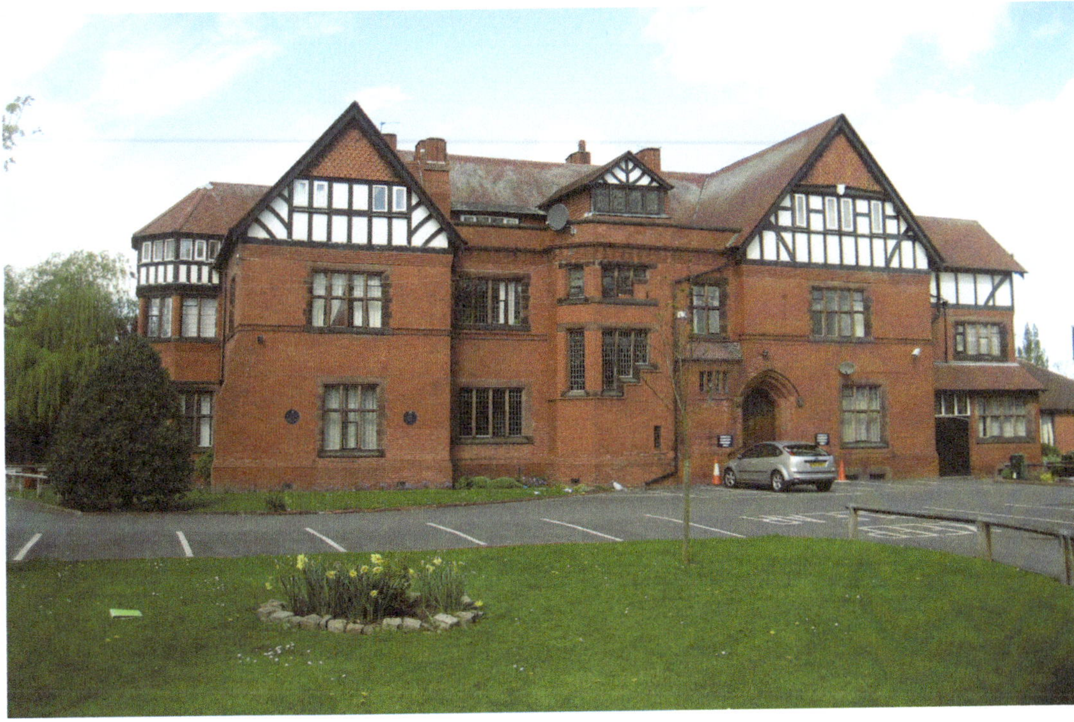

The Sisters of Mercy Convent

Possibly the most famous building in Maghull, the house was built in the early twentieth century, probably by Thomas Martin, a solicitor, and later was the home of Lord Vestey and Frank Hornby, the toy manufacturer. In 1947 it became the Convent of the Sisters of Mercy, and part was used as a school before Maricourt School was opened.

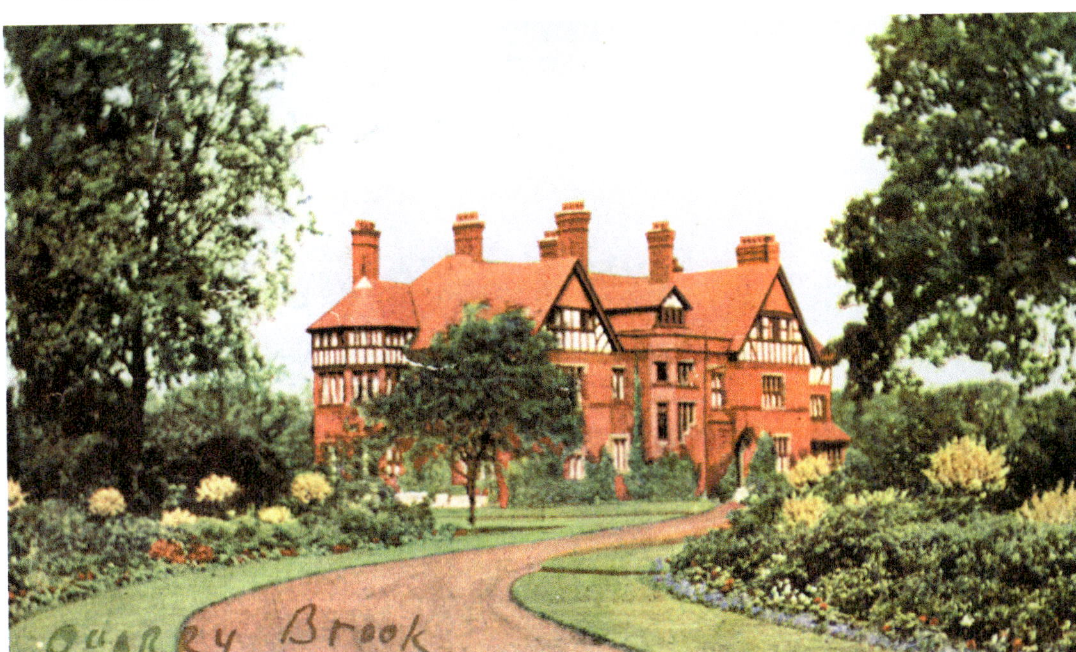

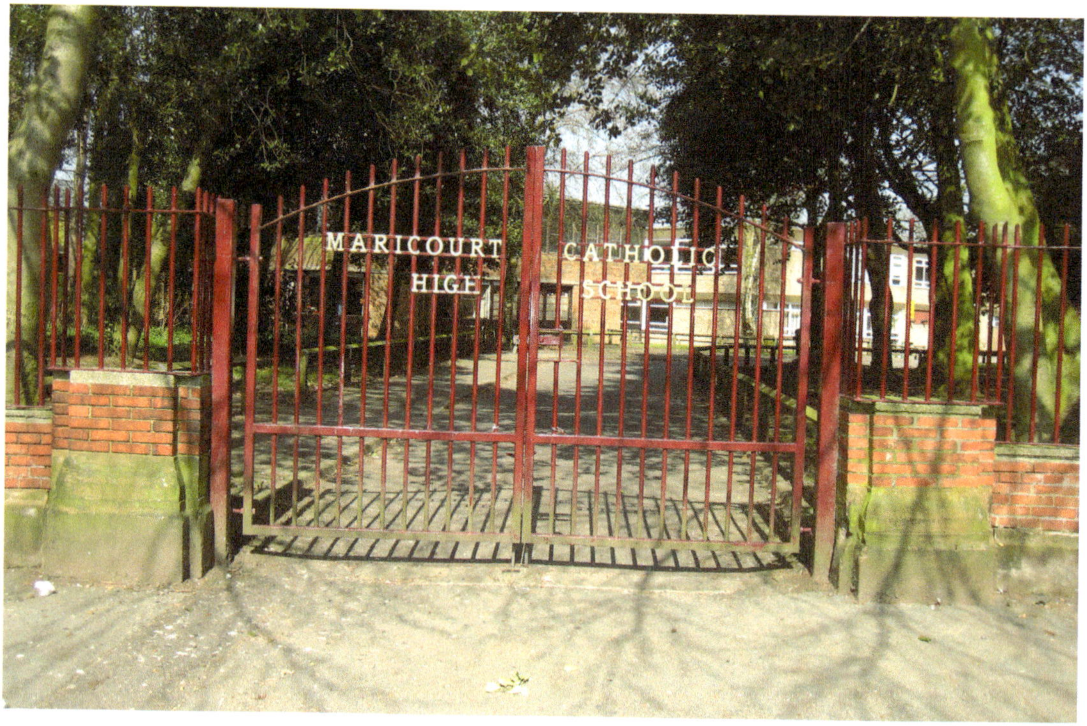

The Gate in Hall Lane

The snow-laden path leads to Quarry Brook House, which can just be glimpsed through the distant trees. Only the bottom parts of the pillars remain, and the new gates reveal the fact that the school has taken over the estate.

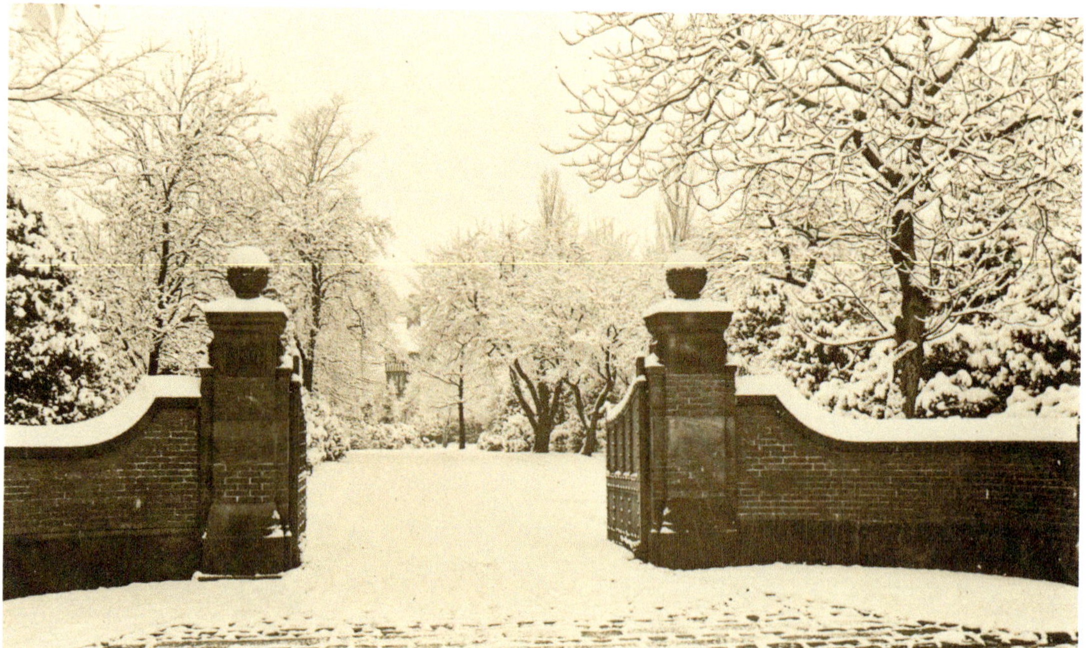

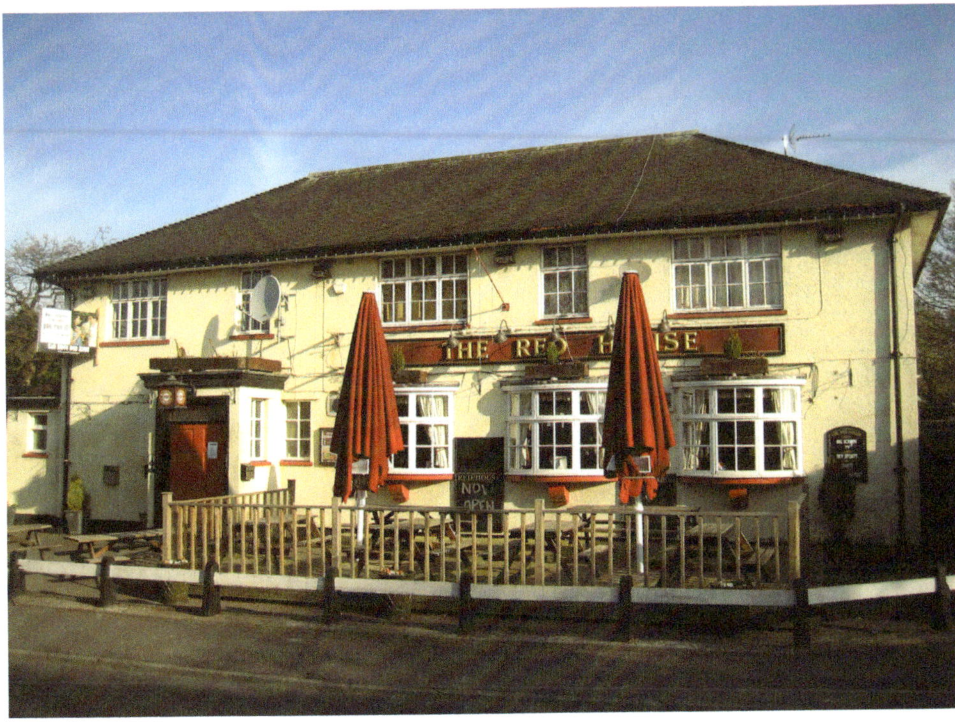

The Red House

It is difficult to realise that this pub was originally a beer house in a small single-storey building, known as the Pig and Whistle, which is seen on the right. It was later named The Red House, and the building was extended in the 1960s.

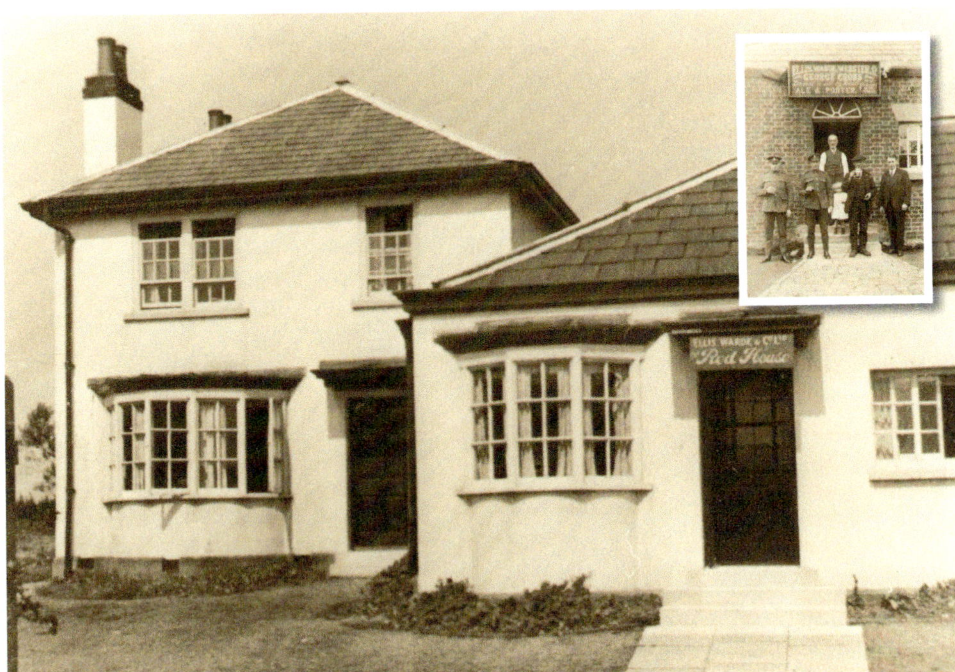

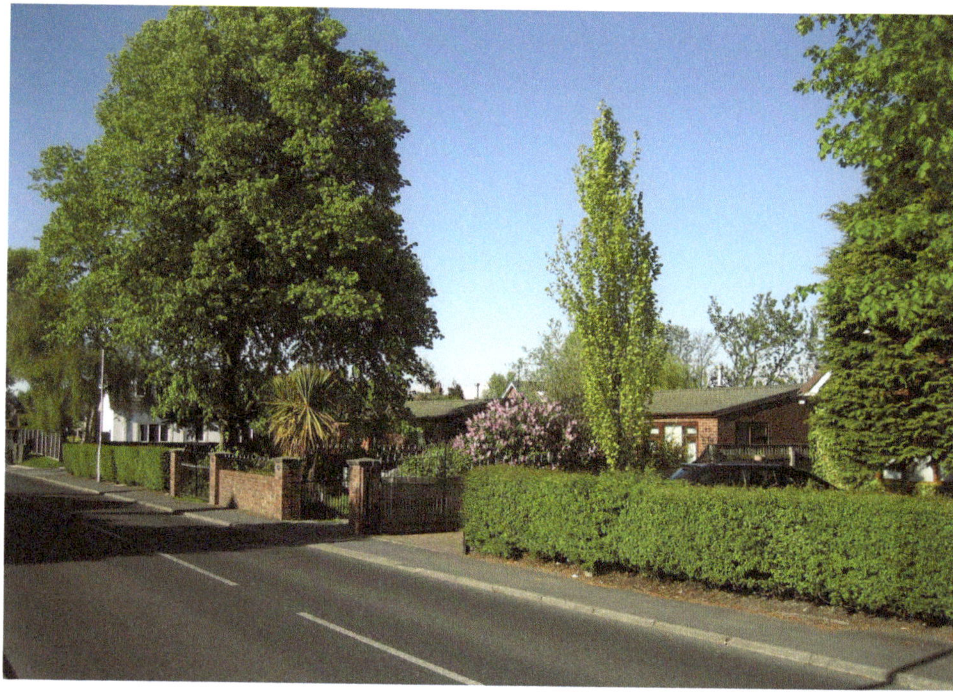

Homes for Heroes

In 1946, the first of the prefabricated homes built to accommodate homeless servicemen and their families after the war was handed over. Some years later the houses were updated, although they remained on the same foundations. Now, with the gardens having matured beautifully, they add to the scene in Foxhouse Lane, and it is difficult to imagine their earlier stark appearance.

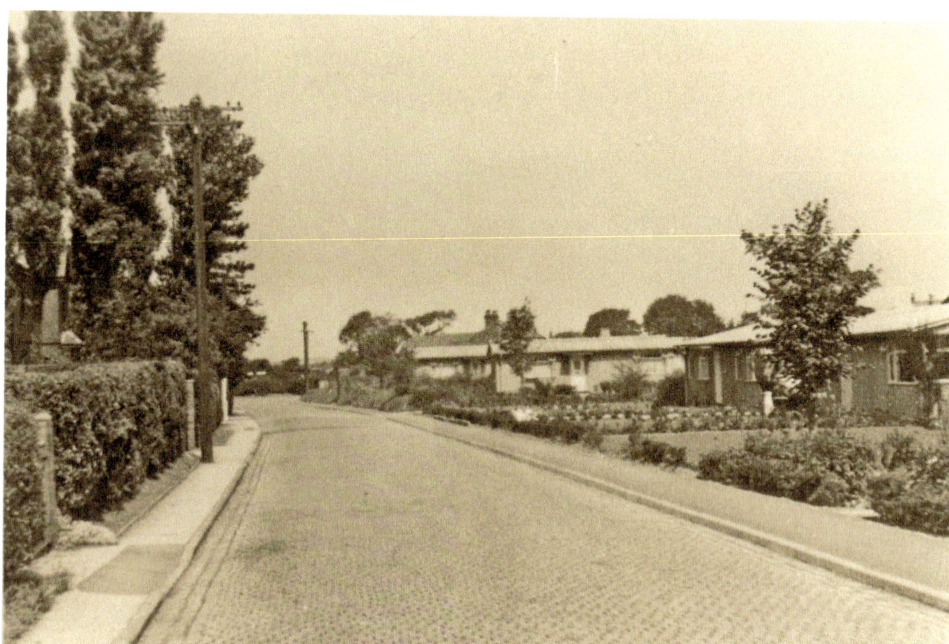

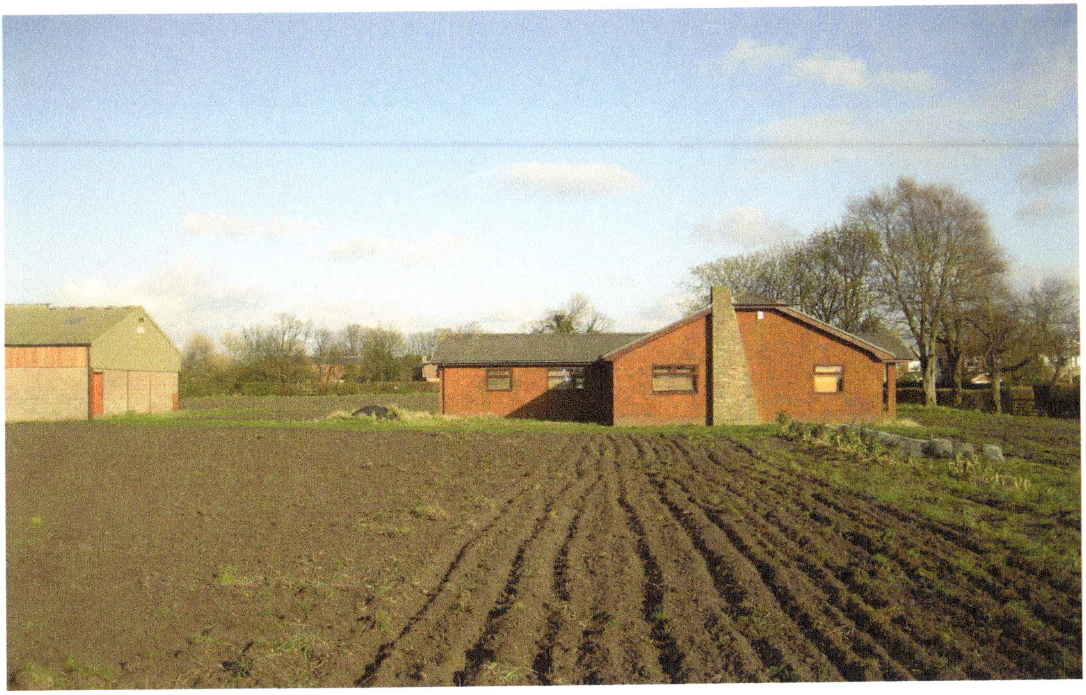

The First Hospital in Park Lane

The Sanatorium was built by Bootle Health Committee for tuberculosis patients from that town, and opened in 1914. It was renamed Maghull Hospital, and was intended for the treatment of female geriatric patients, but when the buildings became unsafe it was closed in 1970 and demolished soon afterwards. The land has returned to agriculture, and a bungalow built on the site has been empty for many years.

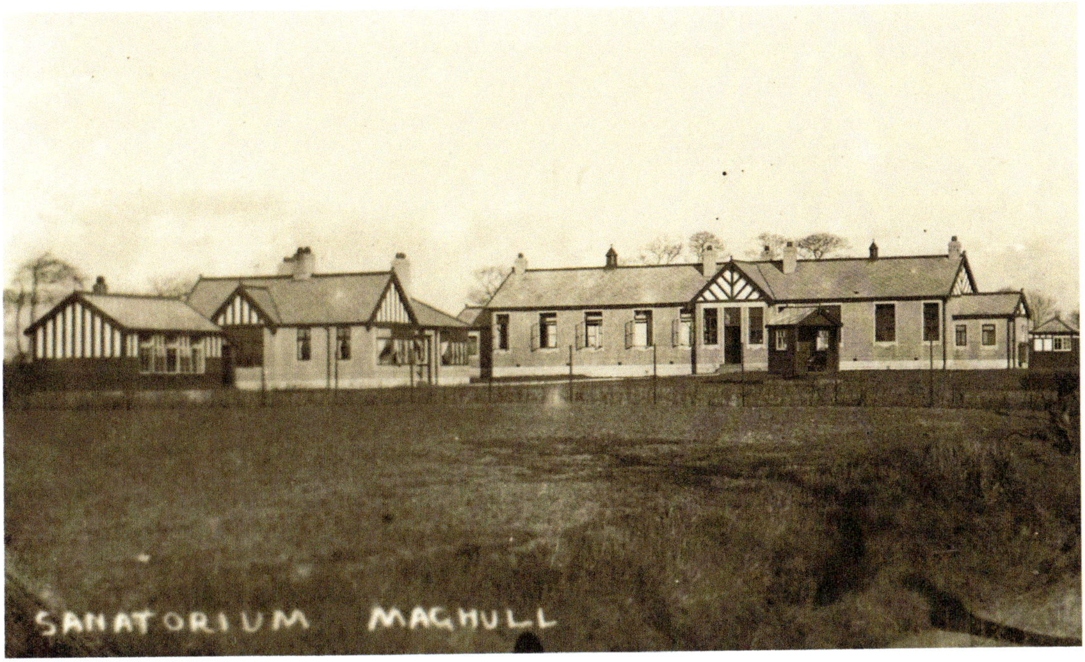

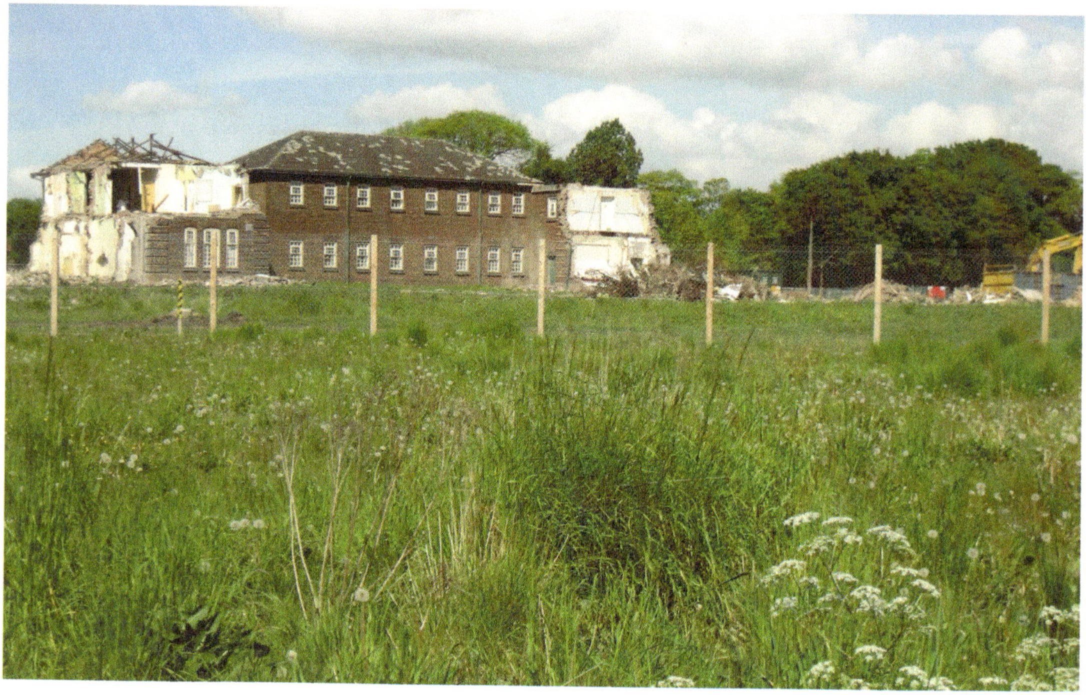

The Demise of a Hospital

For many years Moss Side Hospital, with its conspicuous chimney, was a major part of life in Maghull, particularly when it was a hospital for soldiers. The Nurses' Home, where these young ladies resided, was the large building in the middle. In 2010 the hospital was demolished, and a prison is to be built on the land.

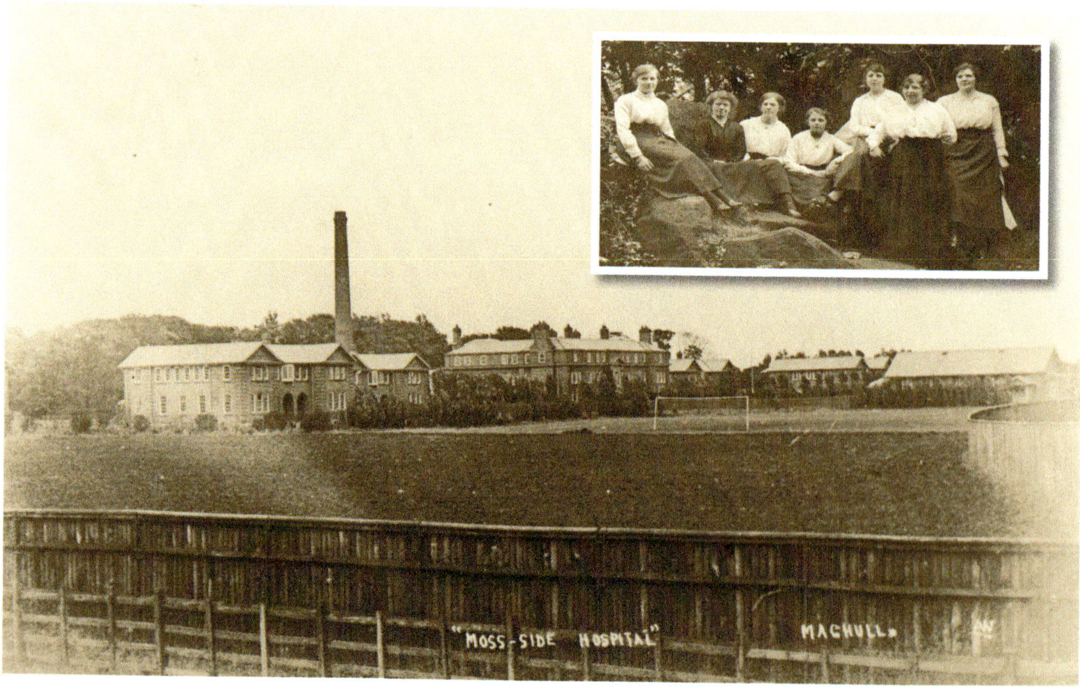

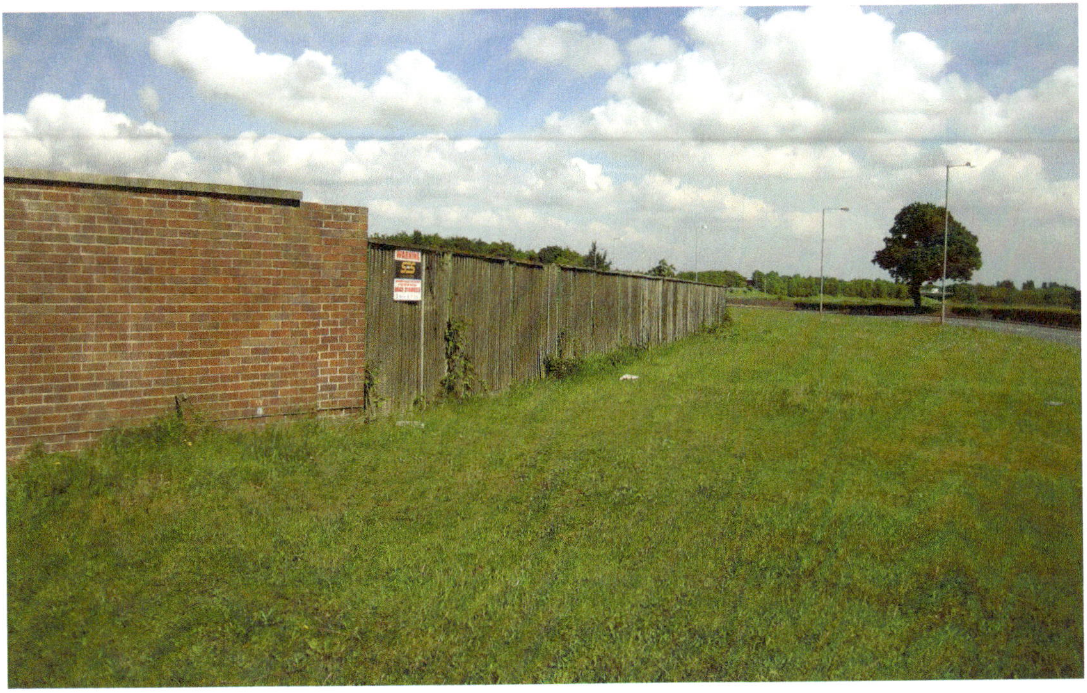

School Lane

This is a very rare photograph of the original lodge to Moss Side House, built by the Harrison family. It was demolished and replaced by a new lodge in the grounds when Moss Side Hospital was taken over by the military in 1914. The direction of the road, which was named after Maghull's first school, has been changed and there is no evidence of the position of either lodge.

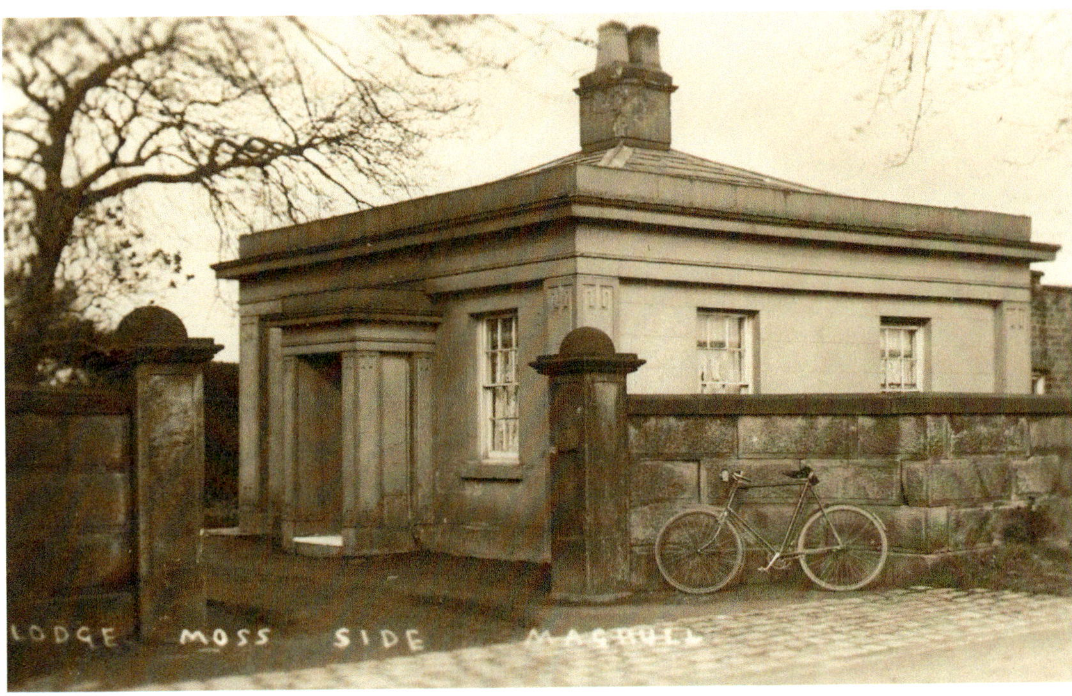

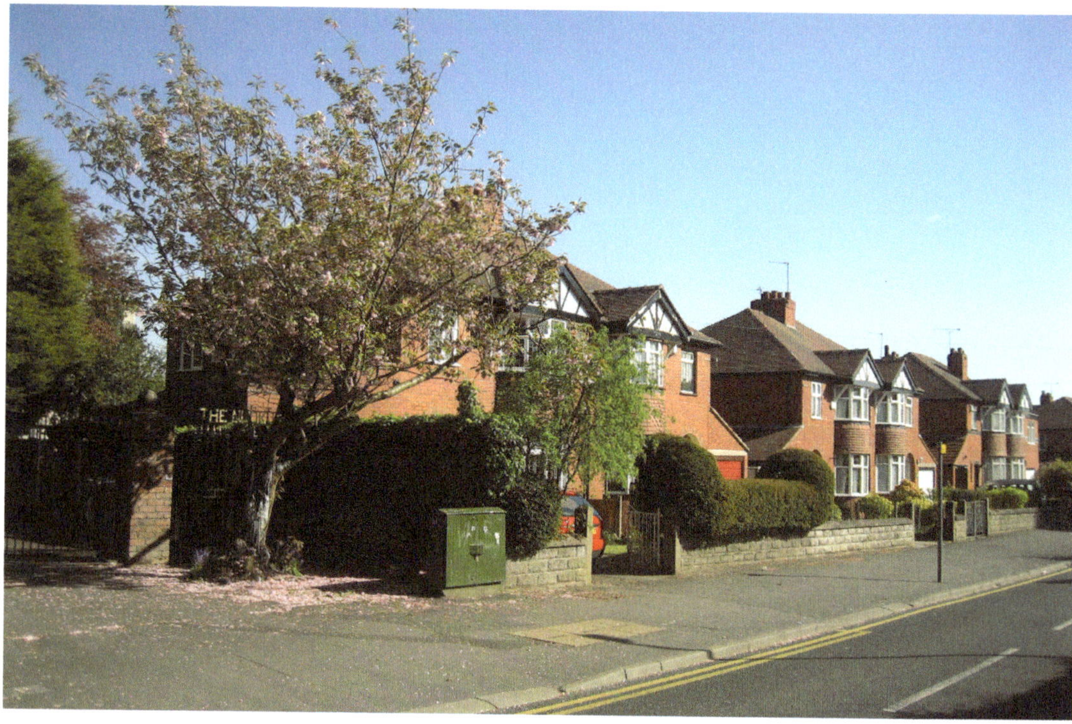

Tailors Lane

This attractive cottage, built in the eighteenth century, was the home of a Dr Thrasycles Clarke, a local general practitioner, and his family for over seventy-five years, but has given way to modern houses.

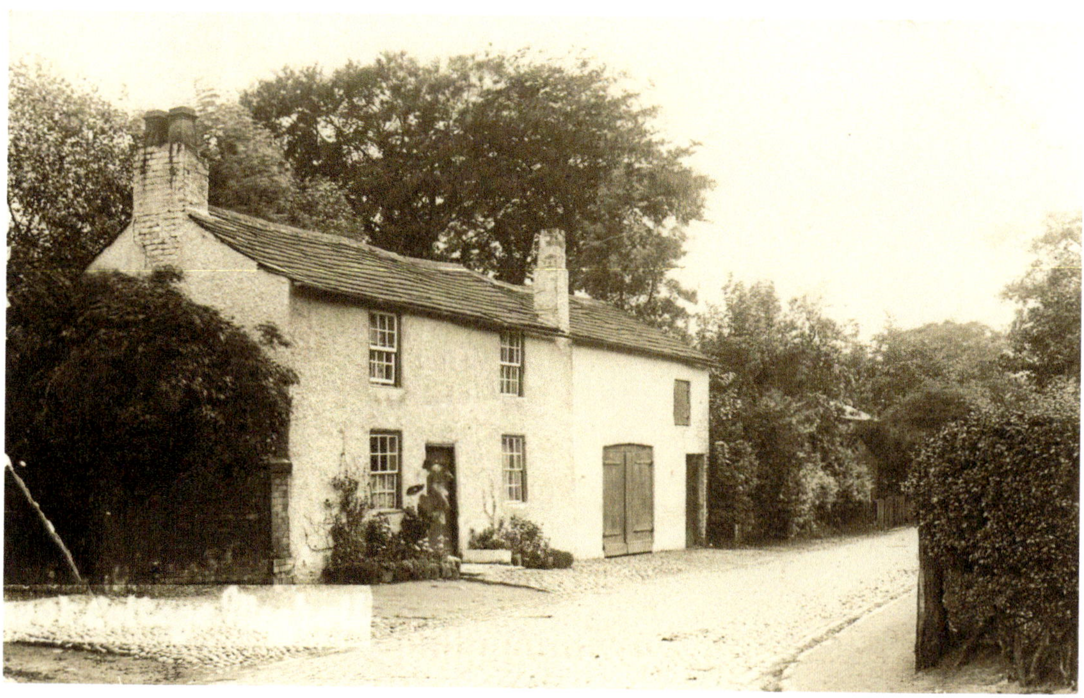

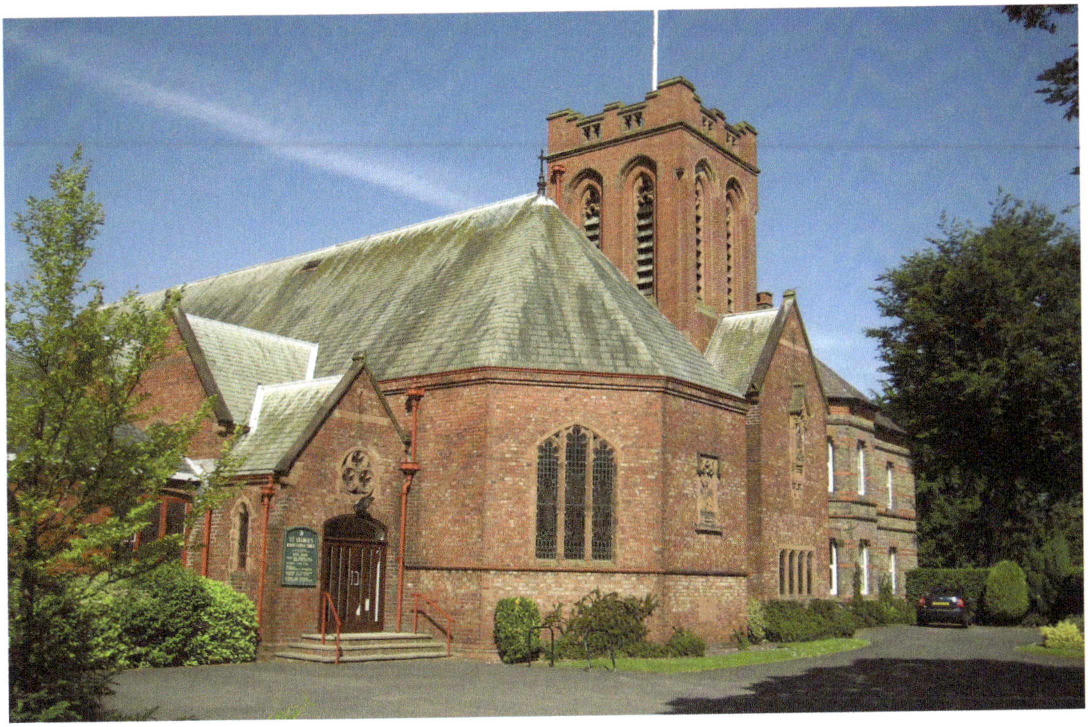

St George's Church in Station Road

The first Roman Catholic services in Maghull were held in local barns, and later in the new school. The Presbytery was built in 1892. It would be another thirty-seven years before St George's Church was built adjacent to the priests' home.

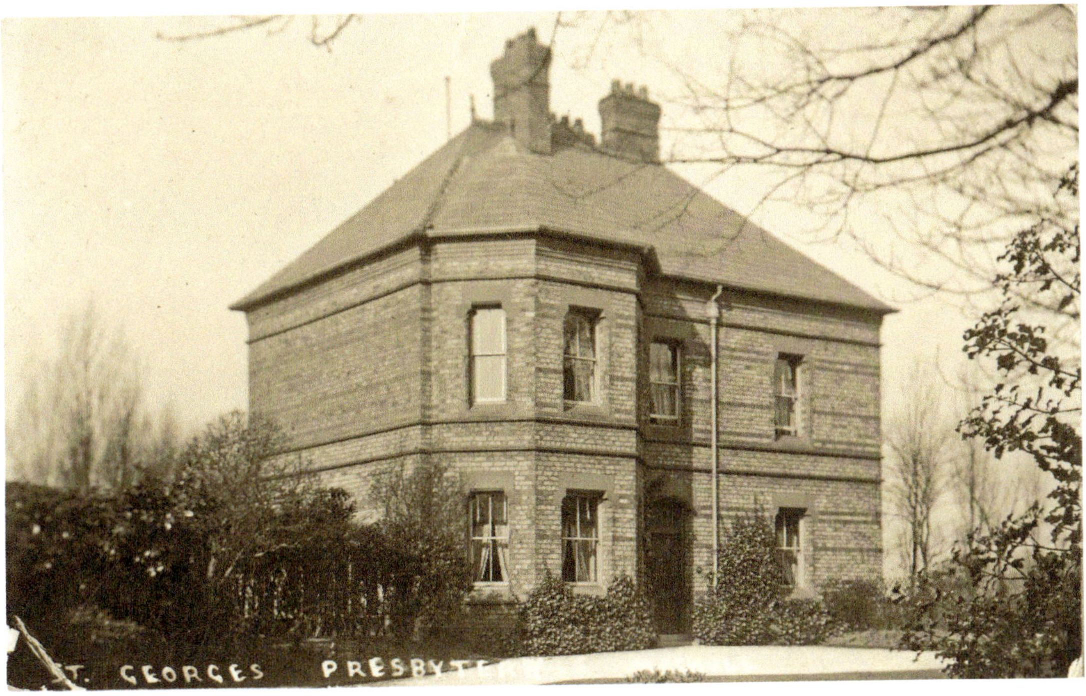

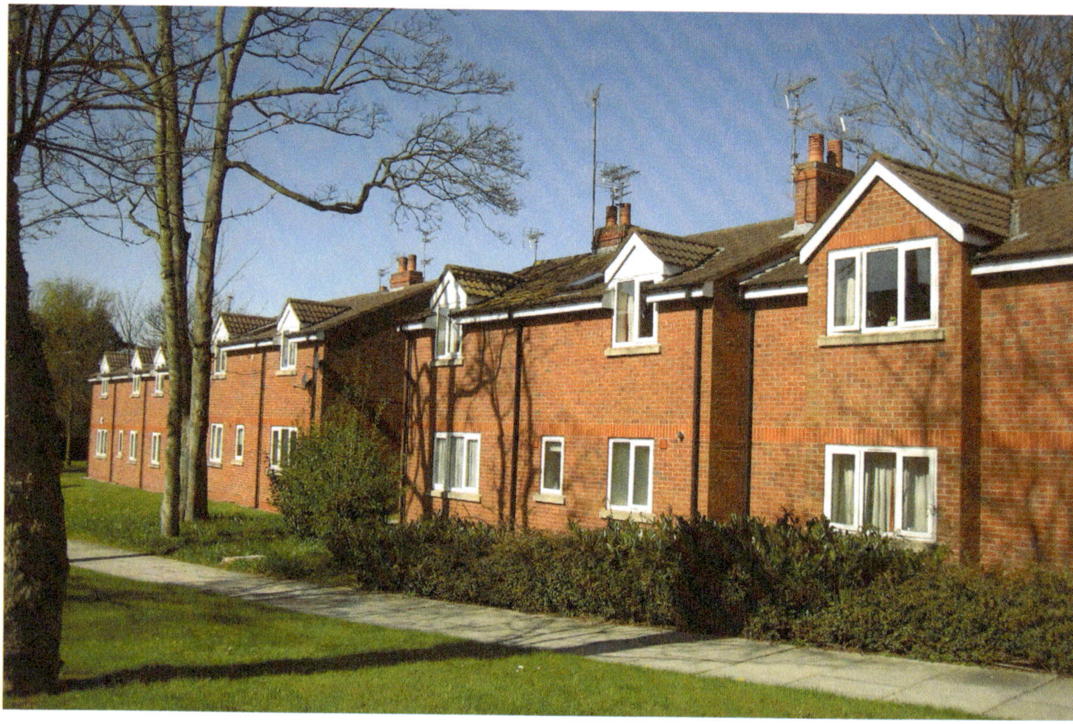

Station Road

St George's Roman Catholic Primary School was built on the land between the church and the canal and opened in 1890, the adjacent teacher's house opening the following year. When the school moved to new premises, the buildings fell into decline and remained empty for many years before being flattened. St George's Court now occupies the site.

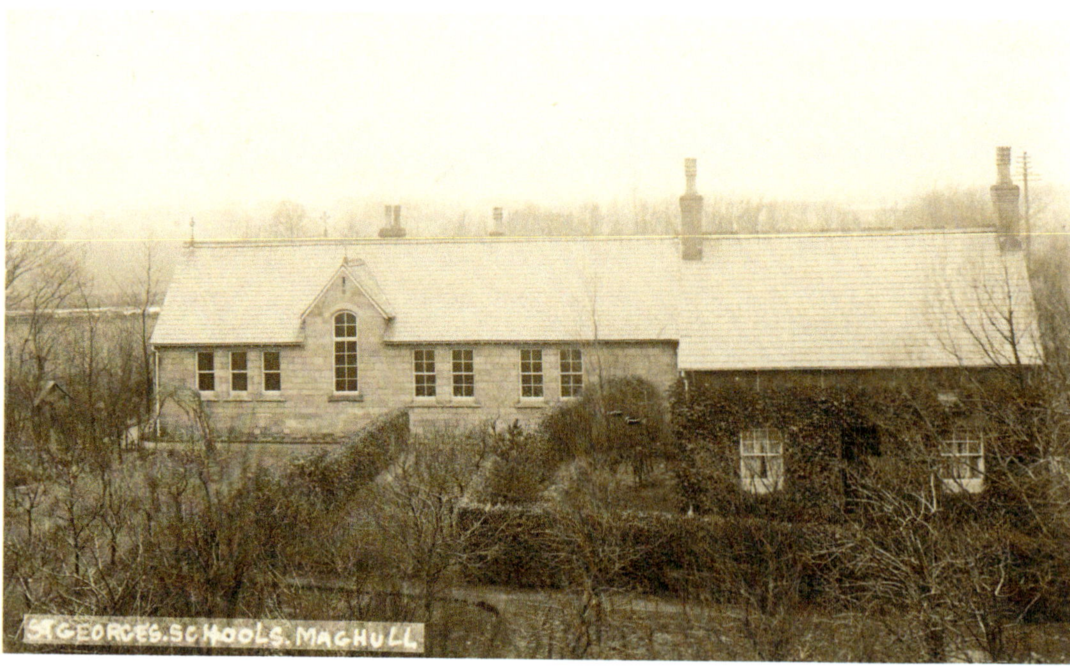

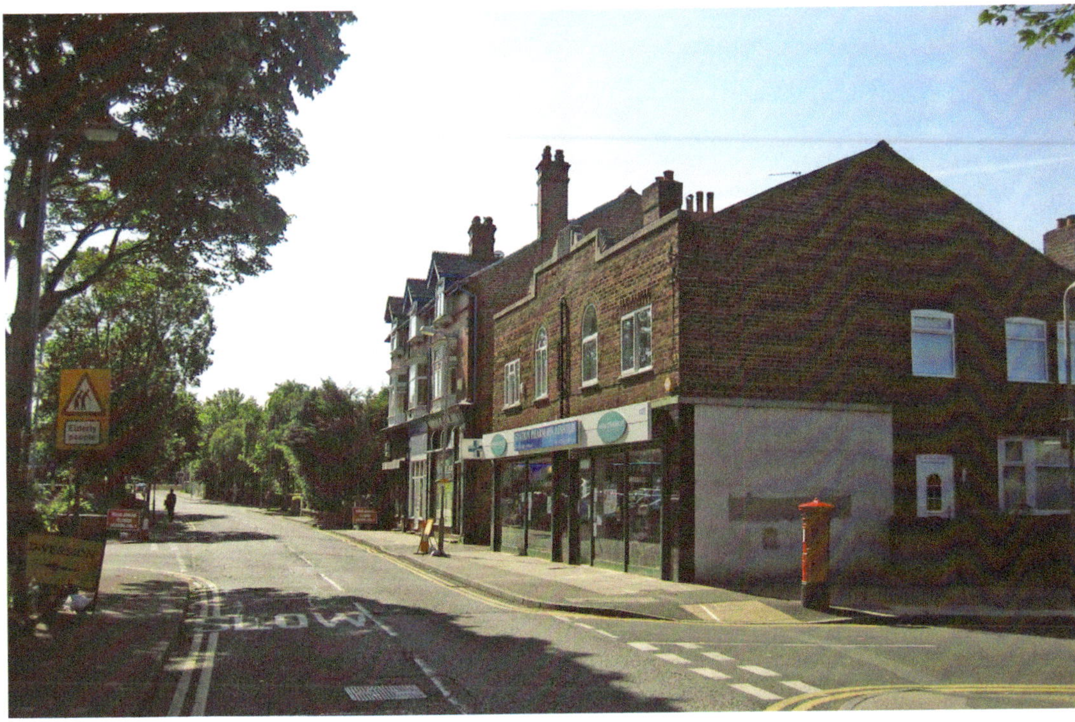

Station Road Looking Towards Maghull Station

The shops are still in use, although the butcher's shop on the right has gone. The wall on the left is replaced by a car park. Bungalows have been built on the open Athletic Ground used by the railway company, and the signal box beyond has been demolished.

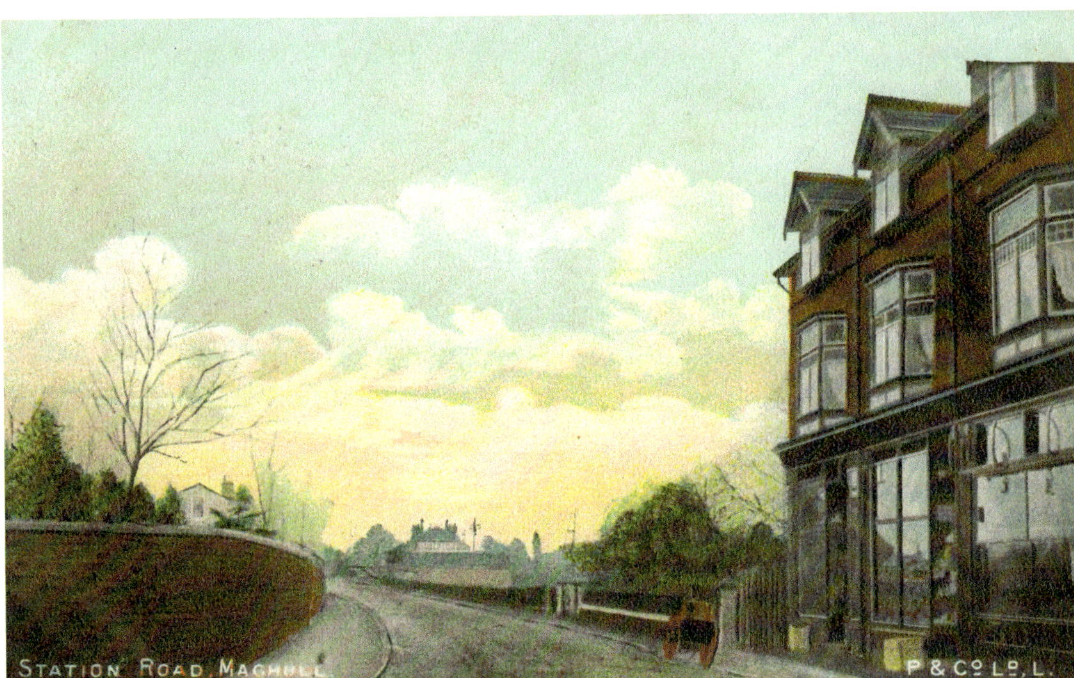

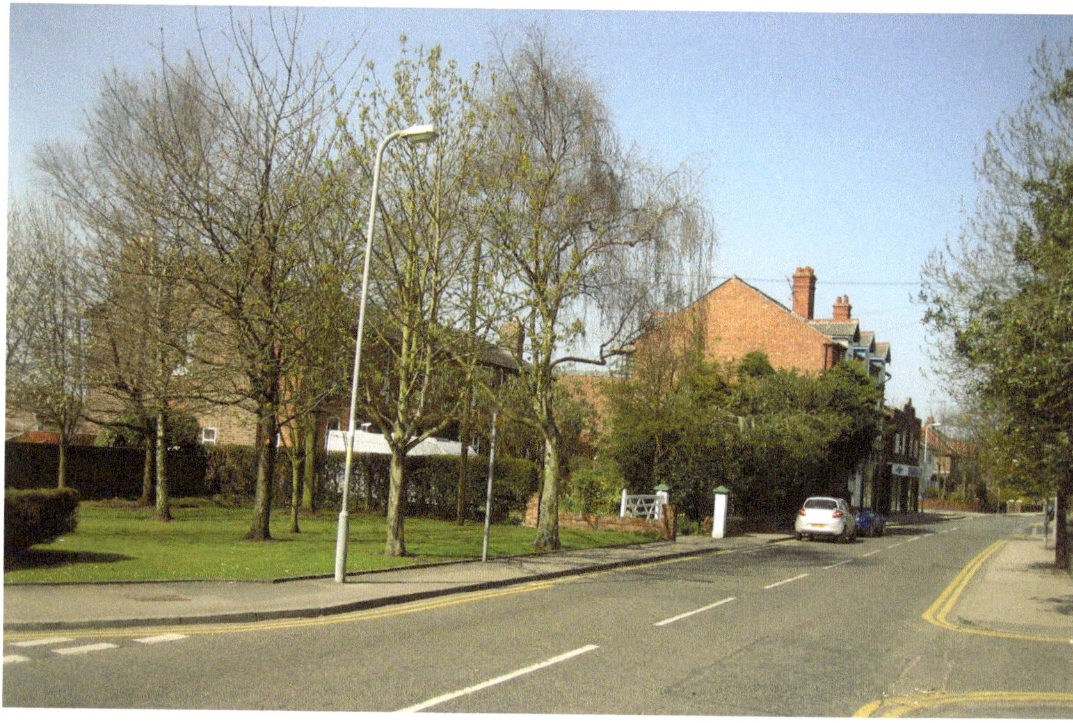

The Toy Maker's Home

Proudly displaying the first Blue Plaque awarded outside of London, the former home of Frank Hornby, the famous toy manufacturer, is now hidden among the trees. The shops next door to Hornby's home appear unchanged, but a chemist shop has replaced the building at the end.

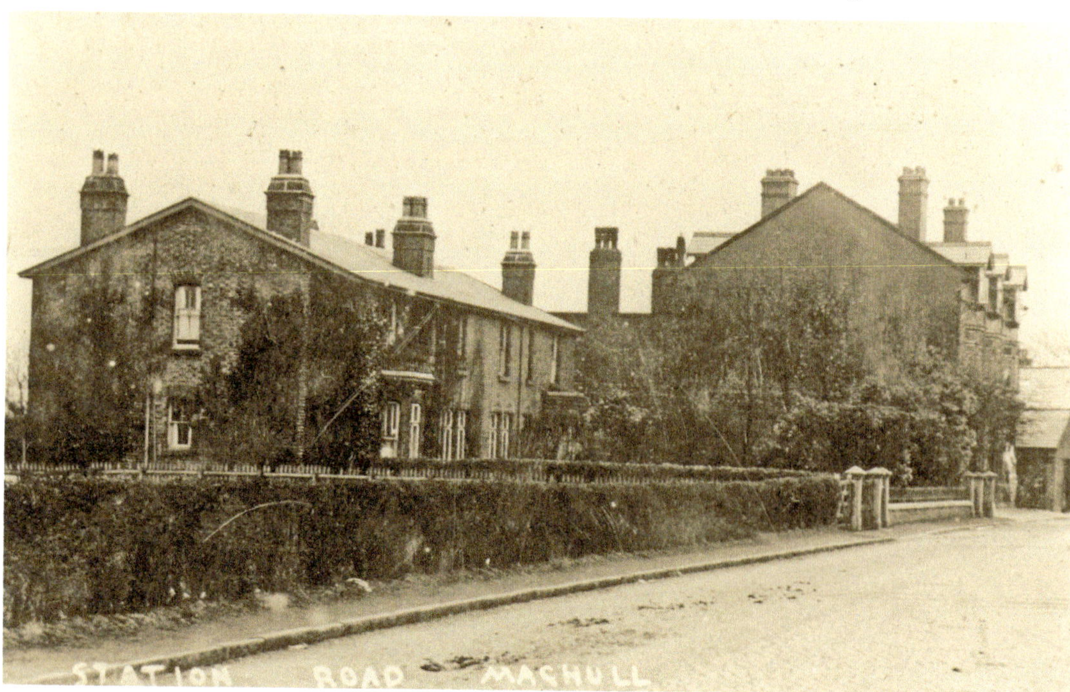

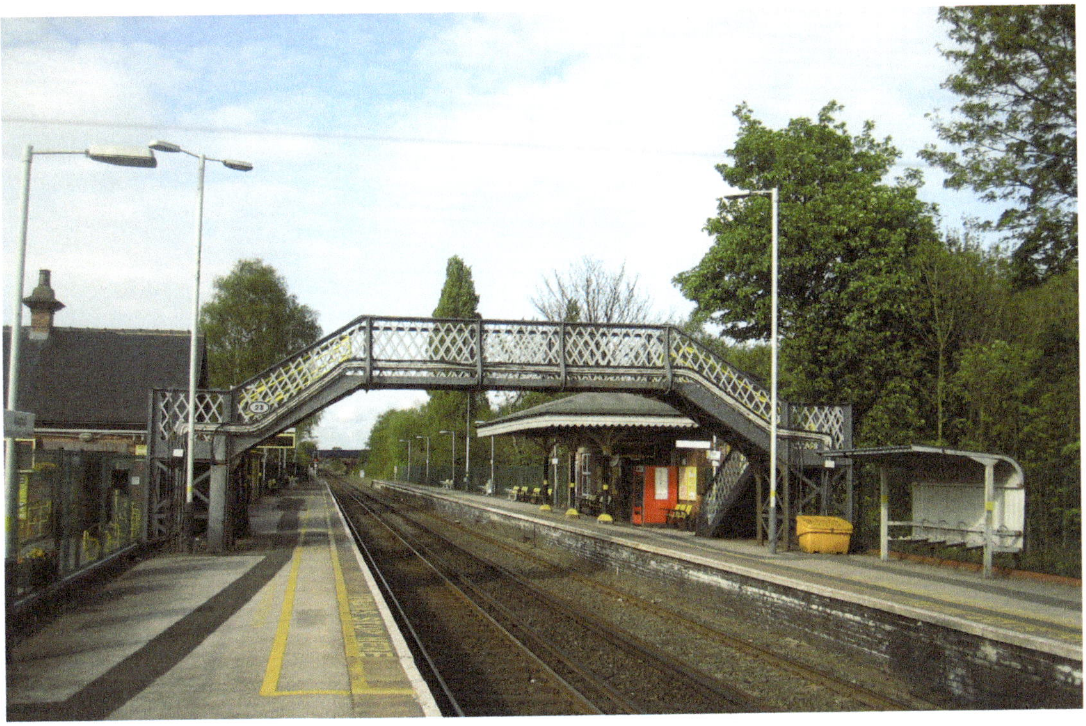

Maghull Station

Opened in 1849 by the Liverpool-Ormskirk-Preston Railway Company, there has been remarkably little change. However, as a sign of the times, the former coal sidings have been made into a large commuters' car park.

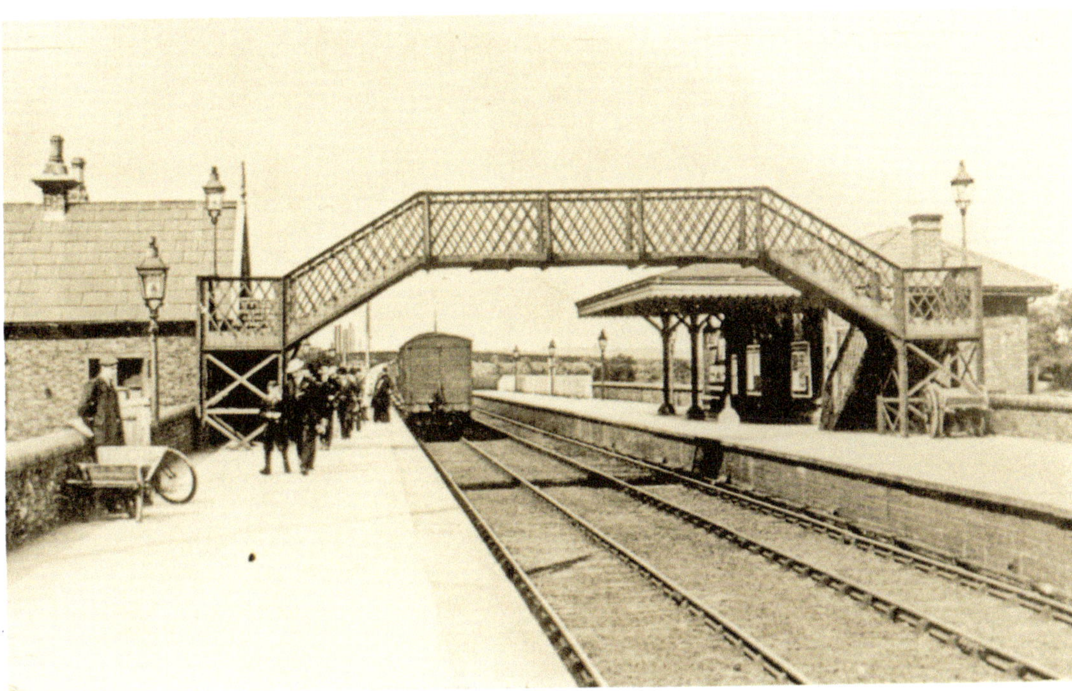

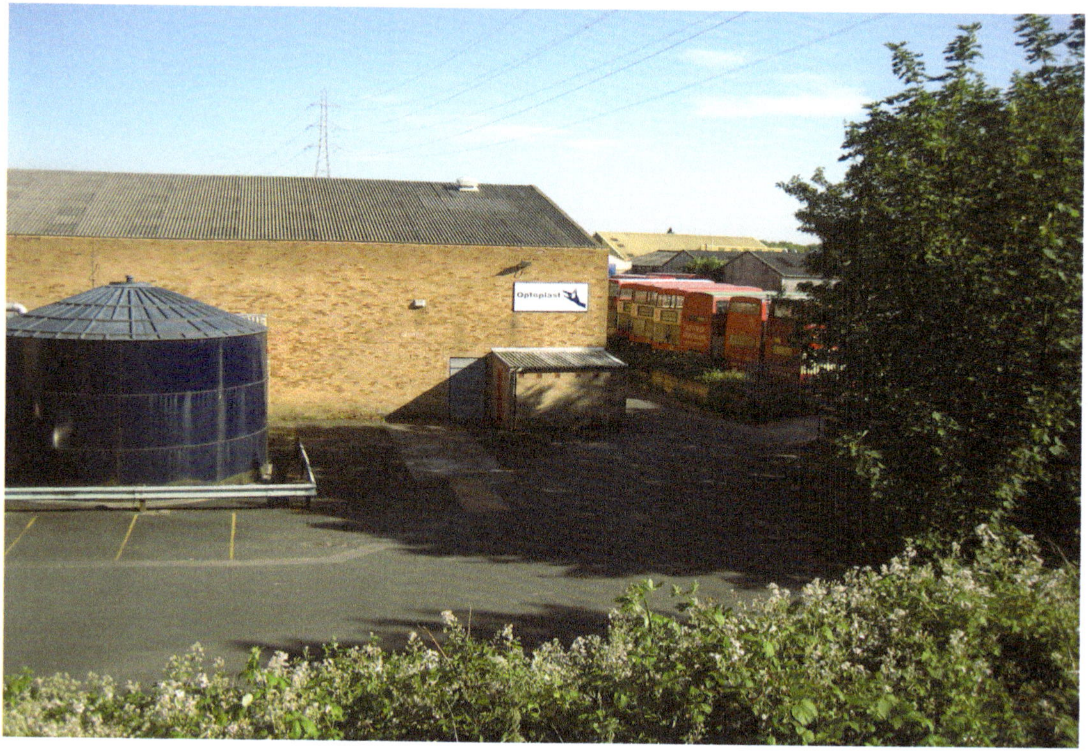

Sefton and Maghull Station

It is difficult to see that the Sefton Lane Industrial Estate stands on the site of Maghull's second station, close to the boundary with Sefton, on the line continuing to Lydiate. The modern view explains why the Trans-Pennine Trail has to take a large detour from the original railway route.

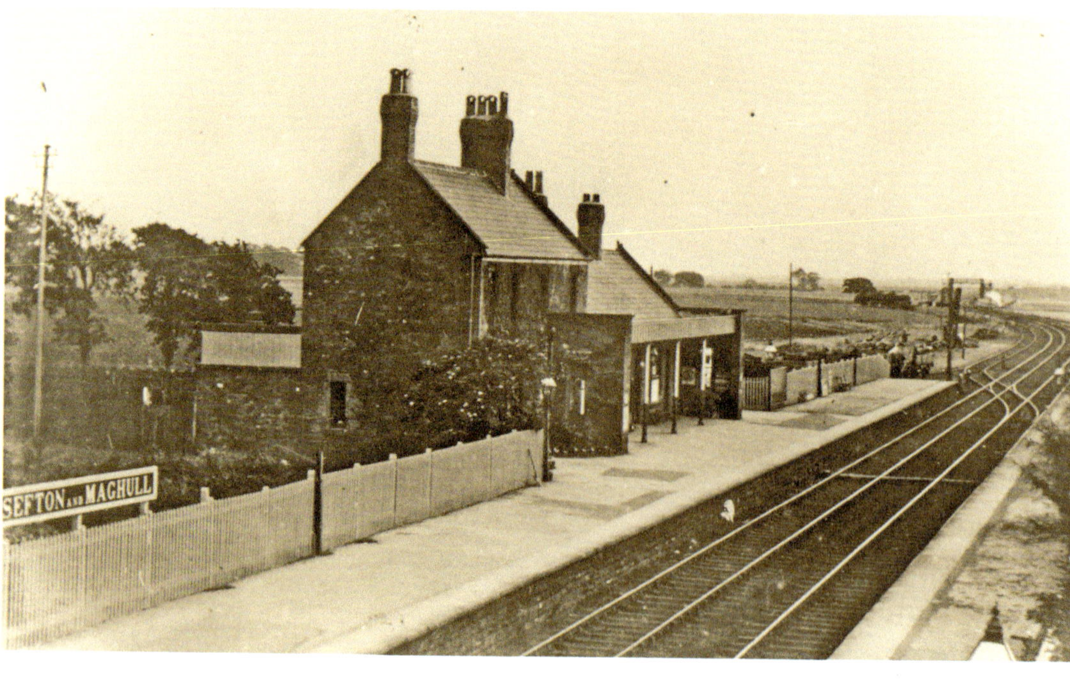

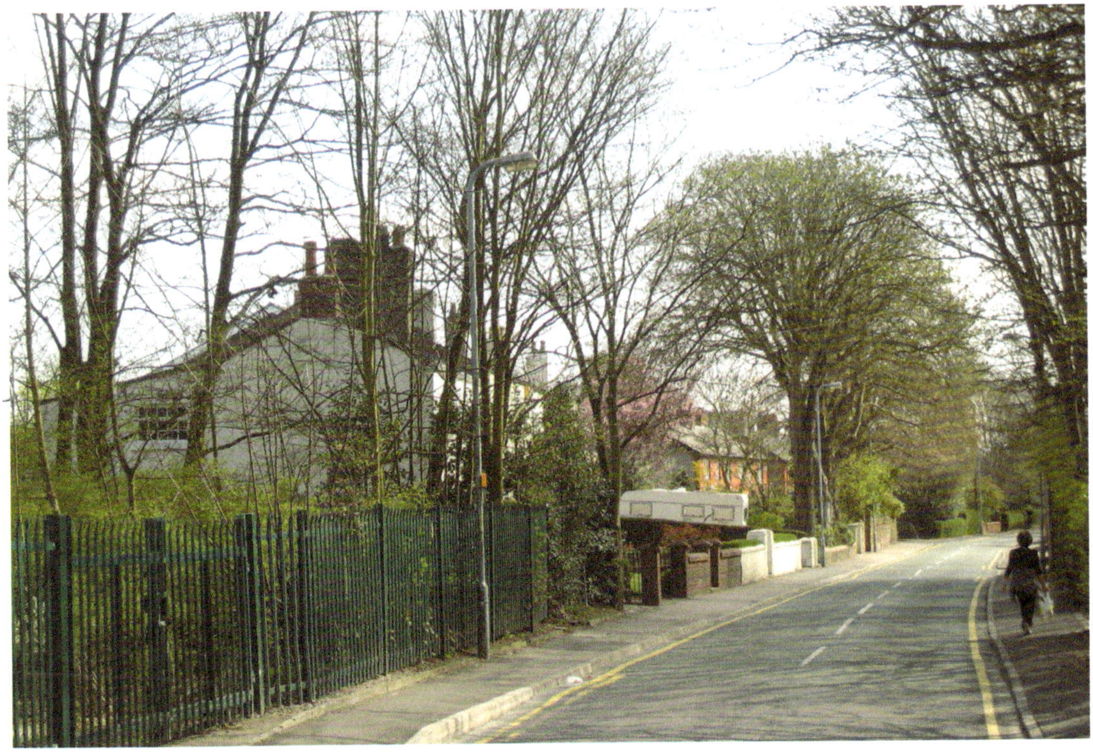

Melling Lane in the 1920s

Now known as Melling Lane, the road out of Maghull is still a narrow tree-lined road, but the railway houses in the foreground have gone and the hidden homes are now just visible through the trees. An estate of modern homes has been built behind the distant wall.

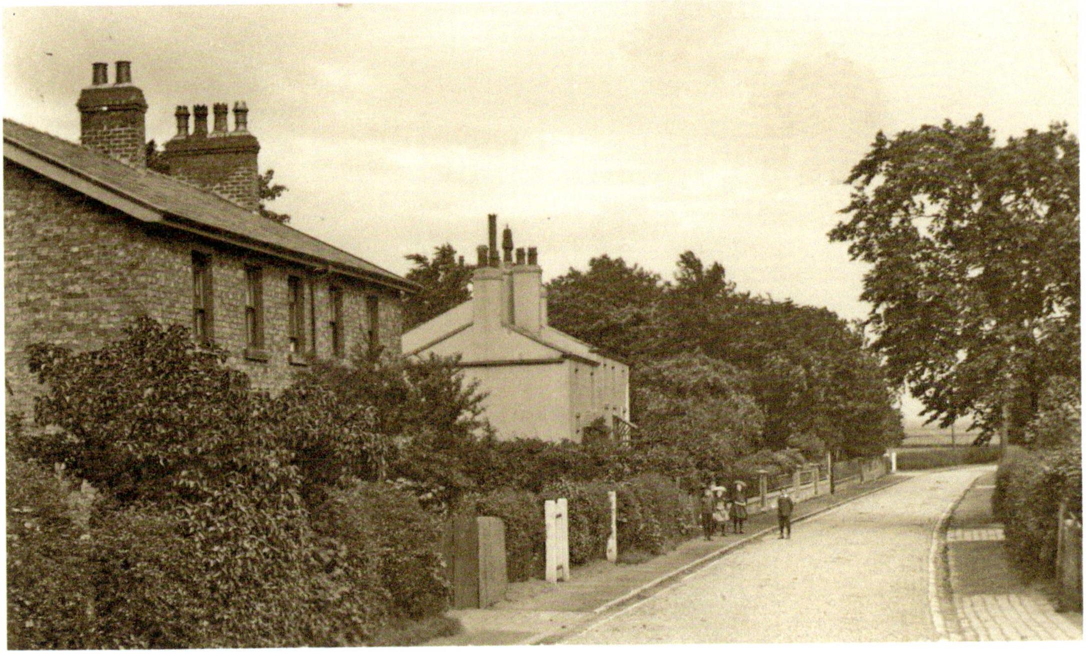

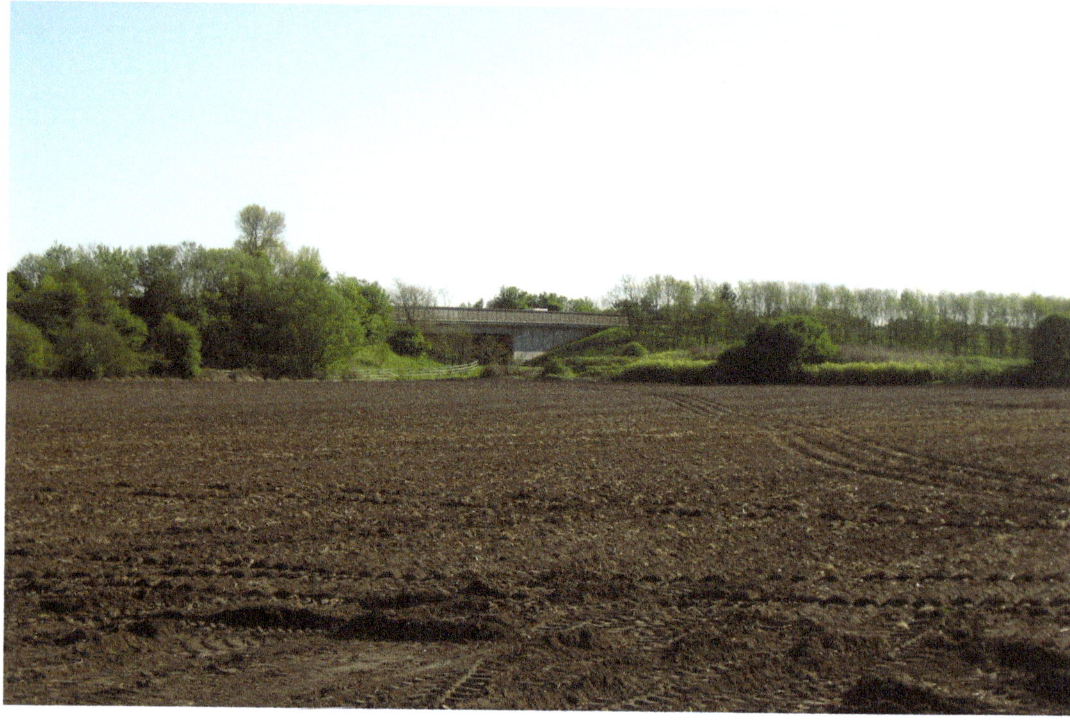

The Visitor Who Came Out of the Blue

It is hard to imagine that this field is the site of one the most momentous events in Maghull's history. In the distance the M58 bridge crosses the canal, and this is the direction from which Samuel F. Cody, who was the first man to conduct a powered flight in Great Britain, flew before landing his aeroplane in the field. A plaque commemorating the occasion is on a nearby house.

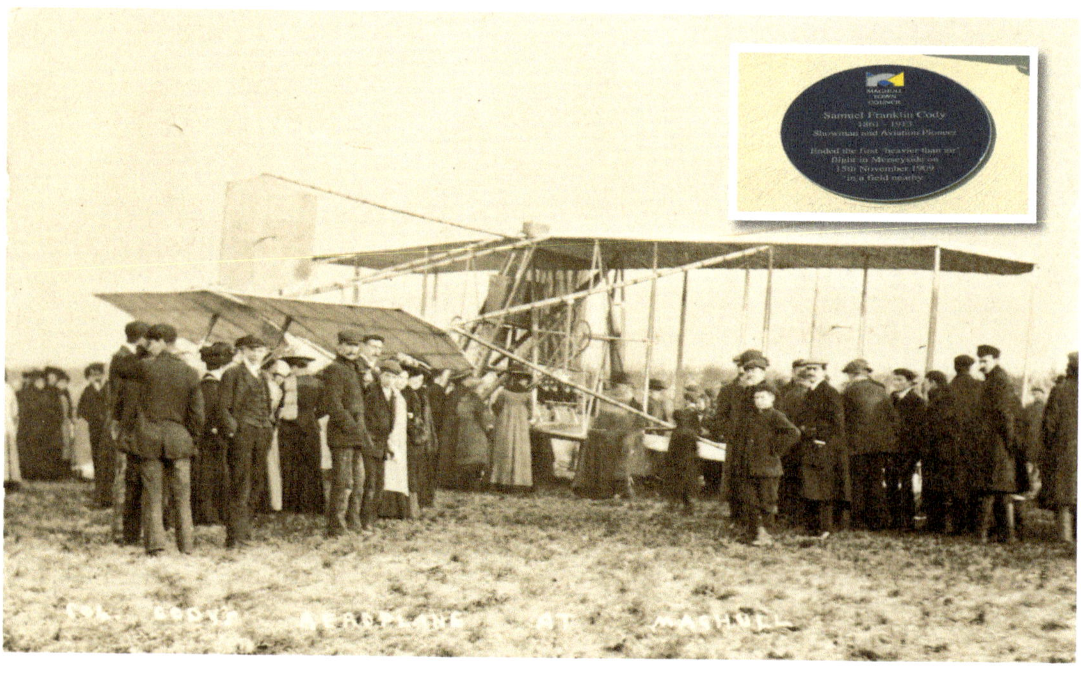